THE PILGRIM PARADIGM

THE PILGRIM PARADIGM

FAITH IN MOTION

André Brouillette, SJ

Paulist Press
New York / Mahwah, NJ

Cover image by virginiabravo/Shutterstock.com
Cover design by Sharyn Banks
Book design by Lynn Else

Library of Congress Cataloging-in-Publication Data
Names: Brouillette, André, author.
Title: The pilgrim paradigm : faith in motion / André Brouillette.
Description: New York : Paulist Press, [2021] | Includes bibliographical references and index. | Summary: "The pilgrimage impulse is a common thread running through multiple religious traditions. Brouillette concentrates on the Christian tradition, starting with its roots in Judaism and going up to the trips undertaken by modern popes from Paul VI through Francis"—Provided by publisher.
Identifiers: LCCN 2021003801 (print) | LCCN 2021003802 (ebook) | ISBN 9780809155415 (paperback) | ISBN 9781587689376 (ebook)
Subjects: LCSH: Christian pilgrims and pilgrimages.
Classification: LCC BX2323 .B757 2021 (print) | LCC BX2323 (ebook) | DDC 263/.041—dc23
LC record available at https://lccn.loc.gov/2021003801
LC ebook record available at https://lccn.loc.gov/2021003802

ISBN 978-0-8091-5541-5 (paperback)
ISBN 978-1-58768-937-6 (e-book)

Published by Paulist Press
997 Macarthur Boulevard
Mahwah, New Jersey 07430
www.paulistpress.com

Printed and bound in the
United States of America

CONTENTS

Preface vii

Introduction 1

Chapter 1: What Is Christian Pilgrimage? The Ideal Type of a Phenomenon 13

1. Defining Pilgrimage 13
2. Pilgrims and *Tutti Quanti*: Contrasting Figures and Shapes 16
3. Approaching Pilgrimage: Toward an Ideal Type 17
4. Three Essential Conditions: Intention, Transcendence, and Memory 20
5. A Geography of Movement: Departure and Destination 30
6. On the Road: Embodiment, Vulnerability, Effort, and Alterity 35
7. Finally: Transformation? 42
8. Conclusion: The Singularity of Pilgrimage 45

Chapter 2: A Pilgrim People and Christ the Pilgrim A Biblical Journey 46

Prelude 46

Introduction 48

1. A Pilgrim People and a Pilgrim God 49

2. Pilgrimage in the New Covenant in Jesus Christ 61
3. Conclusion 88

Chapter 3: The Modern Pilgrim: Identity and Formation in the *Testament* of Ignatius of Loyola 89
1. The "Pilgrim" as Identity in the *Testament* 92
2. A Journey to Be Traveled by Others: Pilgrimage as a Formational Tool 119
3. Conclusion 124

Chapter 4: The Pilgrim Church 126
1. *Peregrinatio* in Augustine's *City of God* 128
2. The "Pilgrim Church" in the Documents of the Second Vatican Council 132
3. The Reception and Diffusion of the *Peregrinitas* in the Liturgy: Pilgrimage in the Eucharistic Prayers 148
4. The Pilgrim Popes: Embodied Symbols of the Pilgrim Church 156
5. Embracing Pilgrimage and Challenging the *Peregrinitas* of the Church 167

Epilogue: Pilgrimage and the Holy Spirit 173

Notes 177

Bibliography 241

Index 253

PREFACE

La Storta, Italy, Holy Saturday 2017. Standing in a little chapel a few miles away from Rome, a few hours away from Easter, I could not help but recall the significance of this unlikely place in the journey of Ignatius of Loyola (1491–1556) and the significance of the day in the Christians' celebration of the life of Jesus Christ.

After years of yearning for a confirmation of God's will for his life, after a pilgrimage to Jerusalem, after long studies, Ignatius was on his way to Rome with two companions to meet with the pope. As he casually stopped to pray in a little chapel on the Via Cassia, the response to his quest was revealed to him in a vision: he was being placed by God the Father with the Son, with the assurance that God would be propitious to them in Rome. The final destination of the journey, which was far from over, was now foretold.

Being in this small chapel while on pilgrimage on a Holy Saturday was also very evocative. I was then in the middle of a research fellowship that initiated the work of this monograph on the theology of pilgrimage. After a few months in Madrid, I had arrived in Rome for some final weeks of research and writing before going back to the United States. My sojourn was coming to an end, my research was evolving, but I still had a long way to go before reaching any final destination. Holy Saturday is this great moment of silence, of uncertainty, too often overlooked, between the utter grief of Good Friday, and the exuberant joy of Easter Sunday. It is grief, but subdued. It is not yet joy, but anticipation of that joy. It is in-between. It is in process. It is a day of journey.

The notion of pilgrimage piqued my interest when I entered the Jesuit novitiate as a young man. While I was reading the founding documents of the Society of Jesus in my first days as a novice, the experience of pilgrimage seemed to encapsulate the choice I had just made to enter religious life. Although a pilgrimage is one of the main experiences planned for novices, I realized mine only later, while I was studying in France, walking and hitchhiking from Paris to Loyola, through Chartres, Tours, Poitiers, Toulouse, and Lourdes. I later went on different pilgrimages, alone or with others, short or long, to World Youth Day, to Santiago de Compostela with colleagues, in Canada on reconciliation with Indigenous people, journeying by canoe, and to urban shrines in various cities.

Years after my post-novitiate pilgrimage, observing both the deep transformation of the Church experienced in a postmodern world and the enduring popularity of pilgrimages, even in their secular incarnations, the notion of pilgrimage emerged more forcefully as an intriguing and challenging metaphor for Christian life. It is by no means a revolutionary idea, but unlike anthropologists, sociologists, historians, or religious scientists, theologians have devoted surprisingly little attention to pilgrimage. Thus, I moved ahead with the project of deepening the theological understanding of pilgrimage.

A research project on pilgrimage calls for some movement. The Pontificia Universidad Comillas in Madrid welcomed me for a time of research as a visiting scholar. I then continued to write between the United States and Canada, presenting along the way some elements of my research to a variety of audiences in French and in English: articles, conference papers, parish talks, retreats. A theological reflection on pilgrimage unfolded on the move.

Along the way, many debts of gratitude have been incurred. At Boston College, I want to acknowledge the institutional support of the School of Theology and Ministry, especially through a faculty fellowship and research grants. Over the years, many exceptional research assistants have contributed to this research by looking at sources, gathering books and articles, correcting my nonnative prose, and offering their honest feedback on earlier versions of this material; my thanks go to Laura Tennenhouse, Grace Agolia, Jeremy Jones, and Scott Molony. Colleagues read parts of the manuscript to offer their assessment and saved me from some mistakes; many thanks go to Marina McCoy, Jeffrey Bloechel, John Baldovin, SJ, Richard Clifford, SJ, Andrew Davis, and Barton Geger, SJ. For their part, I also wish to thank Jérôme Guingand, SJ, Bernhard Knorn,

SJ, Michael Simone, SJ, and Andrea Vicini, SJ, who either answered some of my questions or offered useful references. The personnel from the Boston College Theology and Ministry Library were also very efficient in providing material; may they be thanked!

Some insights of this research have been either gathered or shared at the Communauté catholique francophone de Boston; the "Haltes spirituelles" organized by the Soeurs de l'Enfant-Jésus in Rivière-du-Loup (Québec), Canada; the Symposium for Pilgrimages Studies at the College of William and Mary, Williamsburg, Virginia; the Carmel of Barrington, Rhode Island; the Boston College School of Theology and Ministry Faculty Colloquium; and in the journals *Théologiques* (Montréal), *Nouvelle revue théologique* (Brussels), and *Au Coeur du Monde* (Quebec city). The feedback and conversations were most helpful.

In the last leg of this project, I want to express my gratitude to Paulist Press, and especially to Trace Murphy, who welcomed my book project, and to Donna Crilly, my editor, and their team.

Finally, my gratitude extends to the many people with whom I journey, not simply theologically, but in life: my Jesuit companions, my friends, my parents, and my siblings and their families. I give thanks to the Lord for all of you!

I hope that this book will contribute to a renewal of our theological imagination around pilgrimage, and to new ways to be Christians and to be Church!

Introduction

Pilgrimage is a fitting metaphor for our times. Movement, displacement, discovery, embodiment, and encounter appeal to the contemporary mind. It is not surprising that pilgrimages attract broad interest from travelers, dreamers, and readers. This contemporary interest continues a long tradition.

The connection between pilgrimage and religion runs deep. For millennia, people have been making pilgrimages for religious reasons. Some were done as penance, others to fulfill a vow, and many led to conversion and renewed purpose. They were accompanied by rituals and religious symbols. Their destination was usually a sacred place. They came in all shapes and sizes—from local pilgrimages to nearby shrines to extended international journeys. They cut across social classes. As embodied journeys, they are present in different religious traditions—from Hindu pilgrimages along the Ganges River to the Muslim pilgrimage of the Hajj to the Catholic shrine of Lourdes. Pilgrimage sites can even be shared by multiple religions, as in the case, most famously, of Jerusalem.

Despite the enduring popularity of pilgrimages, Christian theology has not fully engaged this reality. Church authorities have certainly talked about, tried to regulate, and encouraged pilgrimages. They have provided liturgies and prayers. At the Second Vatican Council, Roman Catholicism even adopted the title "Pilgrim Church" as a way to talk about the Church on earth.[1] Nonetheless, on the theological front, the scarcity of reflections has been noted, especially the lack of an explicit *theology* of pilgrimage.[2] From this oversight stems an invitation to consider pilgrimage in theology anew.

Part of theology's uneasiness regarding pilgrimage is because the "action" of going on a pilgrimage usually precedes any discourse about it. The phenomenon comes first and overflows the frame of regular church practices and theological discourse. Pilgrimage is also rooted in popular religiosity, locating it at the periphery of usual sources of theological reflection.[3] Moreover, because pilgrimage is not a religious obligation in Christianity—unlike in Islam—its place is not automatically secured at the heart of faith and theological inquiry. Pilgrimage has also historically been a contentious subject within Christianity, especially in the wake of the Protestant Reformation in the sixteenth century. Consequently, the place of pilgrimage within Christianity can be conflicted.

The aim of this book is to contribute to the embrace of pilgrimage in theology. Pilgrimage can challenge theology and the Church regarding ways to consider God, personal faith, commitment, and community. How can pilgrimage help us rethink the Church and Christian life? Since the language of pilgrimage is so prevalent in Christianity, what does it mean for the Church in her self-definition? The full realization of the Church's self-intuition as "pilgrim" is still ahead of us. My hope is to contribute to that discussion.

A BRIEF HISTORY OF PILGRIMAGE IN CHRISTIANITY

The historical origins of Christian pilgrimage can be traced back to the fourth century.[4] Pilgrimages were not born in a vacuum, since Greeks, Hebrews, and other religious groups were already adept centuries before Christians. The legalization of Christianity in the Roman Empire opened the floodgates of Christian pilgrimages. Although local *foci* of pilgrimage already existed, for example the tombs of apostles in Rome, very few extensive journeys are recorded before that time.[5] Helena, the mother of Emperor Constantine, is remembered as an important early pilgrim who toured the Holy Land in 327, building shrines at the major sites associated with the life of Christ.[6] Emperor Constantine secured relics that were then displayed in the new capital city of Constantinople, enhancing its religious prestige.[7] Helena was followed by prominent individuals, some of whom wrote accounts that have reached us: the earliest by a pilgrim from Bordeaux;[8] then Egeria (or Etheria), one of the most famous;[9] and Sts. Jerome and Paula, who moved to the Holy Land.[10] The first criticisms of pilgrimage go back to that period as well. Gregory of Nyssa was critical of such long and costly journeys, questioning the very possibility of the heightened holiness of a given place.[11] Jerome, on the other side, wrote a treatise to respond to the criticism of the priest Vigilantius, defending the cult of relics.[12] At this early stage, pilgrimages to the Holy Land concerned only a tiny slice of the Empire's Christian population since it was an expensive journey with limited infrastructure available to poor pilgrims.

The Middle Ages constitute the Golden Age of pilgrimage. With the fragmentation of the Roman Empire, the rise of Islam, and its conquest of the Holy Land, Christian pilgrimages took on a distinct European flair. Regarding the Holy Land, the various Crusades and the brief Latin dominance over Jerusalem in the twelfth century kept alive the symbolism of the pilgrimage to sites of the life of Christ and the desire to go there. People from different walks of life were able to undertake the journey and brought back memories and relics. The magnificent Sainte-Chapelle in Paris was built to house some of the most precious relics brought back by King Louis IX from his crusade and subsequent purchases in Constantinople. During the late Middle Ages, the difficulty of reaching the Holy Land led to the development of European sanctuaries acting as substitutes,[13] the most famous being the Santa Casa, allegedly transported from Nazareth to Loreto.[14] Alongside these, a variety of shrines (local, national, or international) sprouted all over Europe: Santiago de Compostela, on the alleged grave of St. James the apostle; Canterbury, site of the martyrdom of St. Thomas Becket; many places graced with miracles or miraculous statues (Montserrat, Liesse, Czestochowa, Rocamadour, Walsingham). The revival of the Jubilee tradition in 1300 by Pope Boniface VIII also gave a new impetus to pilgrimages to Rome. That year, tens of thousands of pilgrims are said to have congregated in the Eternal City.

Pilgrimages took place firmly alongside other popular devotions and became a massive phenomenon. Europeans undertook pilgrimages by the thousands, coming from all social groups, from the destitute to the wealthiest. A network of monasteries and almshouses catered to the throngs of pilgrims flocking to the various shrines. The Church tried at times to regulate such influxes, issuing rules and decrees to distinguish genuine pilgrims from wanderers. Clothing—with staff, shell, and calabash—would signify one's pilgrim identity. Pilgrims would undertake the journey to fulfill a vow, to seek a favor or a healing. Civil authorities also made use of pilgrimage as an instrument of expiation of serious offenses, using the journey of the pilgrim as a means to punish the offender—and perhaps achieve a change in them.[15] Thieves also took advantage of the many pilgrims traveling on insecure roads, making the journey a dangerous one.

Pilgrims were especially drawn to relics or miraculous statues and icons, which would determine a sanctuary's fame. Relics provided an immediate sensory experience of seeing and touching. They also connected the pilgrims with the memory of their forebears. Vezelay and Saint-Maximin-la-Sainte-Baume vied for the honor of harboring Mary Magdalen's body. The body of Benedict, father of Western monasticism, was transferred from the derelict abbey of Monte Cassino to that of Fleury (Saint-Benoît-sur-Loire). Other relics were stolen under cover of night. Pious collections housing thousands of relics were assembled, like the one of Frederick III (1463–1525), Elector of Saxony, in Wittenberg, which Martin Luther saw in his days.

The medieval pilgrimage was a major phenomenon in the Church, attracting its fair share of praise and criticism. Geoffrey Chaucer's *Canterbury Tales*, with the retelling of the mundane intentions of its wide cast of pilgrim characters, testifies to the social and cultural penetration of pilgrimage. The strength of the spiritual movements of the Late Middle Ages, such as the *devotio moderna*, enhanced the dimension of the inner journey at work in the life of Christians beyond the more external devotion of pilgrimage.

The Reformation gave voice to Luther and Calvin's scathing criticisms of actual pilgrimages,[16] as part of their rebuttal of components of popular religiosity and theological developments not spelled out in the Bible. In his explanations of the *Ninety-Five Theses*, Luther argued that there was no need to go far and spend that much money to encounter God, and that charity to the local poor was more worthy than any pilgrimage and procession.[17] Although he recognized a potentially positive outcome for pilgrimages done with faith-filled motives of penance or devotion, he argued that such a result is only attained by very few pilgrims. Erasmus, on the Catholic side, had already mocked pilgrimages in his *Colloquies*, while Calvin followed Luther's lead, and with them went the Protestant tradition. The Council of Trent, while not addressing pilgrimage per se, reaffirmed nonetheless the intrinsic value of the veneration of the relics of saints and sacred images, the usual focal point of many pilgrimages.[18]

The early modern period, through the geographical expansion of the Catholic footprint, witnessed the creation of pilgrimage sites in the New World, Guadalupe and Beaupré in the Americas, among others. It ushered in a new era and new contexts for the medieval pilgrimage tradition. The Enlightenment distracted attention from the popular devotions that pilgrimage represented; bishops even tried to forbid some pilgrimages in the late seventeenth and eighteenth centuries.[19] The elitist and secular *Grand Tour* would cut new roads of discovery across Europe, often culminating nonetheless in Rome, though with a romantic and esthetic emphasis, more than a religious one. But though weakened, the pilgrimage phenomenon would not die.[20]

The nineteenth century saw an increase in accessibility to pilgrimage that continues to our day. With the development of mass transportation, starting with the train, access to various shrines became faster and more convenient for large numbers of Christians, leading to the emergence of shorter pilgrimages to far-flung shrines. The Marian focus is noteworthy among the major pilgrimage centers that materialized at the turn of the century, especially the shrines of Lourdes (1858) and Fatima (1917), which quickly rose to prominence. The political landscape in the Holy Land, in addition to the greater ease of travel, also allowed for a renewed interest in pilgrimages to Jerusalem and its surrounding area, this time even by Protestants.[21]

In the second half of the twentieth century, the rise of the middle class and the greater affordability of travel have internationalized the scope of many pilgrimages. The genre has also been revitalized through a series of initiatives. From the grassroots, the ecumenical community of Taizé has attracted generations of God-seeking pilgrims to a small French village and, more recently, to an annual "European meeting" in a major European city. In Spain, the ancient road to Santiago de Compostela has met with a renewed interest in the last thirty years, both through popular culture (Paulo

Coelho's novel *The Pilgrimage* [1987] and the movie *The Way* [2010]), word of mouth, promotion by the Church, and the financial support of governmental entities.[22] The Camino, as it is known, is undertaken by pilgrims for a variety of reasons, and many of them have an agnostic worldview.[23] In 1985, Pope John Paul II launched World Youth Day, an international pilgrimage bringing together young pilgrims from all over the world to a different location about every other year.[24] The same pope was also behind the Great Jubilee of the Year 2000, for which he himself became a pilgrim to Jerusalem, while attracting millions of pilgrims to Rome.

Today, the name "pilgrimage" is claimed broadly, and is not restricted to its original Christian—often Catholic—religious context. Even the revival of ancient pilgrimage roads that are physically demanding is often driven by reasons other than religious, sometimes even not spiritual. A greater knowledge and openness to the experience of spiritual journeys in other religious traditions has also expanded the contemporary horizon of pilgrimage. The enduring valuation of the pilgrimage experience suggests an ongoing relevance amidst shapes that are transformed. The current strength of pilgrimage in various settings, often independent of religious fervor, suggests that it responds to desires that are deeply rooted in human nature.

DENOMINATIONAL AND CULTURAL PERSPECTIVES

Within the Christian tradition, there are strong denominational perspectives on pilgrimage. Even when not explicitly acknowledged, they loom large in the analyses of pilgrimage—sometimes with polemical overtones. The Catholic and the Protestant perspectives, broadly speaking, are the two main ones, whereas the Orthodox, less present in the academy, is similar to the Catholic.[25]

The Protestant perspective often shows an innate unease with aspects of the pilgrimage phenomenon. The unforgiving criticisms by the Reformers of abuses in medieval pilgrimages led in due course to a purely metaphorical understanding of pilgrimage in the Protestant tradition. It is best exemplified by Bunyan's *The Pilgrim's*

Progress (1678). In an interesting inversion of perspective, the initial *metaphor* of pilgrimage—that is, the Christian's interior pilgrimage to God—becomes the *literal* one, despite the fact that conceptually and historically, the actual phenomenon of pilgrimage predates a purely spiritual understanding of an inner pilgrimage.[26] Zygmunt Bauman observes pithily, "The Protestants, as Weber told us, accomplished a feat unthinkable for the lonely hermits of yore: they became *inner-worldly pilgrims*. They invented the way of embarking on pilgrimage without leaving home and of leaving home without becoming homeless."[27] This "invention" was nonetheless in line with a long spiritual tradition of journey or ascent that was recast as inner pilgrimage. Moreover, as Heather Walton asserts, "What is important to note now is that pilgrimage is not only an incidental metaphor within Protestant piety; it is probably *the* dominant metaphor."[28] From there stems an insistence on the priority of the inner pilgrimage over the embodied one. In another direction, developments of the last century and a half have seen Protestants undertake "study tours" in the Holy Land—much akin in their form to Catholic pilgrimages—and recover an appreciation for the embodiment of the sacred, while often shying away from the historically loaded vocabulary of pilgrimage.[29] These study tours are pilgrimages, but not in name! Protestant scholarship on pilgrimage also tends to focus on Jerusalem, reflecting the priority of Scripture and a lesser regard for the tradition of the Church. For example, in the analysis of the New Testament, it would lead to a specific interest in the diminished role of Jerusalem and its temple for early Christians, to assess the shift away from a theology of place.[30]

On the Catholic side, an uninterrupted practice of pilgrimage for centuries offers a congenial milieu for an academic exploration. However, such continuity should not hide the long stream of criticisms of pilgrimage—from its inception to our days, sometimes from an authoritative perspective—as well as the major transformations experienced by the pilgrimage phenomenon throughout the ages and their great diversity at any given moment.[31] Pilgrimage is seen as a multipolar reality, often linked to the ecclesial structure but sometimes at dissonance with it.[32]

The tension between the inner dimension of pilgrimage and its exterior form—dichotomized in the Protestant perspective—can be eased by the desired conjunction of both. Pope John Paul II displays such a synthesis that combines the embodied dimensions of pilgrimage and the interiority of a faith journey, while launching his Jubilee 2000 initiative:

> A pilgrimage evokes the believer's personal journey in the footsteps of the Redeemer: it is an exercise of practical asceticism, of repentance for human weaknesses, of constant vigilance over one's own frailty, of interior preparation for a change of heart. Through vigils, fasting and prayer, the pilgrim progresses along the path of Christian perfection, striving to attain, with the support of God's grace, "the state of the perfect man, to the measure of the full maturity of Christ" (Eph 4:13).[33]

Pilgrimage is not only an exterior practice, but an invitation to personal transformation.

Regarding the Orthodox tradition, one particular trope distinct from its Catholic counterpart is revealed in the famous *Way of the Pilgrim*, first published in Russian in 1884, which narrates the quest of a wandering pilgrim to pray unceasingly.[34] It depicts vividly the spiritual search of a pilgrim who sets out on a journey on foot after a personal loss, visiting holy places along the way, but without setting his sight on a specific destination since his north star is an inner striving. The Catholic Church, for its part, has always been wary of turning pilgrimage into an actual way of life, condemning, for example, wandering monks, since pilgrimage was understood as a moment in one's life journey from which pilgrims come back to resume, transformed, their life.

Another important often unrecognized bias is that of one's culture, which encompasses language and geography. An English-speaker thinking of pilgrimage would think of Chaucer's *Canterbury Tales*, Bunyan's *Pilgrim's Progress*, or *The Book of Margery Kempe*, while for the Russian Orthodox, *The Way of the Pilgrim* would impose itself. In French or Spanish, no work of literature would come to the fore with such prominence, but local places would—more than for Americans, for example. The French would think of Lourdes first, then maybe Lisieux, Mont Saint-Michel, or Vezelay. Mexicans would have Our Lady of Guadalupe in mind, while Canadians would think of St. Joseph's Oratory, Sainte-Anne de Beaupré, or Notre-Dame-du-Cap. The English would think of Canterbury or Walsingham, but maybe even more of Jerusalem. In a more secular milieu, the Camino of Santiago de Compostela would likely come to mind first. Hence, the mental image that one has of pilgrimage and its geography—literary or literal—is powerfully shaped by one's culture.[35]

TOWARD A *THEOLOGY* OF PILGRIMAGE

There is an increasing diversity of approaches to pilgrimages, with numerous writings. Narratives abound, from Egeria's travel to James Martin's,[36] including countless accounts of pilgrims on the Camino. Devotional material and guidebooks on various pilgrimages are also plentiful. In the academy, various disciplines in the humanities and social sciences have analyzed many pilgrimages, from the perspectives of history,[37] anthropology, especially with the seminal work of Victor Turner,[38] sociology,[39] or philosophy. Even life sciences have lately developed an interest in pilgrimage.[40] Contemporary approaches are often multidisciplinary by nature. An expansion of the horizon beyond the confines of the Eurocentric vision has also gained traction, considering pilgrimage in an international context and in various religious settings.[41]

On the theological front, production is more limited. *Explorations in a Christian Theology of Pilgrimage* (Hants, UK: Ashgate, 2004), a volume edited by Craig Bartholomew and Fred Hughes, did pioneering work by bringing together various theological perspectives to the study of pilgrimage. I will engage with many of its chapters throughout this book. A decade later, the book *Christian Pilgrimage, Landscape and Heritage: Journeying to the Sacred* (New York: Routledge, 2015) by Avril Maddrell, Veronica della Dora, Alessandro Scafi, and Heather Walton, especially the first chapter by Walton titled "Theological Perspectives on Christian Pilgrimage," grappled directly with the theological import of the phenomenon of pilgrimage.

Monographs and theses have also contributed robustly to the field. Christof May's *Pilgern: Menschsein auf dem Weg* (Würzburg: Echter, 2004), a dissertation in theology, touches on the biblical foundations as well as literary incarnations of pilgrimage.[42] Jeffrey G.

Sobosan's *Pilgrimage Theology in the Documents of Vatican II* (ThD Thesis, Berkeley: Graduate Theological Union, 1977), an unpublished dissertation, analyzes the documents from the Second Vatican Council through the lens of pilgrimage. Other monographs, such as J. G. Davies's *Pilgrimage Yesterday, and Today: Why? Where? How?* (London: SCM, 1988), also contributed a more integrated approach to the field. In preparation for the Jubilee of 2000, the Holy See published various documents enriching reflection on the theology of pilgrimage.[43] Another interesting trend is the encounter of pilgrimage with the budding theology of migration, since parallels exist between pilgrim and migrant. Overall, the field of theological research is not yet fully integrated into broader pilgrimage studies and vice versa.[44]

The contribution of this book is located at the confluence of a multidisciplinary approach that benefits from the humanities, while it unfolds on the ground of theological inquiry. The scope of pilgrimages envisioned in this book encompasses only Christianity, since it is already very broad and extremely diverse, but harmonies with other types of pilgrimages are mentioned at times.[45] The main aim of this research is to explore what pilgrimage has to teach about God, the faithful, and the Church. Taking pilgrimage seriously can challenge and enrich theology.

Not all threads will be pursued in this exploration; this book does not aim at comprehensiveness. There is a *propositional* quality to the endeavor, more than an encyclopedic one. Not everything about pilgrimage is covered, but a certain path is sketched that certainly allows for a subjective dimension. In this intellectual journey, four questions are explored that present some overlap but are not forced into a single narrative. The contribution of each perspective is honored for its own sake but allows connections to emerge to enlighten new directions. Various sources are taken into consideration: historical material, biblical narratives, spiritual writings, literary sources, and Church documents. Multiple methodologies are used throughout, in congruence with the objects. Hence, each chapter relies more heavily on a distinct methodological approach. While the book is written with the whole picture in mind, the chapters can be used independently since they each have their own perspective. The wager is that the various angles can contribute to a richer understanding of pilgrimage and trigger avenues of integrative reflection and research.

The journey of *The Pilgrim Paradigm* unfolds in four chapters. Chapter 1 deals with a central question: What is Christian pilgrimage? The question is more difficult than it appears at first. The notion of pilgrimage is claimed broadly, encompassing a variety of realities. Even by limiting the scope to Christianity, the dimensions are manifold. This chapter develops a phenomenologically inspired, ideal type of Christian pilgrimage built around ten characteristics: intention, transcendence, memory, departure, destination, embodiment, vulnerability, effort, alterity, and transformation. In conversation with anthropology, history, literature, and theology, the aim of the chapter is to offer lenses through which discrete journeys can be analyzed and suggest a framework according to which Christian pilgrimage could be compared to other types of pilgrimages, religious or secular.

Chapter 2 explores the pilgrim experience of the people of God in the Old Testament as well as the new orientation to pilgrimage brought about by the Christ event. With the help of biblical studies, some important moments in the history of the people of God as pilgrim are developed to contribute to the theological discussion around the very soundness of Christian pilgrimage. The collective dimension of pilgrimage—in exodus, exile, or mission—the importance of place and movement, and the pilgrimages of Jesus are highlighted. The aim of the chapter is to provide a biblical foundation for the Christian understanding of pilgrimage, addressing the question, "How is pilgrimage connected to Christian Scriptures?"

Chapter 3 focuses on the spiritual pedagogy of pilgrimage for formation and identity through a single, early modern model: Ignatius of Loyola (1491–1556). Through the narrative of the *Testament*, in which Ignatius labels himself "the pilgrim," as well as through the experiment of pilgrimage that he prescribed for Jesuits-in-training, a rich understanding of pilgrimage appears as a lived experience, a literary device for self-understanding, a mystical way of life, and a formational tool used to invite others into the experience of movement toward God. This chapter is grounded in a close analysis of the text of the *Testament*. It addresses the questions of *how* Ignatius was a pilgrim and how he used pilgrimage as a pedagogical tool for others.

Chapter 4 explores the adoption of the expression "Pilgrim Church" (*Ecclesia peregrinans*), which was held up by the Second Vatican Council (1962–65), as an important image to depict and understand the Church. This expression, which finds its roots in Augustine's *City of God*, was later carried over into the liturgy of the Roman Catholic Church. The contours and context of the emergence of the name are analyzed, as well as its embodiment in the teaching and pilgrimages of Popes Paul VI and John Paul II. The fundamental questions are: What is meant by "Pilgrim Church," and has this insight been fully assimilated by the Church?

A brief conclusion addresses the connection between pilgrimage and the Holy Spirit. Pilgrimage, like the Spirit, ultimately escapes us!

Overall, the aim is to explore the richness of the pilgrimage metaphor and reality to see how we can let ourselves be challenged theologically—intellectually and practically—by pilgrim insights. Pilgrimage calls us to journey!

CHAPTER 1

What Is Christian Pilgrimage?

The Ideal Type of a Phenomenon

In the United States, *Pilgrims* first evokes the settlers who fled Anglican England in the seventeenth century to come to the North Atlantic shore of the New World. In a more contemporary key, many books written nowadays about pilgrimages, especially personal accounts, focus on the Camino of Santiago de Compostela. Medieval pilgrimages are carefully studied, pilgrimage courses offered, and the pilgrimage industry is booming. Since the notion of pilgrimage enjoys a positive reputation, its mantle is fashionable, and thus claimed by many.

Through the multitude of pilgrimages over the centuries, it is difficult to establish an agreed-upon definition (with neatly lined characteristics) beyond a generic understanding as journey to a sacred place. However, such attempt is useful to probe at once the various forms of pilgrimages, as well as to see how a given pilgrimage experience could be enhanced by a careful consideration of its characteristics.

1. DEFINING PILGRIMAGE

There are many definitions of *pilgrimage*, and these have evolved over the years. By surveying briefly three important and distinct language groups, English, French, and Spanish, a general landscape of the understanding of the linguistic concept of pilgrimage emerges.[1]

The core component of the definition of *pilgrimage* consists in a journey to a sacred place out of devotion. This is the basic definition of *pilgrimage* in the Christian realm. Some qualifiers can be added. The *journey* can be individual or collective and is usually long. The *sacred place* can be replaced by a place of significant interest. The emphasis on *sacredness* stresses the distinction between sacred and profane spaces. In the French usage, the destination can be equated to the pilgrimage itself—notwithstanding the journey—emphasizing the traditional predominance of the destination over the journey to go there.[2] The *devotional* dimension of the core pilgrimage definition is sometimes expressed through its religious aspect, but at other times omitted. Some more dynamic definitions emphasize the dimension of *quest* at work in pilgrimage.[3]

Insightful nuances and additions can be gathered from further definitions of *pilgrimage*. The first meaning of the Spanish *peregrinar* given by the *Diccionario de la Real Academia Española* is "going to a foreign land."[4] This definition, which does not describe the religious phenomenon, nonetheless uncovers the classical Latin meaning of *peregrinus*, "foreigner," and thus the distance or even exoticism suggested by the notion of pilgrimage.

The more metaphorical definition of *pilgrimage* as "the course of life on earth,"[5] or "life viewed as a journey,"[6] is well attested to in English. It also appears in Spanish for the cognate verb *peregrinar*: "in some religions, to live while understanding life as a road to be travelled in order to reach a future life of union with God after death."[7] According to this definition, pilgrimage undergoes two changes: first, it becomes an interior movement, through an inner understanding of life, and second, it encompasses the whole of life, not only a limited period.

One of the early secular linguistic developments of pilgrimage appears in French, whereas the memorial dimension of the sacred place—associated in Christianity with a particular manifestation of the divine in a person or a place—is extended to other objects of (nonreligious) devotion. Hence, a definition that originates in the nineteenth century depicts pilgrimage as a "trip realized with the intention of giving homage to a place or a great individual that one reveres."[8] In English, we could find also a similar definition as "any long journey, especially one undertaken as a quest or for a votive purpose, as to pay homage."[9] The object is no longer Christ, the Virgin Mary, or another saint, but a place or person important for secular reasons (political, literary, historical, etc.).

A final development is offered by the Spanish substantive *romería*—more specifically used for "pilgrimage" than *peregrinación*. The first meaning of *romería* corresponds to the general definition of *pilgrimage* that we have identified. The other two meanings open up new territories as "popular feast celebrated with food, dances, etc., in the field next to some hermitage or sanctuary on the day of the religious festivity of that place,"[10] then "large number of people who gather in one site."[11] While the latter meaning is derived from the former and is completely secular, the former retains a clear religious connection. It highlights two elements. First, that the pilgrimage entails a festive celebration, especially as one reaches the destination. In that regard, the journey itself is not emphasized, but the proper celebration at the sanctuary. The second element is the communal aspect of such a pilgrimage, with food, dance, and people. These definitions act as a corrective to our initial definition by bringing forward the conviviality and celebration in the pilgrim phenomenon so it is not reduced to an individual ascetical endeavor.

If we were to continue this research into other linguistic areas, new nuances and developments would emerge. Furthermore, in religious or cultural contexts that are strikingly different, other pilgrimage harmonics would play out, hence the importance of not assuming that the core definition of *pilgrimage* is universal. Dionigi Albera and John Eade alerted us to the pitfalls of such shortcuts.[12]

This brief analysis of the definitions of *pilgrimage* in the Western world through three linguistic areas delivers the core definition at work in a Christian mindset, but it also shows that there are already spin-off definitions highlighting some components of pilgrimage or setting it into new directions. The richness and plasticity of the definition creates space for a further exploration of pilgrimage through the delineation of its essential characteristics.

2. PILGRIMS AND *TUTTI QUANTI*: CONTRASTING FIGURES AND SHAPES

Movement defines pilgrimage, but not all phenomena defined by movement are pilgrimages. Anthropologists, sociologists, philosophers, and theologians have compared the figure of the pilgrim to other kinetic figures. The pilgrim can been contrasted with the vagabond, wanderer, or *flâneur* (stroller), who are on the move, but without a clear direction, and do not necessarily display a religious idea.[13] A variation of that figure would be the homeless person, who is on the move, has no place to call home, but is not striving for a destination—they are without a home.[14] The tourist is also compared to the pilgrim; both travel, often to foreign sites, alone or in a group, leaving their home to undertake a journey.[15] The case of the religious tourist is even closer, as the word *pilgrim* is often used as a synonym. The figure of the pilgrim is also linked with that of the hiker, since some adventures on outdoor trails are claimed as pilgrimages.[16] The migrant, and especially the refugee, are also interesting points of comparison to understand pilgrimage, since they share common theological foundations, as well as some features.[17] They both leave home and travel light, but their reasons for leaving, their intention, the risks they encounter, and the welcome they receive—or not—are strikingly different. The concept of pilgrimage can also be likened to the literary odyssey, a long journey engaging one's identity.[18] On the other hand, the pilgrim can be contrasted with the radically stable figure of committed Christian life: the monk.[19] The comparison of the pilgrimage phenomenon with other constituted instances of movement brings to light some dimensions to consider, for example, commitment and length[20] or the relation to the frontier and the center.[21]

Pilgrimages take different shapes. Various religions besides Judaism and Christianity foster the practice of pilgrimage, for example, Islam—for which it is a prescribed pillar of the faith[22]—Hinduism, Shintoism, Buddhism, and so on.[23] Pilgrimage can also take secular forms, for example as a journey to commemorate an historical event or person. Even in the Christian realm, which is that of this research, pilgrimages take various shapes. It can lead one abroad or to a different part of town. It can take months to complete or only hours. It can be done individually or in a group. It can imply an athletic amount of walking or mostly touring by bus. The destination reached can be an ancient and popular site, or a more recent and less crowded location. The contemporary experience of the parish group going to a local shrine, the pilgrims walking from Saint-Jean Pied-de-Port to Santiago, or a couple going on a five-star pilgrimage to the Holy Land would produce distinct experiences and memories, but a common underlying reality of pilgrimage can be deciphered in all of them.

3. APPROACHING PILGRIMAGE: TOWARD AN IDEAL TYPE

The distillation of the essential characteristics of pilgrimage is not an easy task, since pilgrimage is a multifaceted phenomenon that extends over millennia. While some argue that such a task is impossible or cannot produce a coherent result,[24] others have attempted to offer a contribution to theorize pilgrimage.

The anthropologist Victor Turner remains a reference in that regard through a structuralist approach, even as one might disagree with his model.[25] Many key categories of Turner's analysis are now commonplace. Among them, his concept of liminality refers to a "state and process of mid-transition in a rite of passage" in which the pilgrims are "betwixt and between," having shed some characteristics of their previous status (social status, authority) and entered a new realm.[26] Another important concept is that of *communitas* or "social antistructure," which defines the free and fluid connection—and potential communion—that emerges spontaneously among pilgrims—despite their great diversity.[27] French historian Alphonse Dupront also penned an "anthropology of pilgrimage," trying to capture some of its fundamental characteristics. Dupront highlights three characteristics of pilgrimage, grounding the pilgrim phenomenon in the depth of human nature; recognizing: (1) the necessity of the sacred place in the human religious experience, (2) the pilgrimage as an "extraordinary" deed in the human quest for the sacred, and (3) the pilgrimage as a will of power, collective or individual.[28]

A phenomenological approach could be structured many ways. A linear presentation of pilgrimage could equate the various temporal steps of the pilgrimage to its constitutive elements. Christof May proposes in that regard four steps, which he links to an anthropological flow: departure (*Aufbruch*), journey (*Weg*), arrival (*Ankunft*), and return (*Rückkehr*).[29] To these steps, one might add the preparation for the journey. The linear presentation highlights the various moments constitutive of the pilgrimage journey, but they do not uncover all its characteristics. The Vatican document "The Pilgrimage in the Great Jubilee" (1998) similarly uses four steps while adding a clear sense of worship and mission.[30]

Other attempts have been made to sketch the characteristics of pilgrimage. One of the most interesting is that of Martin Robinson through the eleven sections of his anthology on pilgrimage.[31] Robinson's intent was modest: to divide the material he was bringing to the fore in a coherent way. In doing so, however, he already highlighted some essential elements at work in pilgrimage.

A systematic approach to pilgrimage can bear interesting fruit. Taking into consideration the multiplicity of experiences of pilgrimages—a diversity that should be celebrated—the aim of this chapter is to establish the essential characteristics of pilgrimage seen from the perspective of the pilgrims' journey.[32] The approach is flexible enough to embrace the historical, geographical, and cultural diversity of pilgrimages. The pilgrimage phenomena draw on constitutive elements of the human experience, but our reflection is not located only at an anthropological level, since in Christian pilgrimages those elements are channeled through a religious framework and theological discourse. The recourse to the vocabulary of "phenomenon" in this chapter pertains to primacy given to embodied pilgrimages as they appear or present themselves—to dwell on the Greek root of *phainō*. Pilgrimage as phenomenon is a visible, lived experience. From that vantage point, pilgrimage appears first as an embodied reality, though it does not exclude the spiritual dimension or the reflection on the experience.

The delineation of main characteristics implies a task of deconstructing/reconstructing a systematic framework. Such an endeavor is propositional and constructive. An ideal type of pilgrimage thus emerges. As such, it aims to shape a definition of pilgrimage against which any phenomenon claiming the name of pilgrimage could be compared. This endeavor is clearly open to criticism and debate, but it also offers useful anchors to explore in more depth the concept of pilgrimage in its broadest way—even beyond the realm of Christianity. Although the ideal pilgrimage could be an evanescent reality, the working hypothesis is that the pilgrim experience has enough internal coherence to lend itself to systematization despite its multiplicity of forms. The various components are explored in their depth and interrelation, in turn becoming criteria to assess discrete experiences of pilgrimage. While some components are inescapable, others allow for a greater or lesser degree of actuation. The work of definition is achieved more in nuances than in exclusion. Most components taken individually are not exclusive to pilgrimage. Woven together, they constitute the canvas of actual pilgrim experiences. The depth, importance, and obviousness of the characteristics are distinct, but the pace of exposition of all of them is brisk, allowing for a larger view. All the characteristics developed are based on a long tradition and resonate to various degrees with the present experience of pilgrims.

This phenomenology of pilgrimage unfolds in ten core characteristics. In a first part are essential conditions:

1. intention,
2. transcendence, and
3. memory.

The second part encompasses the geography of movement through

4. departure, and
5. the destination.

The third set of characteristics gathers the experience on the road, through the living out of the pilgrimage:

6. embodiment,
7. vulnerability,
8. effort, and
9. alterity.

Part ten explores "transformation?"—the lasting impact (or not) of the pilgrimage experience upon return—hence, the question mark. Together, all ten characteristics sketch the core ideal type of the phenomenon of pilgrimage that goes beyond the basic definition of a journey to a sacred place and accounts for the depth of the experience. We will now explore each characteristic.

4. THREE ESSENTIAL CONDITIONS: INTENTION, TRANSCENDENCE, AND MEMORY

The three essential conditions of intention, transcendence, and memory are present throughout the pilgrimage even before it begins but are not linked to only one temporal aspect of the unfolding. They are foundational in defining pilgrimage through and through, but they are also the most immaterial of categories since they cannot be seen or assessed from outside. They are nonetheless integral parts of the phenomenon of pilgrimage as a whole.

Intention

The first characteristic of pilgrimage is present both as its initial impetus and continuous engine. Pilgrimage is not simply any kind of travel. Because it is not a religious obligation for Christians, the motive is personal, although it could be religiously motivated. One can be a good Christian without ever making a pilgrimage. The intention of being on pilgrimage, both initial and continuous, is intrinsically part of the experience.[33] As a subjective component, it cannot be assessed from the exterior,[34] but it ties in firmly the component of interiority to the pilgrim experience. Pilgrimage is not simply a performance, and the interior and exterior dimensions cannot be kept apart.

The intention holds a *declarative* value. One claims—or recognizes—one's status as pilgrim, as a person on a journey toward a sacred or holy place. To be a pilgrim always requires a personal decision.[35] While the intention could be implicit, unclear in its object or even its voicing, the moment of decision is essential—the decision to undertake not simply a trip or a visit, but a pilgrimage.[36] Brian Brendan O'Malley expresses that choice by saying, "To treat a journey as a pilgrimage is to make it a symbolic act whereby we recognize the transitory nature of our life on earth and that it has a greater goal beyond itself; and whereby we pledge in faith that it is a journey towards God."[37] A value is added to the performance of the deeds.

One can, however, *become* a pilgrim, developing that intention while already on the road. Thomas Merton, in his autobiographical *The Seven Storey Mountain*, relates a visit to Rome as a young man that started as tourism but gradually turned into a pilgrimage, which he could only identify afterward. The inner quest that was aroused led him to prayer, presence, and the beginning of a conversion.

> After about a week—I don't know how it began—I found myself looking into churches rather than into ruined temples....I was fascinated by these Byzantine mosaics. I began to haunt the churches where they were to be found, and, as an indirect consequence, all the other churches that were more or less of the same period. And thus *without knowing anything about it I became a pilgrim*. I was unconsciously and unintentionally visiting all the great shrines of Rome, and seeking out their sanctuaries with some of *the eagerness and avidity and desire of a true pilgrim*, though not quite for the right reason. And yet it was not for a wrong reason either. For these mosaics and frescoes and all the ancient altars and thrones and sanctuaries were designed and built for the instruction of people who were not capable of immediately understanding anything higher....
>
> I read more and more of the Gospels, and my love for the old churches and their mosaics grew from day to day. Soon I was no longer visiting them merely for the art. There was something else that attracted me: a kind of deep and strong conviction that I belonged there: that my rational nature was filled with profound desires and needs that could only find satisfaction in churches of God.[38]

Merton expresses admirably the dialectic between the places visited and the desire that they awoke in him. Uncharacteristically, the visits came first, but the desire to encounter something then grew. He became a pilgrim.[39]

At the heart of the intention, even beyond the core elements of the definition of pilgrimage as journey to a sacred place, lies the quest. The pilgrim, even before undertaking their journey, but also during it, is someone who seeks, hopes, and desires. This yearning does not necessarily have a clear object, but it must inhabit the pilgrim. The object of the yearning could be that of completing the journey, or even of reaching the destination, but yearning consists primarily in a foundational disposition. Without it, no pilgrimage is possible.

Despite the formal similarities between the travel of the tourist and that of the pilgrim, the intention underlining their journey distinguishes them clearly, though not necessarily at a visible level. Turner famously wrote that "a tourist is half a pilgrim, if a pilgrim is half a tourist."[40] That a pilgrim is half a tourist is not problematic. They potentially share many exterior actions: they can visit the same sites, take the same pictures, eat in the same restaurants, and sleep in the same hotels. Even the religious tourist, whose travel focuses on religious sites or events, is different from a pilgrim. They can even share the same bus or the same trip, but the intentionality of their journey is distinct: pilgrims are not simply visiting a place; they bring themselves there on a quest to encounter transcendence. The distinction between tourist and pilgrim could appear immaterial—and it is—but it is essential to the *ethos* of the pilgrimage. These figures are not mutually exclusive, but they are distinct.

In reverse, the tourist is *not* half a pilgrim. Some could be, but one cannot generalize. The pilgrim is fundamentally on a quest. The intention of their pilgrimage could be manifold: a clear desire to connect with a foundational faith event, a desire to break away from the quotidian because of one's dissatisfaction, a hope of something else, a desire to think or pray about some loss, transition, or difficulty. Intentionality is not clear-cut. It could be open-ended, but there must be a desire, as unspecific as it could be. No one *is* a pilgrim inadvertently, although one can *become* a pilgrim. Turner's example of the tourist on the beach desiring implicitly to be part of the *communitas* does not warrant an impetus strong enough to qualify for a robust intention, even as we allow for undefined ones.

It does not follow that pilgrims have a superior status than other travelers, but simply that they are of a different kind.

The intention of the pilgrimage could be tentatively imposed upon the pilgrim. Although such a condition sounds foreign and even deeply problematic to contemporary ears, it was not unheard of in the Middle Ages, when a pilgrimage was sometimes imposed as a punishment by civil authorities—in the hope of transformation.[41] While the materiality of the pilgrim journey can be imposed, its intentionality cannot. A medieval pilgrimage could also be done by proxy, if one was unable to undertake it oneself or wanted to multiply the benefits reaped.[42] In a testament, it was also possible to ask that a certain number of pilgrimages be commissioned on one's behalf,[43] just as one could ask that Masses be celebrated for one's soul. Hence, the intentionality is not only something very personal, but it could be received from someone else—and embraced internally or not.[44]

Even though the intentionality of the traveler, tourist, or pilgrim, cannot be tested exteriorly, attempts have been made to differentiate the pilgrim from other travelers, especially when their condition warranted support and privileges. Although pilgrimage is not an obligation for Christians, Christianity has recognized that condition and sought to cater to pilgrims, and even to protect them, while weeding out vagabonds from the throngs of travelers. Even today, the *Credencial del peregrino* is issued by Church authorities on the Camino de Santiago de Compostela, and its fine print reminds travelers who are benefitting from assistance in their journey (e.g., traveling by car) to refrain from using facilities intended for "real" pilgrims. This example shows at once that the line between the pilgrim and the other traveler—the trekker, for example—is thin and not always visible, but that the intentionality of each of their journeys is quite distinct. The difficulty to enforce the "correct" intention—onto a form that might seem right—is prominent in the issue of the ecclesial approval—or disapproval—of pilgrimage, which has been a point of contention for centuries.[45] Church authorities did not initiate most pilgrimages. These tend to develop by themselves organically[46] and sometimes gain an ecclesial stamp of approval.[47] At other times, Church authorities tried to quell, with or without success, some practices that were associated with pilgrimages and considered problematic.[48] The tensions that surface at times between the ecclesiastical authorities and the grassroots nature of pilgrimage highlight its inner logic that can resist the ecclesial oversight of its intention. In that regard, Dominique Julia talks about the "*anecclésial*"[49] character of pilgrimage—not anti-ecclesial, but at the margins of the institutional Church.

The strong rootedness of the desire for pilgrimage in the life of the individual grounds the preparation that could be extensive. In this sense, desire or intention constitutes the first preparation, leading up to the actual preparation for the journey.

Beyond the initial desire and the decision to start, the intention of the pilgrimage is meant to be treasured, deepened, and thus to act as a continuous desire. The continuous intention would serve as a compass and a criterion for discernment along the way, pilgrims measuring up to their pilgrimage intention the decisions they have to make on the journey. The continuous desire is often exteriorized through a symbol worn (e.g., the shell) as a reminder for oneself and a sign for others.

Transcendence

Pilgrimage is driven by a quest *for* something that lies beyond oneself, for something more, different, potentially ultimate. It goes back to the Latin root of *pilgrim* as "foreigner"; pilgrimage entails a quest for a physical "elsewhere," or a personified "else." It reveals or ushers in a radical openness in oneself, a self-transcendence, since the quest entails searching beyond oneself, recognizing the desire for something that is missing and pursued. Such radical openness would take up one's being and allow for vulnerability, for hospitality, and for conversion. The pilgrimages of Christians have been "a process of conversion, a yearning for intimacy with God and a trusting plea for their material needs,"[50] claims the Pontifical Council for the Pastoral Care of Migrants and Itinerant People. It underlines this openness to change (through conversion), to the divine (by a yearning for God), and to embodied hope (through a plea for material needs).

The object of the transcendence can be diffuse and ungraspable, as a reach for a reconciliation, healing, a *je-ne-sais-quoi* beyond the quotidian flow of life, which seems unattainable by oneself and can remain nameless. Nonetheless, even without a clear object, transcendence animates the journey of pilgrims and keeps it in a tension that moves them ahead.

The object of the transcendental quest can also be clearly defined. It could be the embodiment of a collective human reality (e.g., nation, ethnic group, family), or have clear religious overtones as a divine figure. Hence, the dimension of transcendence does not necessarily unfold in a religious form, although such religious form is fundamental for the Christian pilgrimage. However, the religious sense of transcendence would also show a wide spectrum, ranging from a minimalist option displaying a desire for something "beyond," associated with a spiritual force, to the maximalist option of a committed Christian going on a pilgrimage to encounter God in an explicitly religious quest. A Christian maximalist option entails a transcendence whose object is a God who is a divine person, able to enter into relationship—as shown especially in Jesus Christ. This transcendence is properly divine.

Historically, the phenomenon of Christian pilgrimage is rooted in a fascination for Jesus Christ, since the pilgrimage to the Holy Land is centered on sites associated with important moments of his life and ministry.[51] Since Christ is defined as both divine and human, Christian pilgrims can connect easily with his humanity in the hope of reaching God, in a companionship of radical difference and nearness. The pilgrim's relationship to Christ is often marked either by petition and praise in relation to his divine status, or discipleship and imitation, in which pilgrims indicate an inner commitment to spend their lives walking in Christ's footsteps.[52] In such instances, the transcendental object of the pilgrimage quest is clearly and richly defined.

In the Catholic and Orthodox traditions, the transcendence dimension often takes the shape of the saint(s) associated with a particular pilgrimage site.[53] They become companions on the journey. The saints are constitutively linked to God, from whom they received holiness, but they each highlight different features of the Christian message and are invoked for specific purposes. First among them are the apostles, whose tombs, located close to early Christian communities, constantly drew devotees. In Rome, the tombs of St. Peter and St. Paul have been *foci* of devotion for Christians since times immemorial. Among other saints, Mary, Mother of God, occupies the most prominent place because of her unique role in salvation. The great sanctuaries of Lourdes and Fatima, among others, exemplify the intercessory role of Mary to God that draws millions of pilgrims to those places.

Following the thread of the maximalist option of an explicitly personified divine transcendence, the importance of rituals, especially prayer, emerges. As such, the transcendence dimension of pilgrimage is not simply a far-fetched building block, but a constant presence reinforced through ritual gestures and prayer. It is located not only at the outset of the journey, but in its ongoing actuation. Prayer, as inner movement, weaves the fabric of the pilgrim's relationship with God along the way, keeping in check the initial impetus of the pilgrimage and fostering the inner growth of the pilgrim. In the maximalist dimension of rituals, prayer accompanies them.[54] By themselves, rituals—not all of them religious—mark through ephemeral gestures the space and time of the quest.[55] In pilgrimages undertaken with a clear religious dimension, prayer constitutes a hallmark, either through collective prayer (e.g., Eucharist, Rosary) or through personal types of prayer. This constant encounter with the divine along the way clearly shapes the journey as a pilgrimage, as opposed to a trek or the travels of a tourist.

Through its broadness, the issue of transcendence should not be reduced to the presence or absence of a religious affiliation, which would normally guarantee a transcendental presence. As we mentioned, the object of transcendence could be unspecified, or expressed in a minimalist way. At the other extreme, a religious affiliation does not guarantee a personal quest for something beyond oneself. Religious affiliation could be objectified, whereas transcendence, as part of the essential conditions, requires a personal immaterial commitment to such openness.

Memory

> Every shrine can be seen as the bearer of a specific message, since it vividly makes present today the foundational event of the past which still speaks to the heart of pilgrims.[56]

Pilgrimage is always a return, a return to the site of an event or a return to sources. Such a return emphasizes the collective dimension of the pilgrimage, since the journey can be completely new for someone, but is always inscribed into someone else's footsteps. Hence, a pilgrimage is always inserted in a larger story, and the current pilgrims take their place within it.

Christian pilgrimages commemorate important faith events, people, and places. "A shrine is first of all a *place of memory*, the memory of God's powerful activity in history, which is the origin of the People of the Covenant and the faith of each believer."[57] By visiting the significant place, pilgrims actualize for themselves the collective memory. Even secular journeys claim the title of pilgrimage when they participate in the encounter with a collective memory.[58] This memory could pertain to the family (e.g., ancestors' place of origin),[59] to the country (e.g., a visit to an important historical site, like Gettysburg), a social group (e.g., faith community), or an important figure in history.[60] The embodied contact with a place encapsulating a collective memory allows pilgrims to enliven the consciousness of their own participation in the story, renewing a sense of belonging. This endeavor could be seen as educationally motivated—when information is imparted—but it also fosters an essential emotional connection. Emotions would achieve the personal connection to the storied location visited, reaching to the depth of the person in ways impossible to information, and calling for a personal engagement. Emotions can be positive when the memory pursued is joyful—for example, visiting an ancestor's birthplace—or more difficult, when the memory is heavy. Pope John Paul II mastered the power of emotions when he invited millions of young adults to join him at World Youth Day in a joyful celebration, but also when he called forth the spirit of repentance during the Jubilee Year of 2000 by praying at the Western Wall in Jerusalem.

Memory is history incarnated, history that matters, history with which one feels connected. Not everything that is historical is memorialized. Memorialization happens when the events have bearing in the present and call for a response.[61] To describe interest in a pilgrimage or its destination as purely historical is to miss the personal engagement that comes from the collective memory of events that have an emotional connection with the pilgrims. Visiting another country's capital city can be historically fulfilling but does not command the same engagement as that of a place one feels personally connected to. The interest is memorial, not only historical. In addition, for premodern minds, historical accuracy was not paramount. The origin of some pilgrimages is the material of legend.[62] But just as our own human memories are at times blurred, selective, or even incorrect, a collective memory based on legendary accounts could prove a valuable foundation when it finds an echo in the people's devotion. Memory calls for engagement. Hence, the historical accuracy of the place is less important than the memory with which it is imbued.[63]

The memorial dimension of pilgrimage determines the relative importance and popularity of pilgrimage shrines. In the Middle Ages especially, the more ancient a pilgrimage site, the higher its standing. The importance of the person or event commemorated also plays a role. Thus, the pilgrimage sites of the Holy Land, which witnessed the life, death, and resurrection of Christ, have been prominent since the fourth century. Rome, as the place of martyrdom of the apostles Peter and Paul also gained a prominence, both on account of its antiquity and the importance of its saints. Santiago de Compostela, through its association with the apostle James, also vied for such prominence. The relics in a given place also contribute to nourish the connection between the pilgrim and the story that is commemorated—the ideal setting being one connecting the relics of the saint to the place.[64] Some of the major pilgrimage sites of the last two centuries cannot claim an ancient character, but those associated with important figures of the faith compensate for their novelty. The nineteenth-century sanctuary of Lourdes, for example, compensates for what it lacks in antiquity by its association with officially recognized apparitions of Mary. The fortune of pilgrimage sites associated with less central events or saints fluctuates over the years, and they often reach a more limited audience.

The passive quality of reception that memory entails explains why a pilgrimage cannot be "invented." Attempts at creating a pilgrimage site—often engineered by religious authorities—are usually short-lived or can be simply functional.[65] Pilgrimage destinations *happen*, and popular acclamation sanctions it, as in the popular canonizations of old. Distinguishing the journey from its destination, new routes can easily be created, where an *event* is required to establish a new pilgrimage site that shows it is not simply human-made. Even from the Church's perspective, a pilgrimage site is less created than merely recognized when the foundational event is—often after an initial reluctance and skepticism. Bernadette Soubirous and the shepherds of Fatima were thoroughly examined. Brother André Bessette, of St. Joseph's Oratory in Montreal, and Padre Pio, of the church of San Giovanni Rotondo, were not always celebrated by their respective communities.[66] The apparitions of Medjugorje are still not officially recognized by Church authorities. An exception to that rule of noncreation would be minor sanctuaries established for convenience—out of devotion, certainly, but without pretending that a miraculous event happened.[67]

The memory in play might also be one's own memory, one's own story in a more immediate way. The pilgrim often walks the road with a story in his baggage. It could be a story of remembrance, of thanksgiving, of regret and expiation. The main character of the movie *The Way* completed the journey to Santiago that had been begun by his suddenly deceased son. Others walk to commemorate another journey they began or completed, like a recovering alcoholic I met on his walk of thanksgiving on the Camino. Important anniversaries or transitions give the impetus for journeys of remembrance.

The memorial dimension of pilgrimage mirrors the sacramental practice of the *anamnesis* in the liturgy of the Eucharist. At the heart of the most central prayer ritual of Christianity lies the commemoration of the last ritual meal of Jesus, prefiguring his self-offering on the cross and his resurrection. This core moment of *anamnesis* occupies the central place of the Eucharistic Prayer, as the memorial retelling of Christ's deeds for his people. The Christian eucharistic liturgy is itself heir to the Jewish *berakah* prayer that recounts God's blessings in the movement of prayer. Consequently, this movement of remembrance and reactualization is strongly rooted in Christian prayer and practice. The past events memorialized are those that continue to extend their reach into the present.

In a more personal and less normative key, the spiritual practice of the examen also fosters the consciousness of inscribing one's life in a larger story by summoning to the memory, for thanksgiving or expiation, the events of the day, and seeing them in the light of one's journey with God.[68] This spiritual practice, which requires one to put aside some time, contributes to revisit and deepen the sense of journeying. By taking time from the quotidian, a pilgrimage often functions as an extended examen, allowing the events of one's life that need revisiting to come to the fore of memory. This introspective exercise is sometimes experienced through group sharing and is often complemented by journaling. The examen is also the locus to revisit the intention of the pilgrimage in its continuous desire, and the nature of the transcendental quest in play.

Finally, pilgrimage is a return, because someone else has been there first—God, as well as others. The pilgrimage site is marked by the memory of a special presence of the divine through an event or a person. The pilgrimage is also filled with the memory of fellow pilgrims, from the pilgrims and saints of old to those of our days. We are never the first, but we commemorate.

5. A GEOGRAPHY OF MOVEMENT: DEPARTURE AND DESTINATION

Movement is essential for pilgrimage, physically, or metaphorically. The movement captured in pilgrimage is deeply rooted in an anthropological reality of physical/geographical movement and existential change.[69] Two characteristics of this movement are developed here: the beginning and the end, departure and destination. What happens on the journey itself will be covered in the subsequent section "On the Road," whereas the return and its aftermath will be discussed in the final section on transformation.

Departure

To undertake a pilgrimage, one must leave home, or at least leave mentally if not physically.[70] Pilgrimage entails movement. A departure from one's current location and situation is necessary. Something is left behind, sometimes even avoided, or fled. The main factor at work in departure is the "pull factor" of the destination in its attractiveness, but some elements of "push factor" could play a role—when the pilgrim wants to distance themself from a heavy situation. While refugees are often forced to leave in a haste because of danger and are not drawn by a specific destination, pilgrims usually have time to ponder their decision and prepare themselves. The departure is the moment for pilgrims to put in motion the intention they nurtured of undertaking the journey. Pilgrimage has a beginning, and through it, the intention materializes, and with it the risks of the endeavor. Pilgrims must take this step to start the voluntary and embodied journey.

Leaving entails a separation from the realm of the familiar and the quotidian. The departure can be met with fear and apprehension, or even resistance, while it could also be a freeing moment. The pilgrimage does not only bring a change in scenery, but a different space, and even a different way to inhabit the space. The pilgrim is entering a different time, the favorable time of *kairos*, distinguished from the repetitiveness of the chronological time that flows, *chronos*. The new realm in which pilgrims find themselves opens new possibilities by being less controlled and unfamiliar. The pilgrimage could lead in due time to a transformation, but temporally, it certainly signals first a rupture of the regular flow of quotidian life. Reasons to undertake such a journey show a great diversity, but they often correspond to an important juncture in the life of would-be pilgrims: anniversary, graduation, separation, death, retirement, or other life transitions.

A sense of separation can be more difficult to achieve—or even imagine—in a world as connected as ours, where anyone can be reached almost anywhere at any time, so long as they have a phone and a signal.[71] To ensure the integrity of their experience, pilgrims often must set limits on their communication (even, at times, radical ones). For example, pilgrims might have to turn off their phones. Only then could contemporary pilgrims experience the disconnection of the pilgrims of old, whose journey involved the possibility, for those traveling far, of returning home to a radically different situation, or even to not come home at all. Without a measure of disconnection, the pilgrim would not have left yet, and thus not really entered into the experience of pilgrimage.

Victor Turner's analysis of pilgrimage puts forward the concept of "liminality" to underline the threshold nature of pilgrimage, in which the pilgrim undergoes a transition, akin to rituals of initiation in some cultures. Turner draws on the framework of the rite of passage (*rite de passage*) developed by Arnold van Gennep as a threefold movement of separation (*séparation*), transition (*marge*), and incorporation (*agrégation*).[72] A threshold (*limen*) is irremediably crossed symbolically by the pilgrim—a feat that cannot be undone and ushers pilgrims into a new dimension of their life.[73]

The pilgrim leaves home intent on returning. Unlike the vagabond who has nowhere to return to or does not want to settle, or the refugee who must leave at any cost, the pilgrim plans to come back to their initial location. Medieval pilgrims sometimes ran the risk of not returning because of death, especially during far-flung pilgrimages to the Holy Land.[74] Returning home does not prevent another departure or a new orientation, especially if transformation occurred on the journey. Hence, while pilgrimage has a departure and a destination, it does not necessarily have an end.[75]

Destination

Pilgrimage is described in its most concise definition as a journey to a sacred place or shrine. Hence, pilgrimage is constructed toward a sacred place as its destination. A shrine is "usually the visible goal of the pilgrim's journey."[76] Pilgrims move toward the destination as toward the center, the essential; they are not moving toward the periphery,[77] nor are they simply fleeing their initial location. They are also not wandering without compass, out of *wanderlust* or curiosity; their eyes are set on a destination that holds value.

The Christian pilgrimage site usually has a clear focal point in itself: the box containing the bones of the apostle Peter underneath the *confessio* at St. Peter's Basilica, in Rome, the exact location of the apparitions of Fatima, or the place where Christ's body was laid to rest in the Church of the Holy Sepulchre in Jerusalem. The center is usually located within a larger sacred space and surrounded by other local sacred points of interest, sketching a broader geography of the divine.[78] The sense of the broad diffusion of the divine from its center can be seen by the very name "Holy Land" extended to the region that witnessed the ministry, death, and resurrection of Christ. From afar, pilgrims are overtaken by emotion at the simple view of the Holy City.[79] A clear sense of sacredness emanates from pilgrimage sites, but not in frontal opposition to a profane space. The diffusion of the sacral character around a central focal point into other locations entails a relative progression of such sacredness. To heighten the sense of geographical sacredness, attempts are made to separate the most sacred space from the surrounding spaces with profane uses.[80] In a Christian sense, however, the opposition between sacred and profane space is not the best lens through which to approach what lies at the core of the special character of a place. More than sacredness, a sense of holiness is diffused.

Is the destination sacred or holy? The shift from an indistinct characterization as sacred to a consideration of holiness—which qualifies properly God's own being—is helpful to take into account the criticism leveled against a theology of place that could reify God's gift. Sacredness and holiness both pertain to the divine, but while sacredness highlights the separation from the profane in a quasi-material or geographical way, holiness stresses its personal source, namely, God. It is only in relation to the divine that a place or object can be deemed holy. What lies at the core of the holy place pertains to the very source of holiness, which Christians see in God and his presence.[81] God alone is the Holy One, as the liturgical hymn of the *Sanctus* declares.[82]

Yet God chose not to limit holiness to Godself, but to impart it to creation, through the act of creation itself[83] and through redemption.[84] Human beings are explicitly called to correspond in their lives to God's holiness: "You shall be holy, for I the LORD your God am holy" (Lev 19:2). For Christianity, the event of the incarnation marks a moment in history where God himself dwells on earth in an embodied and personal way. The Holy One dwelled among human beings. The diffusion of holiness and the multiplicity of holy places it causes run contrary to the prior intuition of the uniqueness of the holy place in late Judaism. The Hebrew Scriptures bear witness to a centralization of holiness in the tablets of the Law, the ark of the covenant, and eventually the Jerusalem temple, to the exclusion of any other site.[85]

By their association with Christ, women and men share in the holiness of God through their lives, and sometimes through their martyrdom.[86] The Council of Trent underlines the divine source of the holiness of the martyrs and saints whose relics are venerated.[87] A multitude of places recall Christ's deeds, and many more those of his faithful followers throughout the centuries. Despite a multiplicity of pilgrimage destinations, the source to be encountered in each place is one and the same: God himself, through his holiness. A healthy tension is then set between worship proper, which is due to God alone, and the veneration of the place. A theology of place, or even of material relics, could still uphold both God's incomparable holiness, and the value of material witnesses through God's own gift, memory, and sacramentality. In a Christian perspective, despite the multiplicity of potential destinations for pilgrimages, the ultimate *telos*, as destination and finality, is Christ himself. From him was bestowed holiness, and to him is rendered worship from various points; no saint, no sacrament, no sanctuary can be understood independently from Christ. When the *telos* of pilgrimage is understood as encounter with God incarnate, the relationship from the literal pilgrimage to the metaphorical one, from the actual pilgrimage to the interior one, becomes natural, as they share a destination. The shrine as destination is then properly seen as the "Tent of the Meeting" where human beings and God encounter each other in a renewal of the covenant.[88] As testimonies to the imprint of God's holiness in the lives of so many saints and in the world, pilgrimage destinations are holy places, inviting the pilgrims to share themselves in that holiness.[89]

A pilgrimage is more than a place; it is a movement toward that place, an attraction to a holy place. A tension emerges in the understanding of pilgrimage between the journey itself and its *telos* in a place. Dominique Julia noticed how the papers of a conference on pilgrimage emphasized the journey over the destination,[90] a trope that is characteristic of the contemporary world. Is the process more important than the result, the search more than the truth? The necessary dialectic between the two poles should not be resolved too easily by collapsing one into the other, as in the trope, "The journey is the destination." The destination has its own value as a center embodying holiness. The journey to reach the destination also has its intrinsic value, as we will uncover in the subsequent pages. Regarding the journey, especially if it is arduous, the attainment of the destination can be experienced as an achievement, but it could also be experienced as anticlimactic and even too hasty. Nowadays, after reaching Santiago de Compostela, many pilgrims continue their journey toward Finisterre, on the Atlantic coast, finding for a few days the quiet rural landscape that eluded them in the city of James. By doing so, they set a new destination beyond the traditional one of the tomb of the apostle. The inadequacy of the destination might signify a dichotomy between the outer pilgrimage brought to completion and an inner pilgrimage not as settled.

The destination is essential. The vagabond travels without destination, but the pilgrim always has one, even if it is not clear. But even the destination does not signal the end of all journeys. A different journey continues beyond the destination, as we will see in our ultimate point.

6. ON THE ROAD: EMBODIMENT, VULNERABILITY, EFFORT, AND ALTERITY

Pilgrimage unfolds as a journey, in the time and space from departure to destination. From the lived out unfolding, *embodiment* stands out as the involvement of the body in the experience of pilgrimage, *vulnerability* as the openness to encounter or to be hurt, *effort* as the taxing involvement, even in pain, and finally *alterity*, as the constitutive presence of others along the way.[91]

Embodiment

The dialectic between the journey and the destination creates a dynamic in which a particular occupation of the space is sketched out through the movement of one's body on the journey. The inhabitation of body (my own) and space (by my body) unfolds at the microcosmic and macrocosmic level.

Pilgrimage fosters a distinct occupation of space. Pilgrims experience an extension of their horizon; they left, journeyed, reached the destination, and then came back. The journey let a different space unravel, while the destination was not intended to become home. The space is inhabited as it is passed through, leisurely, attentive to the fleeting details, but not to be grasped. From a collective perspective, pilgrimages devise a new network, new connections between various points, drawing out a distinct use of the space. Through each step a road is sketched by thousands of people over the years. Pilgrimage roads crisscrossing the continent cemented Europe, bringing about contacts among different peoples, alongside artworks, architecture, and ideas. The pilgrimage route to the Holy Land also opened the road of Jerusalem to later crusaders.

Recent scholarship has highlighted the role of the landscape in the pilgrimage experience.[92] As the architecture of nature, it can convey a message to the pilgrim, for example, remoteness, height, serenity. The architecture of sanctuaries also attempts to foster the experience of the pilgrim through signals in the stones. The embracing arms of Bernini's colonnade at St. Peter's Basilica in Rome, or the simplicity of the grotto of Lourdes, each want to embody the message conveyed in their midst.

In a more intimate key, pilgrims experience in an inescapable way the strengths and limitations of their own body, their own finitude. The body plays a central role in the experience of pilgrimage. For more athletic pilgrimages, people prepare themselves for months, buying special gear and clothes, getting in shape, and training. Along the way, when the body is tired, sick, wounded, the rhythm of the pilgrimage must be adapted. In pilgrimages that involve walking long distances, footwear, fatigue, and blisters are a constant topic of conversation and even mutual care among pilgrims. The monotony of walking anchors the pilgrim in the body and opens a space for reflection. There is no escape from the body. The centrality of the body fosters a more physical type of proximity. In *albergues* on the Camino, simple lodgings bring people in proximity, while on World Youth Day, people congregate by the hundreds of thousands to sleep in a single location on the eve of the final day, in conditions reminiscent of medieval pilgrimages. Pilgrimage essentially entails being there, presenting oneself wholly with one's beauty and frailty. It is taking the step, literally, to come to the place of holiness.

The dimension of embodiment in pilgrimage is also at work in rituals performed in which the body is intrinsically involved. Diverse rituals, old and new, mark the paths of pilgrimages. Traditional rituals include walking on one's knees,[93] reciting the Rosary in procession,[94] kissing or hugging a statue,[95] even dances,[96] in addition to participation in sacramental rituals, like confession, or the Eucharist.[97] New rituals whose significance is sometimes less obvious also develop over time, such as leaving a stone in a certain location, a picture of a loved one, a cross on a fence, or shoes next to a mile marker. Those rituals testify to the need to perform something tangible as part of one's journey. While some rituals are formally connected with a transcendental meaning, many are not, but all involve a performance of the body.

Pilgrimage is also about seeing and touching. The memorial dimension is not sought only as a pure idea, but with a desire to see and touch for oneself, as a way to actualize the memory and make it one's own in an embodied way. In that regard, the importance of relics for pilgrimage cannot be overstated, especially in the medieval period. As Alphonse Dupront asserts, "Even today, in the Western world, there is almost no pilgrimage, even a minor one, without relics to be venerated."[98] The bodily involvement is a reason for the success of pilgrimage, by allowing a more direct connection to the divine,[99] but bodily involvement has also been shunned by many ecclesial authorities and theologians, who have favored a more cerebral expression of the experience of faith. Relics are tangible to the pilgrim's body, available to be touched or seen.[100] As body parts of saints for most of them, relics constitute a link across the centuries between the deceased saint and the pilgrim, between the Church on earth and the Church in heaven. They testify in a material way to the truth of the claims of their faith. Because of the sacredness associated with them, various powers have been attributed to relics, such as intercession or healing.[101] Representation of Christ, the Trinity, or the saints through statues, paintings, or icons also participate in the experience of openness to the divine through the senses. Although major relics constitute the heart of the shrine, pilgrims throughout the ages tried to bring mementos back home under the form of lesser-class relics.[102] Nowadays, pilgrims can easily buy trinkets that they can bring home and share to serve as mementos of their experience, investing them with the memorial quality of an immaterial experience. Today, selfies function as "digital relics," reminding pilgrims and showing the world that they have been there, have seen, and touched.

A culmination of embodiment in Christian pilgrimage lies in the celebration of the Eucharist. Christof May connects with sacramental action the quest for the places of Christ, "The Christian pilgrim searches for the places associated with the life of Jesus in order to encounter (*vergeganwärtigen*) there an embodied presence in the celebration of the Eucharist. This way, through the pilgrimage itself, faith becomes an embodied event."[103] The pilgrim's embodied journey toward a tangible and visible trace of God's holiness encounters in the Eucharist the commemoration of Christ's gift of himself, up to the very life of his human body, to nourish and bring life to those who will partake in this sacred meal and gather them into his sacramental body. The memory of Christ becomes sacrament.[104] Paradoxically, Christ's body, more precious than any relic,[105] is eaten, echoing the physical void left by Christ's ascension. Places that house material testimonies of God's dwelling are then inhabited briefly by the active celebration of a community of believers in the sacramental body of Christ. Hence, the Eucharist echoes and reinforces the bodily dimension at work in the pilgrimage; a fallible human body encounters a eucharistic body.[106] The Eucharist also makes the pilgrims a community by gathering them visually, in their diversity, and inviting them to become the one Body of Christ.

The embodiment in pilgrimage, both through the journey and the destination, calls forward the immanence of God. While I emphasized earlier the transcendence at work in the quest for something "outside" that calls the pilgrim forward, the dimension of immanence suggests that the response to the quest is to emerge along the way. God is not simply at a distance but is also to be sought through all creation and creatures.

Finally, the dimension of embodiment will be prolonged in the final category, that of the hoped-for transformation.

Vulnerability

The "quest" dimension of pilgrimage establishes an openness, which is then actualized in vulnerability. Hence, vulnerability is at once a theoretical *condition*—as openness—and a concrete *consequence*, as one reaches an unfamiliar terrain, and needs to be met by others, hence open to hurt and pain. Pilgrims experience a form of vulnerability. They lack control over the environment around them.[107] On the journey, they cannot bring everything they own or consider important or useful. In fact, even in the most generous conditions, the number of things one could carry along is limited. Pilgrims walking without assistance are certainly paradigmatic in that regard, since they can only bring what can be carried on their shoulders. By leaving behind most of their belongings, albeit only for a time, pilgrims undergo a voluntary dispossession, a radical downsizing. For a while, pilgrims put their lives in a single bag—or a few suitcases. Any superfluous item soon appears to be an unnecessary burden.[108] Pilgrims uncover what is essential.

The pilgrim is laid bare. They are exposed to their limitations, the limitations of what they are or own, the limitations of the knowledge of the environment, the limitations of the languages they know. In the most extreme forms of journeys, pilgrims experience simplicity, if not outright austerity, staying in rudimentary accommodations and exposed to the elements on the road. They might not even know where they will sleep the following day. Pilgrims experience their incompleteness. They might need to ask for directions or even beg for something.[109] As strangers, they need to be received, to be shown hospitality. The solo pilgrim would face vulnerability more acutely, but even as part of a group, each pilgrim needs to find their place among their peers.

The use of one's time opens another venue for vulnerability. In crowded places and in large traveling groups, one does not control one's schedule; there are people to wait for, lines, and so on. Even well-laid plans do not always unfold the way they were supposed to. On a walking pilgrimage, the empty time can bring boredom, or even numbness. Outside of one's usual routine and milieu, the pilgrim can face loneliness, the vulnerability of facing oneself unfiltered. However, the vulnerability deployed in time also opens one up to inner reflection, or even to listening. Silence is both a risk and an opportunity. In a civilization that promotes an ever-increasing personal control over one's environment, from what one hears, sees, or constantly communicates, pilgrimage offers an antidote of openness to what "happens": the inner chatter—which can be uncomfortable—the surrounding noise, the possible chance conversation.[110] Vulnerability entails receptivity.

Vulnerability fosters encounters—because no one is self-sufficient—and contributes to the recognition of the need for others. When one feels in control, in a familiar environment, the *need* for encounter is not as present, although the desire for it might be. In instances of vulnerability, however, encountering one's neighbor becomes a necessity. Vulnerability opens a "breach" in oneself into which the other can reach out. By being welcomed by the other, the pilgrim experiences hospitality—that of a fellow traveler in conversation, or that of someone offering shelter, food, or simply information. This encounter could even lead to God, since by the pilgrims' acknowledgment of their vulnerability, prayers of petition can emerge, but also, when vulnerability is not threatening, the discovery of God's providence. The openness of pilgrims in their vulnerability invites them to care for others too. They are not simply on the receiving end of hospitality; their vulnerability opens them up to encounters in truth and humility.

Effort

A famous saying by Pierre Corneille proclaims, "*À vaincre sans péril, on triomphe sans gloire*,"[111] which could be adapted, in the pilgrimage context, into, "If the journey is effortless, the achievement is unnoticeable." Pilgrimage requires effort, often repeatedly.[112] Such effort can be financial, physical, affective, spiritual, or simply temporal. Effort does not turn pilgrimage into a joyless experience, but powerfully ingrains the intention into its actual embodiment.

A pilgrimage can be a taxing endeavor, especially a long trek. In her *Pilgrim Stories*, Nancy Louise Frey captured the way that strenuous effort and physical achievement are viewed by contemporary pilgrims on the Camino as hallmarks of genuine experience.[113] The more sweat, the better.

In the medieval period, the effort required by pilgrimage could bring one to the verge of death because of the risks involved in long journeys. Turner even suggests that the medieval pilgrimage was understood as a form of *via crucis*, a Way of the Cross.[114] In his advice to young pilgrims in 1546, Simão Rodrigues also underlined the connection that the pilgrim can trace with Jesus's own life of labor:

> I will remember that Christ did not go round with his flesh swathed in cotton. If my hands and feet are hurting me, so his hurt him: indeed, they were pierced with nails. If my body hurts me, I must remember how he was scourged; if I sweat, he first sweated drops of blood; if I am thirsty, I must remember his thirst; if I do not find lodging, "the Son of Man has nowhere to lay his head"; if I am tired, "Christ too, tired out by his journey, sat by the well."[115]

The effort here reaches the point of pain and suffering.

Unsurprisingly then, as a popular devotion, pilgrimage has penitential roots.[116] In Christian thought, pain has often been presented as a means to expiation and redemption: "The trials of the journey... contribute to the purification of the pilgrim's body and soul when he offers these sufferings in a spirit of penance and redemption."[117]

Effort and penance were meant to be markers on a journey of conversion. Many rituals accompanying pilgrimage are destined to strain the body: the regular exertion of physical activity (although this should not be the aim) or more specific rituals like climbing stairs or walking on one's knees. For medieval pilgrims, the hardships experienced on the road contributed to the atoning value of their endeavor. The hardships underlined the costly dimension of pilgrimage.

Alterity

One does not travel alone. Others play a role in pilgrimage, even when undertaken alone. Transcendence is already an alterity when its object is a personal God.

Any pilgrimage induces encounters. It could be meeting people for a first time, sharing part of the road with them. It could be deepening one's knowledge of a fellow pilgrim. Many chance encounters of people we might never meet again happen along the road. Some encounters can bring distress and pain, like the thieves that were feared on medieval roads.[118] Many more would comfort, guide, and help. Most encounters would be ephemeral, lasting a moment, while others may be memorable. Groups of fellow pilgrims can take shape, even for those journeying solo. Through encounters, even an individual pilgrimage becomes a collective enterprise. The border between individual and collective is blurred since, as Dupront states, "the pilgrim gesture is essentially a collective one."[119]

In a group dynamic, the constant presence of fellow travelers could be a hindrance, just as it can be helpful when the pilgrims share a similar intention and help each other. Victor Turner identifies the recomposition of the social space brought by the pilgrimage as a distinctive component of the phenomenon; this is what he calls the *communitas*.[120] The *communitas* upends the previous social order, and replaces it with a new one, albeit temporary. Pilgrimage can be a great social equalizer. In some instances, the presence of others is warranted at all stages, from the preparation to the return. In his study on the *Bailes religiosos* (Religious Dances) in the region of Arica, in Chile, Nelson Peña Antil details the customs and social organization of groups who plan during the year the dances that they perform annually on their pilgrimage.[121] Planning involves the creation of costumes and the rehearsals of the music and choreography.

These groups remain stable over the years, members acquiring new roles according to their age and experience. The performance at the shrine requires in an absolute way the collaboration of others. It cannot be individual.

Pilgrims also experience themselves as "other." They are not on their turf; they are venturing outside of their comfort zone. As "others," sometimes in need, they call upon the openness toward them of those they meet. They can face rejection, or even harm, but they can also find hospitality along the road, the literal hospitality of a place to stay and eat, or the hospitality of a moment of fellowship. Such hospitality can be experienced even as the pilgrims and the "hosts" do not share the same outlook on the experience of pilgrimage. Leo Agung Sardi, writing about the experience of young Jesuit novices on pilgrimage in Muslim Indonesia, emphasizes the value of such interreligious encounters for pilgrims.[122]

Finally, two other sets of "others" populate the pilgrimage: those left behind (at home) and those who preceded the pilgrims on the way. Beyond the physical absence, the presence in thought and through communication of those who have been left behind can be felt. Many people inhabit the memory of pilgrims: those who have departed this world and are grieved; those who have hurt or been hurt and need reconciliation; those who have entrusted prayers to the pilgrim, and all those in need of prayers. The sense of communion can be enhanced by the absence and the quiet pondering of relationships it allows.

Communion is also experienced, more subtly, with generations of saints and sinners who have walked previously on the same path, converging to a common holy place. Through the doctrine of the Communion of the Saints, catholic theology emphasizes that they, also, are part of the Church. These others have stretched a path now traveled toward the absolute Other.

7. FINALLY: TRANSFORMATION?

Transformation stands on its own as the last category. More than simply a return or conclusion, it stretches beyond arrival and harkens back to preparation.

Transformation?

This last characteristic is more a question than an affirmation. Is transformation necessary? On returning from the journey, the pilgrim can experience a host of feelings: disappointment, difficulty readapting, excitement, new purpose, and renewed energy. Be they positive or negative, the feelings experienced prompt the question of the lasting effects of the pilgrimage on the individual or the group. How can the movement of the pilgrimage morph into transformation upon the return? Although the pilgrimage represented a departure from the quotidian realm and the entrance into a new time and space, it could easily be reduced to a simple parenthesis that brackets the experience of the pilgrimage and limits its impact on the subsequent life of the former pilgrim. Here lies the difference between pilgrimage and other kinds of travel. While travel can transform—a French saying attests that *les voyages forment la jeunesse* (travel shapes the young)—travel's main aim is not necessarily to transform.[123] Not so for pilgrimage. In a narrative about his pilgrimage to the mission churches of California, Richard Roos writes that one constant question he was asked after his journey was about his transformation.[124] "The pilgrim's journey is an ellipse; it is complete when the devotee has returned home with a new understanding of themselves and their God that is embodied."[125] Such transformation upon return is nonetheless left to be experienced by the pilgrim in a very subjective—and sometimes isolating—way since the moment of reintegration (or incorporation) of van Gennep's rite of passage is often underdeveloped.[126]

The issue of the transformation arises during the pilgrimage proper, but even more upon the return, and especially in its aftermath. Muslims who have completed the pilgrimage to Mecca obtain the title *hajji* which distinguishes them as "permanent pilgrims" (*pèlerin permanent*), bestowing upon them a new social status.[127] On the Christian side, one could hope that the striving for the destination and the holiness it entails would spill over the quotidian realm. The call of conversion, *metanoia*, resonates powerfully in the Christian tradition. However, one of the most common criticisms addressed to large modern-day pilgrimages like World Youth Day is that they are mere moments without long-lasting consequences.[128] Another trend is the endless accumulation of "pilgrimages," which suggests an insatiable longing—and potentially a longing for the wrong reasons.[129]

The figure of the pilgrim is used as a symbol of the transient nature of life, and a sign of the new type of religiosity in the postmodern world. In that regard, it is portrayed as an unsettledness, a lack of rootedness, often in opposition to more stable institutions like the parish.[130] However, one can also experience a single pilgrimage as a radical life-changing experience, which transforms their very identity. Pierre-Joseph-Marie Chaumonot (1611–93), one of the early Jesuit missionaries in New France, made a stop in Loreto, Italy, as an unruly youth on his way to Rome. He was physically healed and transformed, even adding "Marie" to his name in thanksgiving, and later became a religious, a priest, and a missionary.[131] A great example of transformation and modeling of one's own identity through pilgrimage is that of Ignatius Loyola (1491–1556), who would even style himself "the pilgrim" in an autobiographical narrative, an example we will explore in depth in chapter 3.

Pilgrimage can also have some outward-looking consequences. In the reflection on the shrine by the Pontifical Council for the Pastoral Care of Migrants and Itinerant People, three consequences are noted for the encounter made through the shrine as the endpoint of the pilgrimage: awe and adoration (directed to God), then thanksgiving,[132] but also sharing and commitment to others.[133] In this perspective, the privileged experience of pilgrimage culminating at the shrine in a heightened encounter with the divine cannot but lead to a renewed encounter with the world through service, especially of the poor.

The question of the transformation reflects on that of intention, the first characteristic of pilgrimage named. If the quest was sincere and has been continuous in its desire, a transformation would naturally arise along the way that would blossom upon the return. The God who was sought even unknowingly in that transcendental thrust would be better known. As Graham Tomlin writes, "A common outcome of good, healthy pilgrimage is a renewed and strengthened sense that God can in fact be found, not just in so-called 'holy places,' but anywhere."[134] In that place, the inner pilgrimage and the embodied one do meet.

8. CONCLUSION: THE SINGULARITY OF PILGRIMAGE

Pilgrimage is a plural reality. Establishing a "standard" through these ten characteristics does not imply that any pilgrimage fits the bill perfectly. There is a singularity to each pilgrimage that is linked to the pilgrim's personal circumstances and the broader context (historical, religious, etc.) in which the pilgrimage is made. Armchair pilgrimages, travels by planes and buses, or long treks do amount to diverse experiences, though each could have a claim at being a genuine pilgrimage. From the core experience, analogous phenomena developed that stretched the pilgrim experience or even went beyond. The usefulness of a normative ideal is to offer a common ground to wrestle with when assessing a particular experience that claims to be a pilgrimage. In each instance, some elements of the pilgrim ideal might be emphasized, others missing altogether. The attempt is not to weed out phenomena from the realm of pilgrimage, but to compare, challenge, and deepen their analysis. This could also play out in the case of pilgrimages that are held as paragons of the pilgrim experience. In their case, a deepening of the pilgrim characteristics could lead to a fruitful renewal of practices. With the characteristics of Christian pilgrimage at hand, comparisons in ecumenical and interreligious settings can be made. Different traditions emphasize distinct elements.

In the next chapter, we will explore the deep connection of pilgrimage as lived out in Christianity with essential elements of the Christian faith seen through Scripture. Although pilgrimages predate Christianity, their important historical role in the popular experience of that faith suggests a strong correlation even at a theological level.

CHAPTER 2

A Pilgrim People and Christ the Pilgrim

A Biblical Journey

PRELUDE

The visitor venturing to the end of a wing in the Musée Jacquemart-André in Paris is seized at the sight of an extraordinary chiaroscuro by Rembrandt in the dim light of the library, the last room.[1] *Les pèlerins d'Emmaüs* (The Emmaus Pilgrims), as they are traditionally called in French, are depicted at the precise moment in which something had happened during their meal. The table is set with bread and wine, and the silhouette of Jesus is sketched in black by the light coming from beyond. The disciples affect strikingly different positions; the one in the center of the painting displays his bewilderment in full view, while the disciple in the foreground is prostrated at the feet of Jesus and shrouded in darkness. In the background, a servant carries on with her tasks, unaware of the event taking place next to her. The crux of the journey of these disciples is encapsulated in that sudden recognition of the transformative identity of a fellow pilgrim. The Lukan story of the disciples on the road to Emmaus (Luke 24:13–35) indeed offers a wonderful setting to explore the theme of pilgrimage, since it constitutes at once a voluntary anti-pilgrimage and a Christian pilgrimage par excellence.

Two disciples were on the road. They were leaving Jerusalem and the other disciples, turning their back on them in sadness (Luke 24:17). The death of Jesus on a pilgrimage feast had dashed their hopes (v. 21). The testimony of some women and other disciples about the empty tomb earlier in the day (vv. 22–24) did not alleviate their sense of loss. Hence, they took to the road, this time in the opposite direction than a few days earlier. They walked away from Jerusalem, away from the other disciples, away from the rumors of Jesus being potentially alive. They walked and they talked.

Despite their grief, the disciples were able to make space for the stranger (*peregrinus*) who was a fellow traveler.[2] They welcomed him in their midst, shared their pain with him (Luke 24:17–24), listened to him (vv. 25–27), and even prodded him to stay with them that night in Emmaus (v. 29). Despite moving away from God's place, they showed themselves to be pilgrims welcoming of others, disposed to encounter their neighbor wholeheartedly.

Their encounter reached its greatest depth when they sat at table, and Jesus "took bread, blessed and broke it, and gave it to them" (Luke 24:30). They recognized him through that eucharistic sign[3] as "he vanished from their sight" (v. 31). The presence of the risen Christ that had begun much earlier but was not acknowledged (v. 15) became clear through that new way of presence foretold by Jesus at the Last Supper (22:14–38).[4] Hence, Emmaus became the end point of the disciples' journey. They had reached a destination—although they did not know before that it was to be such—insofar as they encountered God there.

The pilgrims of Emmaus give witness to a genuine transformation experienced in the journey. First, they returned to the place they had left. They returned but their short journey was far from a parenthesis; they were radically transformed. Although they had settled for a rest on their journey away from Jerusalem, after realizing that they had encountered Jesus, they returned at once, showing their haste to take a different direction (Luke 24:33). They were transformed in their desire to rejoin the community of the disciples and share with them the great joy of the presence they had experienced during their journey. Their previous commitment to the way of Jesus was enlightened and renewed.

The Emmaus disciples also highlight how the realization of the transformation often happens after the fact. It is only after they recognized Jesus in the fellow pilgrim that they were able to seize what had already happened to them. "Were not our hearts burning within us while he was talking to us on the road, while he was opening the scriptures to us?" (Luke 24:32). It is only after the climax of the experience was reached that they realized the full scope of the progressive transformation of what became a pilgrimage.[5]

INTRODUCTION

The Bible abounds in elements pertaining to pilgrimage, either directly, like ancient pilgrim rituals in Israel, or more subtly, like the missioning of the disciples of Jesus. While the reality of pilgrimages in the Old Testament is well attested, it does not carry over into the New Testament untouched. On the contrary, pilgrimage is deeply transformed by the Christ event and the subsequent evolution of the Christian community. At the same time, there is no absolute break, either in practice or in theory, between ancient Jewish pilgrimages and the Christian experience of pilgrimage, but it is in light of Christ and of the Christian understanding of pilgrimage that this biblical journey will unfold.

Our aim here is to uncover essential biblical resources that ground the phenomenon of pilgrimage. In many reflections on pilgrimage, the biblical dimension is treated in passing by mentioning eminent figures like Abraham and Jesus, as well as the exodus and the incarnation. This chapter seeks to explore some biblical harmonics of pilgrimage, in order to move forward theological reflection on pilgrimage for today. This biblical journey encourages us, for example, to reclaim elements of the Old Testament experience of pilgrimage that are less obvious today: the collective dimension of a pilgrim people, as opposed to the individual pilgrim, and the ethical concern especially, since the welcoming of the otherness is at the heart of the Jewish faith because of having been welcomed as foreigners.

Pilgrimage is consonant with the Christian faith, and from the core of the biblical witness, a theological coherence can be deployed. The biblical material that we dwell on constitutes steppingstones in that path to make sense of pilgrimage and to be challenged as further dimensions are emphasized. This chapter is not a complete history of pilgrimage according to the Bible, nor is it limited to the strict vocabulary of pilgrim and pilgrimage, which is not particularly prevalent in the New Testament. Our approach is twofold. First, to hear echoes from our systematic phenomenological inquiry into pilgrimage from the previous chapter in biblical material. Second, to listen to the distinct contributions of the biblical moments brought to the fore. Through the various biblical material explored, a certain narrative emerges, which forms this chapter.

The chapter is divided in two main sections. In the first section, on the pilgrim people and the pilgrim God according to the Old Testament, the figures of Adam, Eve, and Abraham are explored in relationship to pilgrimage, followed by the exodus event that established a covenantal people, and revealed a God on the move. The second part pertains to the pilgrimage in the new covenant in Jesus Christ. Pilgrimage is first looked at through the prism of its practice—literally and metaphorically—by Jesus, through the figure of "movement." Then around "place and person," a theology of embodied holiness is sketched out, drawing on Jesus as embodied holiness—versus the holy place of Jerusalem. This holiness later extends to others, the saints at first, and thus to other places and people. A reflection on the nexus of the Eucharist will also emerge here. Then the missionary dimension of the pilgrim "sending" is explored in relationship with apostolic work. At the end, we will look at further pilgrim *theologoumena* in the New Testament that have played an important role in the Christian imagery and discourse on pilgrimage.

1. A PILGRIM PEOPLE AND A PILGRIM GOD

The Old Testament does not lack vantage points from which to explore pilgrimage. It contains many examples of pilgrimage rituals, journeys, songs, and destinations.[6] From such wealth, we will explore three key moments that are structurally important for Christian pilgrimage. First, the archetypal models of Adam, Eve, and Abraham, who provide strong individual foundations as foremother and forefathers of pilgrims. Second, the central experience of exodus as establishing a people in the journey toward the land of the promise. Finally, the striking characterization of God as on the move.

Adam, Eve, and Abraham: Way Out, Way To

The stories of Eve and Adam and of Abraham are a study in contrast. Both are foundational to the understanding of pilgrimage from a biblical perspective. With Adam and Eve, we find anti-pilgrims who are exiled from an ideal location. With Abraham, we encounter one who heeds God's call to set out for another land, becoming the forebear to countless migrants and pilgrims.

Expelled from the Garden of Eden (Gen 3:23–24), Adam and Eve set the stage for pilgrimage by carrying the memory of paradise lost. Theirs is the wistful twist of "pilgrimage," with no hope of ever regaining lost ground. Theirs is a perpetual exile. They had experienced a dwelling provided to them by God (Gen 1—2). They had experienced closeness with God. They had experienced a perfect setting on earth. But now this place is forever closed to them; only the forbidding memory would live on, the remorse of having lost it, and, maybe, the desire to find it again.[7]

Through the loss of the place shared with God on earth, Adam and Eve became enablers of pilgrimage since pilgrims are set on a journey of desire fundamentally awakened by memory. Symbolically, Eden represents a place or state to be sought, desired, recovered, the aspiration to a renewal of the original state of closeness to God, and inhabitation of divine space beyond the failure of sin and exile.[8] Paradise represents the restoration of the place of intimate union between God and human beings, and is, as such, a worthy goal.

Regarding their physical destination, Adam and Eve illustrate an anti-pilgrimage because they are moving away from the ultimate destination. By the same token, they also mark the beginning of a history, of a (long!) "path of conversion and return."[9]

While Eden represents the imprint of the place of desire, Abraham personifies the positive call from God that sets it in motion. Abraham is not only the father of all believers (cf. Rom 4:11); he is the father of all pilgrims:

> The LORD said to Abram, "Go from your country and your kindred and your father's house to the land that I will show you. I will make of you a great nation, and I will

> bless you, and make your name great, so that you will be a blessing. I will bless those who bless you, and the one who curses you I will curse; and in you all the families of the earth shall be blessed." So Abram went, as the LORD had told him.... (Gen 12:1–4)

Abraham is a man journeying toward an unknown land. While the destination is unclear, the one who sends him is not, being the Lord himself. God is the one who sets forth the invitation to journey. Abraham responded to that invitation by setting himself in motion, bringing with him all his possessions (Gen 12:5). He trusted in the word said to him. His faith is attested in the very movement of his being.

A promise accompanied the invitation to undertake a journey, a promise to be made a great nation, a promise of blessing. The continuous action of blessing Abraham, and of blessing others through him, suggests a close presence of God along the way. Hence, the invitation to journey is accompanied by a promise, and opens the horizon of a quest for Abraham: the quest for land, quest for progeny. Abraham's gaze is toward the future. He is not looking back nostalgically at a lost divine place, but toward a new place and a new relationship with the Lord.

The nature of the promise highlights the collective dimension of Abraham's journey. Not only is he bringing all his belongings, cattle, servants, and household, but as a childless husband, he is promised, repeatedly, that he will become a great nation (Gen 17:4). Isaac is the first fruit of that central promise, his only son by his wife Sarah (18:10), living proof of the value of the promise upon which Abraham established his radical life choice. His journey extends beyond himself. The transformation of pilgrimage takes the shape of generativity. This proleptically fulfilled dimension of the promise is even more important because the promised land would not belong to Abraham's descendants before generations had passed.[10]

Abraham is rightly seen at the intersection of the figures of pilgrim and migrant.[11] Those two figures have many things in common, despite fundamental differences.[12] Abraham is specifically pilgrim because of the divine impulse that launches him on a quest, a quest for the land shown to him by God, though still unspecified. Yet Abraham is typically migrant because he leaves the place he called home in a radical way: with his belongings, without plans or hope to go back. There is no horizon of return; Abraham had irrevocably set his sight on a new future home.

Despite the assurance of the divine promise and Abraham's trust in it, Abraham and generations of his people endure the radical experience of being sojourners in someone else's land. The experience of being outside of one's home and one's land as a people deeply marked the religious consciousness of the Hebrews. They journeyed in a land that was not theirs yet. They experienced oppression in a foreign land before making their way to the promised land. Later they would also experience dispersion, exile, and return. This experience shaped a profound reverence for the hospitality to be extended to travelers, especially because of the great story of the exodus.

The Exodus: The Constitution of a People

The promise of progeny to Abraham was fulfilled in Isaac, Jacob, and their descendants. The nucleus of a great people grew in Egypt (Exod 1:7), but it was through the exodus that the individual call of Abraham gained its full collective value in the pilgrim experience of a people.

The exodus is of paramount importance in the religious experience of Israel. Even today, Jews retell its story every year at the Feast of Pesach (Passover). In the last century, liberation theologians dwelled on this fundamental experience of God's liberating power in order to comprehend God's relationship with his people through the struggles of our age.[13] For a theology of pilgrimage, the exodus story offers the foundational template of a rich religious experience of movement, initiated by God and lived with his people.

Pilgrim Features of the Exodus Experience

Dire conditions led to the exodus. The Hebrews were living as slaves in a foreign land, crying out to God (Exod 3:7). Moses, the leader chosen to lead them out of Egypt, had killed a man and was living in exile (2:12, 15), and Pharaoh was in a mood for confrontation: he did not want to let the Hebrews go (7:13). The stage was set for a dramatic struggle before they could undertake the journey: wonders, plagues, death. This dramatic background underlines the nature of the journey as one of moving *away* from the current location—a clear "push." God was not only leading his people somewhere; he was also liberating them from a wretched situation. The journey was one with no return, unlike a normative pilgrimage. A strong sense of *telos* in the earthly destination is at work in the exodus story. The people are marching toward the land of promise. Harking back on the promise of old made to Abraham, a clear destination is set on God's terms. The memory here is not yet one of living on the land but the remembrance of the promises made to them by God from Abraham onward, reversing the expulsion of Adam and Eve from the Garden of Eden. The sacredness of the destination of the Hebrew people is founded only on the promise that it is God's intended land for Israel.

This "exodic pilgrimage," to borrow the expression of the Pontifical Council for the Pastoral Care of Migrant and Itinerant Peoples, constitutes a total experience. It became paradigmatic for the experience of divine liberation. It was not devoid of struggles:

> The various stages—which included the departure, wandering in the desert, the trial, temptations, sin, entering the promised land—have become the exemplary model of the history of salvation itself. This includes not only the gifts of freedom, of Revelation in Sinai and of divine communion, expressed in the Passover ("passage") and in the offering of the manna, water and the quails, but also infidelity, idolatry, the temptation to go back to slavery.[14]

The "infidelity, idolatry, [and] the temptation" underline the effort—even failed ones—required along the way. Although the exodus would finally be brought to a successful completion, the journey met with internal resistance and setbacks among its participants. The great gifts and accomplishments should not obscure the genuineness of the challenges.

An essential part of the march toward the promised land is time. Time to atone for unfaithfulness to God, but even more, time to move from one place to another, from one state to another, from slavery to become fully God's people. Such change could not happen overnight, nor even quickly. Time is necessary to cross the desert;

a long, empty time in which complaints and "murmurs" can arise and be atoned for.[15] A time to be formed as a people by living out the Law entrusted to them. A time to nurture the desire for the destination, the inhabitation of the land promised by God. Those who began the journey did not reach its end; Moses passed the baton to Joshua, and a new generation brought the journey to its conclusion (Josh 1—4). In that feat, the journey became at once open-ended and intergenerational.

The viatorial experience of the Hebrews entailed an experience of God's ongoing care. Through the guidance by the column of smoke or by light (Exod 13:21), the people were directed firmly toward their destination. Along the way, God miraculously provided water and food for them (Exod 16—17:7). The relationship between the Lord and his people grew deeper, based on the trust that such daily care fostered. The action of God was no longer to be seen in the demonstration of power of the initial events leading to the journey, but in the inconspicuous normality of providing food and guidance.

Despite the towering figure of Moses and his position of leadership, the journey is eminently collective, not even simply that of a sum of individual experiences, but a journey that would shape the Hebrews into a *people*, God's people. Here lies the most striking contribution of the exodus story to a theological understanding of pilgrimage; the endeavor is not only that of an individual, but a collective journey that creates a new reality. This reality surpasses the temporary *communitas* experienced by pilgrims along the way, since the community has a vocation of permanence forged in the movement toward a land, but not yet land based. The coming together of Israel as a consequence of the journey constitutes a formidable instance of pilgrim transformation. A practical condition contributing to the experience was its shared quality, in isolation from other peoples. This transformation was epitomized by the establishment of a covenant, sealing at once the association of the people unto itself, as well as its union with the Lord. As such, it constituted a response to the events of the journey. As they reached the promised land at the end of the journey, they were literally a transformed reality. Although the journey was clearly a physical and geographical one, the inner dimension was also essential: the journey was one of inner transformation.

The Law and Ethical Commitment

As part of the covenant and the process of community-building, the bestowal of the Law cemented the unity of the people on the move and gave them a clear identity as God's people and as a people living under a particular moral code. Departure from Egypt and reception of the Law on Mount Sinai go hand in hand in the Book of Exodus, since "the entire purpose of God's liberating action was to make a covenant with Israel and thus lay down norms for her to follow in order to be a free nation at his service."[16]

As part of the gift of the Law during the exodus itself, beyond the Decalogue (Exod 20:1–17; Deut 5:6–21), the exodus experience became a powerful ground to generate a strong ethical commitment to hospitality toward travelers, migrants or pilgrims: "You shall not wrong or oppress a resident alien, for you were aliens in the land of Egypt" (Exod 22:21).[17] The experience of being sojourners rooted an ethical leitmotif in Hebrew Scriptures about the necessity to welcome foreigners through the reminder that "you were aliens" (Lev 19:34). Hospitality as a moral duty to the pilgrim and the migrant is founded in the experience of having been at one time, through one's forebears, a migrant and pilgrim in Abraham, in Egypt, then in exodus. In Exodus 22, immediately after the command to care for the foreigner, words of warning from the Lord use a language similar to the beginning of Exodus, when the Lord heard the cry of his people: "You shall not abuse any widow or orphan. If you do abuse them, when they cry out to me, I will surely heed their cry" (22:22–23; cf. 3:7). The Lord listened, not only to Israel's cries of old, but also to the potential cries of aliens in the midst of Israel. From this remembrance emerges an ethical commitment to the traveler. The pilgrim experience generates moral implications toward fellow travelers.

Focusing, Revisiting, and Ritualizing the Experience

The foundational quality that the exodus gained for Israel led to a constant reassessment that refined its value and meaning and ensured its lasting impact as a template of subsequent events and rituals.

A first element in that regard is the specific focus that the geographical destination of the exodus gained. Although the initial sight is on the destination as *land*, upon arrival, the focus eventually narrowed down to a city, Jerusalem, which came to epitomize the promised land, as its center and the location of the ark of the covenant (2 Sam 5—6), and later of the temple. This shift from land to city allows for a clearer destination in which a central location embodies a *telos* that can then radiate to other points. This shift would have a great impact, since in the history of Israel—and up to our day—Jerusalem captured the religious imagination of Hebrews.[18]

A most central element of reinterpretation of exodus touches upon the further experience of exile. The later periods of exile, away from the promised land, were opportunities to revisit the covenant that constituted Israel as a people in exodus, especially through the challenging preaching of the prophets such as Ezekiel and Jeremiah. The periodical reembracing of the desert experience of waiting, this time after having inhabited the land, entails in return a sense of unsettledness, of nonpossession, even in times of presence in the Holy Land. The experience of exile brought to the fore the fragility of the covenantal relationship and the ongoing purification of desire necessary on the part of God's people. The dwelling in the Holy Land could not be severed from the striving for God's holiness that it requires from the people called to be God's people (Lev 19:2). The prophets already called attention to the connection between the moral failure of the people and the discontinuation of their habitation of the land of their destination.[19] The inhabitation of the place provided by the Lord cannot be only a physical reality; an inner disposition must accompany it. A correspondence between God's gift and the human disposition to receive it must be attained—as in the experience of the wait in the desert—or retrieved—as in the call for conversion heard in exile and beyond. As the Cameroonian theologian Jean-Marc Éla wrote, "The roads of exodus and exile are the necessary way to reach life in plenitude."[20]

The connection between the inner life and the spatial journey of pilgrimage is also underlined in the Psalms, according to McConville, as those who ascend to the Lord's mountain shall do so with "clean hands and a pure heart (Ps 24:3–4)," being required to walk in the ways of the Lord (Ps 81:13).[21] Pilgrimage calls for a purified pilgrim.

As part of the constant vigilance about the covenant and the striving for God, and as a testament to the importance of the exodus story, two essential rituals of remembrance emerged. The first was the ritual reenactment of the preparation for the Passover meal, which marked the beginning of the flight from Egypt: eaten hurriedly, loins girded, sandals on, and staff in hand (Exod 12:11). This meal illustrates the preparedness expected of a people on the move, ready to heed God's call to liberation. As an annual commemoration involving body and family, the Passover meal enfleshes anew in the individual and the community the fundamental deed of the exodus of the people of old.

The second ritual, tied to the first one, is the annual pilgrimage to Jerusalem, at the *telos* of the journey with God that became the stable place of encounter.[22] The ritual meal of Passover was to take place during the festival. Even after the destruction of the Jerusalem temple in 70 CE, and the later expulsion of the Jews from Jerusalem in the second century, the aim of undertaking this yearly pilgrimage of remembrance remained. Even today, the Passover seder concludes with the wish "Next year in Jerusalem." In the pilgrimage to Jerusalem, or the ritual expression of the intent to undertake such pilgrimage, the desire to live at last at the destination is refreshed and kept alive in God's people, evoking *ipso facto* a movement similar to that of the exodus journey. Hence, two instances of remembrance are called forth by the rituals. On the one hand, the Passover meal recalls the deeds of old. On the other, the pilgrimage to Jerusalem—and even more the sole desire for it—looks toward a future of proximity with the Lord.

By extension, the presentation of the three main festivals in Deuteronomy 16, in the wake of Passover, highlights not only the memory of the Lord's deeds for Israel (vv. 1, 12), but also the inclusiveness of the gathering and its celebratory character. The inclusiveness is expressed by the explicit mention of children, slaves, strangers, orphans, and widows (v. 14). The feast is not only Israel's but extends to foreigners. In addition to memory and inclusiveness, the gathering entails "grateful worship, assembly, [and] rejoicing."[23] As McConville concludes, in this pilgrimage

> there is so much more here than a call to make a journey. The law is a vehicle for Deuteronomy's portrayal of the people in its truest nature—a unity created by its common experience of the salvation of Yahweh, resisting all

> divisions created by inequality or oppression, giving back to God as he has given to them and, in all this, rejoicing. Here is holiness theology turned into nothing less than a vision of the kingdom of God.[24]

The Exodus as a Grounding Experience for Pilgrimage

In the words of the Pontifical Council for the Pastoral Care of Migrants and Itinerant People, the importance of the exodus is inescapable:

> Exodus acquires a permanent value. It is a "memorial" that is always vital and comes up again even upon the return from the Babylonian exile. This is sung by the Second Isaiah as a new exodus (Cfr. Isa 43:16–21), that is commemorated each time Israel celebrates the Feast of the Passover and is transformed into an eschatological representation in the book of Wisdom (Cfr. Wis 11–19). The final aim is in fact the promised land of full communion with God in a renewed creation (Cfr. Wis 19).[25]

This perspective propels the exodus experience to its ultimate eschatological consequences of fullness of communion with God, and renewal of the whole of creation—that it has already anticipated. The transformation hoped for in pilgrimage would then be achieved in the most splendid way.

In addition to the many features of pilgrimage that the exodus highlights, its major contribution to the study of pilgrimage is its strong emphasis on the collective dimension of the experience. In exodus, pilgrimage is fundamentally the experience of people, but even more than that, it is an experience that creates a people. The ritualization of the experience also contributes to keep God's people united covenantally with God and one another through the constant remembrance of their historic journey with the Lord. The common experience of exodus, and its ritual commemoration, also implies an ethical commitment to foreigners, especially those amid the people. Such care illustrates the genuine transformation effected through pilgrimage.

God on the Move

The exodus story does not only concern God's people and its pilgrimage; it revealed a God on the move. Ancient Near Eastern religions usually connected a deity with a particular place where a temple housed the statue(s) of the god(s).[26] The links among the worshiping people, its temple, and its deity were straightforward. Moreover, the deity was closely associated to its personification as a statue.

The religious experience depicted through the exodus story and its immediate aftermath tells a different story. As the Hebrews embark on their journey, the Lord is presented as close to them, or even in their midst, but not under the guise of a statue: "the Lord himself is a pilgrim with his people."[27] The Lord not only cares for his people along the way but joins in their journey. Although the Lord is near, he is not graspable.

In terms of depiction, the concomitant events of the bestowal of the Law (Exod 20:1–17) and the (reproved) worship of the golden calf (Exod 32) stress a common point: the radical unsuitability of depicting God. God cannot be encapsulated in a single object; the Lord radically evades depiction. Therefore, a dialectic of presence and absence animates at once the relationship of God with his people: he is present, and an objectified focus is provided for worship, but the dissimilarity of the depiction underscores the absence of a proper image of God; God is not contained there, though he is really there to be encountered. The presence of God is indeed very fluid.

While the God of the Hebrews is strongly connected to a people, he is not located in a single place since he accompanies his pilgrim people along the way. Throughout the exodus, the presence of God amid his people is symbolized by a tent, the tent of the encounter, where Moses meets God in an abode made for travel, and not permanence. At its center, when at rest, lies the ark of the covenant containing the tablets of the Law, the most sacred religious possession of the Hebrews, although not a depiction of the divine. These tablets and the ark containing them acted as proxy for a nonexistent statuary depiction of the Lord. Located at the center of the camp (Num 2:2), they signified God's presence, and were also taken out of the tent and onto the battlefield (Josh 6). As ark and tent, they testify to God's own mobility. The God of a people in movement was a God on the move, not the God of a place. The holy place is mobile, and the core of the holy destination is a fluid image, and both illustrate the tension in the "place" and embodiment of the holy. Holiness is located, but its core lies in a presence.

Even upon the arrival of God's people into the promised land, the issue of God's dwelling would not be settled easily. The ban against depiction remained. The installation of the ark in a more permanent abode did not come about quickly. For the Lord to have a temple in the holy city, Jerusalem, would be normative since important deities were usually housed in such buildings. The exchange between the Lord and David is instructive in this regard. Whereas David wanted to single-handedly normalize the accommodation of the God of the Hebrews by providing a suitable abode for him, the Lord was not willing to let himself be deprived of his agency in such matters and be limited to the enclosure of a sanctuary (2 Chr 17:2–6). David's son Solomon would be the one who built a splendid temple of stone to house the ark (2 Chr 5). Even there, the installation of God in a single place would not be complete, since the heart of the temple, the *sanctum sanctorum*, would not house a depiction of the Lord, but the mobile ark of the covenant. On the other hand, the realization of the Jerusalem temple did focus the religious imagination of the Hebrews into a single stable place, a far cry from the early mobility of a God on the move with his people for decades. Now, it was time for the people to come in pilgrimage to the Lord and his temple. The subsequent destruction and rebuilding of the temple reinforced its centrality as a place of God, but without erasing its previous "nomadic" history. It maintained the distance between the temple and the Lord by not housing an image of God. Even while apparently settled in a place, the Lord could not be seized by a place.

Conclusion

Pilgrimage was an institution in ancient Israel, and it evolved in its practice, also reaching the time of Jesus. Some structural highlights are important for a consideration of subsequent, and even contemporary, pilgrimages. The nostalgic abandonment of a place for Adam and Eve. The forward-looking movement of Abraham through a divine promise whose full realization he would not see.

The centrality of the exodus as the bedrock of the religious experience of Hebrews, constituting them as a covenantal people, going through the desert toward the promised land. The collective dimension of their pilgrimage can be challenging to contemporary minds. The ethical commitment that accompanies the pilgrimage and its memory speaks of the radical transgenerational transformation hoped for in this experience. The exodus is also a foundational experience commemorated in embodied rituals of pilgrimage, and even meal, making present anew the memory of the event. Throughout, a sense of located holiness is infused, as a dwelling presence of God, but a presence that is mobile, and fluid. With the Christ event, a new light would be added to the experience of a pilgrim people and a pilgrim God.

2. PILGRIMAGE IN THE NEW COVENANT IN JESUS CHRIST

At first sight, pilgrimage does not play a major role in the New Testament. It is not a religious practice required of the community in the same way that pilgrimages were ingrained in Jewish religious life. However, there is more continuity, especially in the life of Jesus, than might first appear. In addition, many pilgrimage tropes are transformed or developed. Hence, an exploration of pilgrimage can be significantly inspired by important moments in the New Testament. This exploration will proceed in a narrative way along three key moments. First, *movement*, through Jesus himself. How did the Jesus depicted in the Gospels experience Jewish religious pilgrimages, and what role did pilgrimage play in his proclamation? The very life of Jesus can also be read in a narrative way as a pilgrimage. Second, *person and place*, which moved from divine holiness to embodied holiness in the incarnation. Pilgrimage in the Old Testament fostered a clear sense of place as destination of pilgrimage, from the lost Eden, to the promised land, and the presence of the Lord through the ark and the Jerusalem temple. The sacred "placeness" was already not unidimensional, but the incarnation and its aftermath of diffusion of holiness would bring a new dimension to a theology of holy "place" and persons. The third moment is that of *sending*, from the disciples onward. A "pilgrim style" marks the sending of Jesus's disciples, connecting the pilgrim *ethos* firmly to the proclamation of the gospel, under the guidance of the Holy Spirit. Finally, we will look at some of the other pilgrim *theologoumena* present in the New Testament that played a central role in subsequent reflections on pilgrimage.

Movement: Jesus the Pilgrim

The Pilgrimages of Jesus

In the Second Temple Judaism, pilgrimages to Jerusalem were largely practiced by the Palestinian Jewish communities during the important festivals of Passover (conflated at that time with the Feast of the Unleavened Bread), Shavuot (Pentecost), and Sukkot (Feast of the Tabernacles).[28] Both Passover and the Festival of Tabernacles commemorate the exodus experience of Israel, in which the people of God was led out of Egypt.[29] These festivals lasted many days, and Roman Jewish historian Flavius Josephus mentions the large crowds at the Passover festival.[30] Of these three festivals, the New Testament signals the attendance of Jesus at both the Feast of Passover and the Feast of Tabernacles, and adds the Feast of the Dedication (John 10:22).[31] From an early age, and until his last days, the devotional praxis of Jesus is portrayed as one of faithful accomplishment of the Jewish religious pilgrimages. By his own regular journeys to the city of Jerusalem, as the focus of the religious festivals, Jesus condoned the practice of pilgrimage.

In the Gospel according to Luke, Jesus famously went as a twelve-year-old on the yearly pilgrimage (of Passover) to Jerusalem "according to the custom" with Mary, Joseph, and a large group of relatives and friends (Luke 2:41–52). This is the only recorded instance of Jesus and his family attending a festival. This is also the first encounter with pilgrimage as a group event, in a set time in the life of Jesus. A previous mention in the same Gospel of a journey to Jerusalem was cast as a fateful presentation of the infant Jesus to the temple (2:22–39). The Passover pilgrimage to Jerusalem of the young boy Jesus follows a clear pattern of journey, important event at the destination, return, and further growth. It is also the only descriptive instance of the agency of the young

Jesus in the canonical Gospels. From a pilgrimage perspective, two elements of the story should be highlighted from this experience of Jesus in Jerusalem. First, Jesus is engaged in a genuine quest; he stays behind to discuss with teachers amazed by his wisdom (2:47), seeking the truth by listening and asking questions (v. 46). This is the action that the narrative puts at the heart, both spatially and temporally, of Jesus's personal sojourn in Jerusalem. The second element is also extremely important. Jesus makes the bold claim to his distressed parents that the temple is home for him, that it is his Father's house, his things (2:49). Hence, the real home is the destination of this journey, not the place the journey started from. Moreover, the claim of Jesus hints at the special connection between himself, the temple, Jerusalem, and God as Father.

In the Gospel according to John, pilgrimage plays a different role: it marks the rhythm of the life of Jesus throughout his ministry.[32] Jesus preaches, heals, is seen during Jerusalem festivals. His journeys to the holy city are always occasioned by attendance at a religious festival. They are religious pilgrimages. Jesus never condemns pilgrimages, but condemns vehemently the commodification of offerings that could threaten and distract from the holiness of the temple (John 2:13–22).[33]

In the Gospels according to Matthew and Mark, the only instance of pilgrimage mentioned is that of the final Feast of Passover attended by Jesus (Matt 26:17; Mark 14:1–2). This ultimate pilgrimage appears in the other two canonical Gospels as well (Luke 22:1; John 12—13). The final ascent of Jesus to Jerusalem is cast as a participation in the most important Jewish religious feast, overflowing with symbols. The journey to Jerusalem echoes that to the promised land, and the ritual killing of the sacrificial lamb to be shared by relatives and neighbors is a motive applied to Christ himself. The Last Supper itself was performed as a ritual meal prescribed for the Feast of Unleavened Bread. Hence, the last meal of Jesus was a highly ritualized pilgrimage meal, and Jesus was arrested, tried, and died while accomplishing a pilgrimage, having reached its destination in Jerusalem. Place is significant. The culmination of each Gospel and of Jesus's life unfolds during a final pilgrimage.

Other important instances of pilgrimage in the New Testament are the pilgrimages *to* Jesus. In Roman-period Hellenistic culture, and in later rabbinic Judaism, a frequent *telos* of pilgrimage was a living individual, great teacher, or holy person.[34] The same was also true in early Christianity.[35] In the Gospels, we see people coming to Jesus, as on a pilgrimage, sometimes even from or through Jerusalem, foretelling the upcoming shift from Jerusalem to Jesus as the most authentic destination for pilgrimage, from the holy city to the Holy One himself.

The most elaborate instance of pilgrimage to Jesus concerned the Magi, who journeyed from a foreign land, went *through* Jerusalem, to finally reach Jesus and adore him (Matt 2:1–12). Theirs was a long and arduous journey from the distant east, following a star, stopping first in Jerusalem before continuing to Bethlehem. Overjoyed at reaching their destination, they saw Jesus in Mary's arms, bowed down to him as a sign of respect, and worshiped (*proskyneō*) him. They also brought gifts to him, before taking the road again to go back to their land by a different route. The magi foreshadowed generations of pilgrims who would leave their land to set off on a journey to encounter Christ—maybe *through* another place—and who are overwhelmed with emotion at the conclusion of their pilgrimage as they worship him.[36]

Throughout the ministry of Jesus, especially after he gained a reputation as a healer, many would come from afar to revere him in the hope of healing or instruction—or simply out of curiosity. "Great crowds followed him from Galilee, the Decapolis, Jerusalem, Judea, and from beyond the Jordan" (Matt 4:25),[37] signaling the extent of the journey that some were willing to make to come to the presence of Jesus. Similar crowds had been flocking earlier to another holy man, John the Baptist, while he was in the desert.[38] Teachers of the law also made the trek from Jerusalem to Jesus to converse with him (Matt 15; Mark 7). When they reach him, Jesus welcomes their concerns and desires. As an embodied destination, he receives his pilgrims and engages with them.

Both the perspective of the pilgrimages *of* Jesus and the pilgrimages *to* Jesus illustrate how actual pilgrimages shaped the life and ministry of Jesus. He embodied at once the personal praxis of "pilgrimaging," and the status of being the destination of other people's pilgrimages already in his lifetime.

Christ's Life as Pilgrimage

Pilgrimage is also structurally built into the fabric of the gospel narratives. In the Gospel according to John, the multiple pilgrimages of Jesus to Jerusalem give the narrative of his ministry its rhythm. Luke's Gospel proceeds differently. After the early visits of Jesus to the temple as an infant, as a young boy, and potentially annually, Jesus is tempted in Jerusalem after the devil brings him there (Luke 4:9). Throughout the narrative of his ministry, the movement toward Jerusalem is a constant leitmotif[39] and shows Jesus's singleness of purpose, as well as his strong teleological bent.[40] The ascent to Jerusalem is portrayed along the way more as an ascent to a place than an ascent to Passover. Such a strong impression of pilgrimage in gospel narratives of Jesus's life opens the door for a broader reading of Jesus as pilgrim.

A retelling of the life of Jesus highlights the pilgrim resonances of his existence. Jesus was born while his parents were on the road, visiting the city of Bethlehem from their home of Nazareth (Luke 2:4). Since they were traveling, they had to find lodging, but failed despite Mary's pregnancy. Consequently, Jesus was born outside the comfort of a home. Soon after, fleeing potential danger and threat to the child's life, Joseph and Mary went to Egypt as refugees, starting Jesus's life in exile from the Holy Land (Matt 2:13–23). Later, as a young boy growing up in Nazareth, the only reported event of his youth was a religious pilgrimage to Jerusalem.

Jesus's ministry was itinerant. He went from village to village, preaching, healing, welcoming. The matter of his home—or lack thereof—is left in flux in the canonical Gospels. In John, Jesus had a place to which he brought his early disciples (John 1:39), whereas in the Synoptic Gospels he tells an inquirer that the "Son of Man has nowhere to lay his head" (Luke 9:58).[41] Home or not, Jesus is portrayed as on the move, welcomed into friends' homes,[42] and inviting himself into strangers' homes![43] As an itinerant preacher, as a pilgrim, Jesus had to rely on the generosity and support of people willing to show him hospitality.

Jesus was going up to Jerusalem,[44] inexorably attracted by the holy city and its temple, in a tension between his ongoing ministry and the teleological "hour" (*hōra*),[45] the moment of the revelation of his being in its fullest extent through the cross and resurrection. His journey was also an attentive and progressive search of the Father's will marked by prayer.[46] This quest deepened in him a desire to know and live something that went beyond him, exemplifying in his daily life how a transcendental dimension acted as both a source and the object of a quest.

Jesus's invitation to those who want to know him is not only to listen, or to believe, but to come and see, to come and follow, or to be sent to testify.[47] His invitation is not only cognitive, but existential and embodied. The people encountered are either called to follow or sent on their own journey, even when they want to follow.[48] The very call of the disciples to follow him entreats them to a movement that would consume their whole being and life. They are called not simply to trust, to believe, to assent, but to risk their whole life, their body, their commitment, their hopes, by walking in the footsteps of Jesus.

Jesus wants to form community, both in the fraternity of transient encounters, and in a new community of companions, called and sent, sometimes welcomed by others, sometimes rejected (Luke 10:1–12), gathered in a last meal around bread and wine, during a final moment of the pilgrimage to Jerusalem.[49]

Throughout his journey, Jesus did not spare his effort, until the end, not shying away even from pain and suffering. Pilgrimage can be arduous. The pilgrim must travel light and can face needs and pain along the way. Jesus suffers, dying on the cross, an apparent failure. The cross tells the story of a complete emptying, a kenosis, a self-gift that reaches to the gift of one's life itself, death—and death as a man rejected by the community, brought outside the city walls. Does the journey end in Jerusalem?

Traversed by the unspeakable suffering of death, God nonetheless transcends that suffering in resurrection for Jesus. This marks the ultimate transformation for him, a renewed life, a vindication of his witness, and a great hope for his disciples. Resurrection is the pinnacle of transformation at the completion of a pilgrim journey.

The apparitions of the risen Christ carry on his pilgrim existence. Christ appears in different places, even to disciples who were on the road (Mark 16:12; Luke 24:15). To those who were enclosed out of fear, he breaks into their midst despite walls and closed doors (John 20:19). Inviting them to go to Galilee (Matt 28:10), he sends them to all nations.[50]

The ascension, as the departure of the risen Christ from earth, is at once a return and a promise of return. The theme of the return is important for the phenomenon of pilgrimage; a pilgrim returns home. Where is home for Christ? The authors of "The Pilgrimage in the Great Jubilee" emphasize the return of the eschatological pilgrim Jesus as his coming back on earth,[51] completing the pilgrim journey he had accomplished there. Such reading highlights the human nature of Christ's pilgrimage. On the other hand, from a divine perspective, the pilgrimage of the Son who started in Godself[52] is brought to completion by returning to the Father's side. Therefore, the dual nature of Jesus Christ leads to a dual reading of the completion of his pilgrimage and the signification of his return(s)—heavenly home versus earthly one.

Place and Person: A Theology of Embodied Holiness

The pilgrimages of Jesus and to Jesus, and the importance of Jerusalem as a holy place in Judaism, raise the question of a theology of place, or even whether any place could be deemed more sacred or holy than another. Are there holy places that are such ontologically and not just functionally? The nexus of the issue lies with the concepts of holiness and embodiment.

The concept of embodied holiness that I put forward relies on the distinction between sacred and holy explained earlier.[53] It conveys the idea that while holiness pertains to the divine realm, it is not ethereal and can be embodied, although not reified. Contrary to sacredness, which is based on the clear separation from the profane, holiness is *orientational*, insofar as it is oriented toward God, but also allows for growth. The prime locus for embodied holiness is the human body, that of Christ first, then of other Christ-like figures, then of physical traces of their embodied holiness. The (divine) source always has precedence, just as the (moving) body has over the place it inhabits or traverses.

Two complementary approaches to the question can be pursued. On the one hand, a view of the radical shift of the holy place from Jerusalem to the person of Jesus Christ, signaling a transition from a located to an embodied holiness. On the other hand, a theology of holy place can be seen from the starting point of the incarnation, which expended the realm of divine holiness into humanity. This, in turn, calls for the reassessment of the role of holy places, and the examination of the other forms of embodiment of holiness elicited in bodies and community.

From Jerusalem to Jesus: Embodied Holiness

As the major author in the New Testament, Paul does not show a particular devotion to Jerusalem—or even Judea and Galilee for that matter—as the place that witnessed Jesus's life, ministry, and death. He certainly and emphatically raised funds to support the brethren in Jerusalem, and visited the apostles there,[54] but his letters show no nostalgia for Jerusalem, or even an inkling toward a potential value for believers, even Greeks, to undertake a journey there to see the Jerusalem temple or the locations associated with Jesus's life.[55] The preaching of Paul is focused on a person, that of Jesus Christ, and not a place. Paul himself was geographically forward looking, ultimately setting his eyes on Spain as he was writing to the Christian community in Rome (Rom 15:24).

With the destruction of the Jerusalem temple in the year 70, a clear reconsideration of the status of such a highly centralized place of God's presence ensued. Already in the Gospels, some utterances of Jesus flagged the *hubris* that accompanied the temple and foretold its upcoming demise,[56] a criticism that was used against him at his trial (Matt 26:61; Mark 14:58). Jesus challenged the easy self-assurance that the temple and its sturdy buildings seem to provide, in oblivion of its genealogy marked by the mobility provided earlier by the tent, and the nonfiguration of the central focus of the ark of the covenant. In his discussion with the Samaritan woman, written down decades after the destruction of the Jerusalem temple, Jesus prophesizes that people would no longer worship in the temple in Samaria or in that of Jerusalem, but in truth and spirit (John 4:23). The stream of nonreification of the presence of God would be renewed through the ministry of Jesus, and the destruction of the temple. Neither Jesus himself nor the early Christian community offer any surrogate Christian building for the Jerusalem temple.[57] In Christianity, no place could ever play a role equivalent to that of the temple in early Judaism.

The early Christian deemphasis of the Jerusalem temple should not be too quickly equated with a condemnation of a pilgrimage to a place. The praxis of Jesus himself did not warrant such interpretation. Although historically pilgrimage—to the Jerusalem temple or elsewhere—has never been a requirement in Christianity, the early believers did not abandon altogether the Jewish practice of praying at the temple, as is recounted multiple times in the Acts of the Apostles[58]—which does not depart in that regard from the Gospels. Multiple factors played into the later desertion. One was the geographical distance from many Christian communities, a factor that was already at work in contemporary Jewish communities, for which the pilgrimage to Jerusalem had become a sign of devotion more than an obligation.[59] Moreover, since Christians were driven out of Jerusalem because of persecution (Acts 8:1), the "center" of the community moved away from Jerusalem, and ever more distant from it.[60] While Judaism had experienced a centuries-long process of centralization of worship, Christianity experienced from the start a diffracted development—best exemplified by Paul's ministry and letters. The integration of non-Jews into the fold led to a reconsideration of the observance by new Gentile members of Jewish religious practices. Only the most essential were kept.[61] Religious pilgrimages to Jerusalem were not among them. Finally, the destruction of the temple and its aftermath evidently put an end to a certain era of Jewish—and potentially Christian—pilgrimages to Jerusalem. But that did not stop early Christians from going to places, albeit different ones. Hence, visiting the tombs of the apostles is a very ancient custom, and Christian pilgrimages to Jerusalem would be undertaken some centuries later under new conditions.

At a theological level, a deeper transition occurs for the holy place from that of the Jerusalem temple to Jesus. The core of holiness shifts from the divine presence in the *sanctum sanctorum* of the temple to the very person of Jesus Christ. Peter Walker, for example, exemplifies the rejection of the "place" by stating that for Christians, Jesus becomes the true center of worship; hence, it is no longer Jerusalem or its temple,[62] or by extension any other place.[63] Likewise, John Paul II writes that "in the New Testament, this 'concentration' of sacred space reaches its summit in Christ, who is, in his person, the new 'temple' (cf. John 2:21), in which dwells the 'fullness of Godhead' (Col 2:9)."[64] Therefore, there is a strong continuity between the temple and Jesus because both express a divine presence. The distinction in terms of the place is that in the temple, the divine presence is *located*—though not reified—in a building, whereas Jesus is a person, and as such, he *embodies* the divine presence, signaling at once a greater intimacy of the connection, but also a fragility—inherent to the body. In the Synoptic Gospels, the shift between the two is symbolized by the tearing down of the veil of the temple at the hour of the death of Jesus on the cross.[65] From another perspective, the shift from temple to Christ lifted the ban on representation of the divine person. Not only was representation possible, but it was open to multiplicity, while not falling back on the type of worship offered to statues or images in other religions. Christ thus achieved a rupture in the holiness of the place by becoming the embodied holy one par excellence. Consequently, the theological source of the phenomenon of pilgrimage is not necessarily a return to or revival of Jerusalem but lies in Christ's holiness, which is *stricto sensu* beyond place. Hence, the Jerusalem focus of a Christian theology of place is misguided.

There is a greater continuity between the Jerusalem temple and the person of Jesus Christ than one would first see. The move is one from holiness to holiness, from a *located* holiness to an *embodied* holiness. The holiness of the Jerusalem temple as a place relied on the divine presence according to the ark of the covenant. For Christians, divine holiness has been incarnated in the very flesh of Jesus Christ. Hence, in Christ, the importance of holy place(s) is not abolished but recast. Christ points to a recentering of the holy place, from place to holy. This holiness is itself relational, capable of encounters, located in the frailty of the body, and later in the memory and promise of that body.

From the Incarnation to the Saints: Embodied Holiness in Others

The main theological foundation underwriting Christian pilgrimage is the doctrine of the incarnation.[66] The Word was made flesh and dwelled among us (John 1:14). In Jesus Christ, God is made visible. He can be touched, heard, seen, or even pictured. He has a body, constrained in time and space in his earthly life. The distance and elusiveness that had been experienced in the Hebrews' relationship with God in the dialectics of presence and absence through the tent and the temple was now reordered to a primacy of embodied presence. A connection was established between God—and his holiness—and the material realm. God was literally moving through the space of creation. As John Paul II writes, "The mystery of the Incarnation therefore reshapes the universal experience of 'sacred space,' on the one hand relativizing it, and on the other hand underlining its importance in new terms. The very 'taking of flesh' by the Word (John 1:14) is in fact a reference to space."[67]

The implications and definition of the embodiment of God in Jesus Christ would lead to centuries of struggle before being refined theologically through crises and discussions. The disconcerting aspect of this new embodied divine reality should not be overlooked. Walker notices the accrued interest in the fourth century for the actual places that witnessed Christ's life, through pilgrimages to the Holy Land.[68] This century was also that of great christological debates at the Councils of Nicaea (325) and Constantinople (381). Interest in the theological definition of the person of Christ and in the physical places where he lived were concomitant. The task of defining the nature of Christ, which extended to the Council of Chalcedon (451) in particular, was settled in the acknowledgment of his being both truly human and truly divine. These two natures of Christ, and the belief in his continuous presence, opens an interstice of divine presence in the material world. Such potentiality for beholding the divine enhances the value recognized to the material world. The tension between a divine holiness and embodiment must be kept in check nonetheless to avoid a pure reification.[69]

The empty tomb, but even more pointedly the ascension, meant that the divine and human body of Christ disappeared from the surface of the earth. The only material trace of its earlier presence rested in the places where he dwelled, but the holiness (*hagiotês*) of God that was resplendent in Christ would not be absent. Early Christians called themselves the saints (*hagioi*),[70] and the apostles would unceasingly call them to holiness (Rom 1:7; 1 Cor 1:2). This holiness is not based on one's personal merits, but on an adherence to Christ himself, who is the bestower of the holiness that is God's quality. Just as through the incarnation the holiness of God dwelled perfectly in the human body of Jesus, in the saints, the holiness of God is also present and active. Their embodied holiness is mediated through the holiness of the Holy One, Christ himself. Through their life, ministry, and onto their death, the saints have carried holiness to a multitude of earthly places. The holiness ascribed to these places would nonetheless always be referred to the single holiness of God revealed fully in the world through Jesus Christ.

The continuity between the holiness of the Holy One and the holiness of the saints as holy people is achieved through the Holy Spirit, Spirit of the Father and of the Son, Spirit of holiness. The same Spirit that led Jesus in his earthly ministry, from the incarnation to the resurrection, had been imparted to the disciples, as promised. Called to be "temple[s] of the holy Spirit" (1 Cor 6:19), they can hold the very source of holiness in their mortal bodies. By this connection with the Spirit, saints enact through their lives the diffraction of holiness that would result in due course, at their deaths, in the multiplication of holy locations associated with them.

From Embodied Holiness to Holy Memorials

Instead of hindering the possibility of a pilgrimage destination, the absence of the physical body of Christ after the ascension led to a multiplicity of holy sites associated with his life in the Holy Land. With the embodied holiness also exemplified in innumerable saints, a multiplicity of holy sites is unavoidable in the diffraction of so many saints whose relics were kept, related either to their bodies or to locations of events of their lives. This holy diffusion reenchants the world and stresses that "the presence of God by its nature cannot be restricted to any one place, since his presence, which has its fullest expression and communication in Christ, pervades all space."[71]

Through the lens of the divine presence, the importance of specific places shines. Holy places, or shrines, act as memorials, material witnesses, to the holiness that comes with God's presence, even through human beings. Such memorials do not constitute only museums of past events but actualize in the present the revealed holiness. Considering the special reverence given to the Bible in the Reformed tradition, the styling of the Holy Land as a "fifth gospel"[72] also illustrates an attempt to recognize the high significance of its locations. The role of holy memorials is to make divine presence more alive, more accessible to human beings, who are embodied beings after all! A holy place is a place that has been sanctified, but it is not a reification of holiness. Shrines are sometimes dubbed "thin places,"[73] places where God seems closer, where the distance of human beings to God is decreased. The operating principle of a holy memorial is the memory of a holy presence. It is through the memory of God's embodied holiness in an event of the life of Christ or in the deeds of a saint that the holiness of a place is recognized.

No place can encapsulate holiness, but many can express and foster it. Holiness is not in a place, but in a person, Jesus Christ, and in the many people he inspired throughout the centuries, starting with the saints revered as such, whose memorials of earthly life stimulate devotion. The role of the memorial is to foster the encounter of the pilgrim with the very source of holiness. The shrine, by inviting one into participation in the memory of God's dwelling in a person and a place, also questions the pilgrim in return: How do you embody God's holiness yourself?

Embodied Holiness: The Nexus of the Eucharist

At the beginning of this chapter, we explored the story of the disciples on the road to Emmaus. The culmination of their (anti-) pilgrimage was the realization at the (eucharistic) breaking of the bread that the risen Christ was present among them. The Eucharist, with its deep roots in both the Old and the New Testament, offers a meaningful *locus* to cap a reflection on embodied holiness in place and person.

The Eucharist is eminently embodied. At its heart stands the sacramental body of Christ, memorializing the risen body of the Lord. Such a body allows for accessibility and mobility. It is confected from the simple element of bread. The host as body of Christ is also not limited to a single location, inhabiting many places, numerous communicants, and even tabernacles. But the body of Christ is not only located in the sacred host, it is constituted also by the assembled community of believers who partake in the divine meal, as a community in prayer.[74] Jesus said to his disciples that when two or three of them are gathered in his name, he is there among them (Matt 18:20).

The central event of the Eucharist is the concrete encounter with the divine presence, facilitated by the physicality of both the community and the host received. The Eucharist sacramentally celebrates the life of Christ offered for our redemption, calling to memory his words and deeds. The Eucharist constitutes a collective and eschatological memorial. The place and time of the eucharistic celebration manifests, constitutes, and renews the Church as holy Body of Christ.

As memorial, the Eucharist acts as an intangible place. Its physical location is usually that of a shrine, church, or chapel; it is not *any* place, but it could be anywhere.[75] The holiness of the place is induced by the memorial ritual, the prayerful presence of the believing community, and the divine presence celebrated and actualized. The memorial can also be on the move, as in processions in which the eucharistic elements are carried. What is happening in the place is what makes the place holy. Even in a shrine—already memorializing holiness—the Eucharist enhances the "presentification" of holiness by reactualizing it in a community.

The Eucharist finally highlights the further embodiment of holiness. Already through the saints—the Church in heaven—the divine holiness revealed in Christ is made more broadly visible. Through the Eucharist a further diffusion of holiness is achieved in the partaking (and constituting) of the holy body. Embodied holiness is potentially multiplied. Such "increase" in holiness—if quantifying language is appropriate—is realized by the Holy Spirit, as it is prayed in the Eucharistic Prayers. After the first invocation of the Spirit over the gifts of bread and wine, the prayer calls for the transformation of the assembled community into the Body of Christ. Therefore, by partaking in the eucharistic celebration, the believers express the desire to let the sacramentally embodied holiness of Christ lead them to be "places" of embodied holiness themselves. In the collective prayer of the living community gathered as Church shines the holiness[76] of the Body of Christ, to use the Pauline imagery relayed by the Second Vatican Council.[77] This invitation is expressed powerfully in the universal call to holiness in the documents of this Council.[78] The hope of the Eucharist is that the participants will be radically transformed by their communion with the one holy Body of Christ,[79] just as the Hebrews were called to be ethically transformed in the aftermath of the exodus. The embodied holiness wished for in the partakers of the Eucharist would lead them to a concrete care for bodies in need: the poor, through social justice, or even the earth, through environmental concerns.[80] The Eucharist as embodied encounter with the divine presence calls for a total embodied response.

Sending: The Disciples in Mission and Pilgrimage

Our journey in the New Testament led us this far to see the pilgrimage praxis of Jesus and the pilgrim narrative arc of his life, then the embodied holiness at play between place and person. This third part pertains to the pilgrimage "style" of mission of the apostles, and its connection with the Holy Spirit. The connection between pilgrimage and mission is made explicit in many contemporary ecclesial documents about pilgrimage.[81] While it might appear at first to be an imposition on the phenomenon of pilgrimage, the connection is actually strongly established in the New Testament through the sending on mission of the disciples by Jesus in a pilgrim-like manner, as well as by the subsequent dynamic diffusion of the Christian message by itinerant missionaries—an impetus subsequently carried over as a Christian ideal in religious apostolic communities. Hence, the pilgrim way colors strongly the style of Christianity in its apostolic dimension.[82] Such "pilgrim style" does not necessarily carry all the characteristics of pilgrimage identified in chapter 1, but its connection is strong enough to suggest an insightful inquiry.

Sending on Mission

An important anchoring point of the theology of pilgrimage in the New Testament is the initial sending in mission of the disciples, already in Jesus's lifetime. Jesus, after having spent time with the disciples, chose the ones he wanted to send, making them "apostles"—etymologically, the ones "sent." This sending anticipates the mission entrusted to the apostles and the Church after the resurrection and ascension of Christ. Luke's narrative of the sending of the seventy-two emphasizes the pilgrim-like dimensions of the mission but also introduces some complements that enrich the normative pilgrimage experience (Luke 10:1–24).[83]

The narrative begins with Jesus already on the road. He had set his sights clearly on Jerusalem and had started to move toward that destination (Luke 9:51). While he was on the road, questions were asked of Jesus that gave him the opportunity to clarify the meaning of following him (vv. 57–58). The sending of the seventy-two disciples happens in a "nowhere," an unspecified location between the Samaritan village that did not welcome the disciples (v. 52), and the village of Martha (10:38).[84]

Jesus sent the disciples in pairs (Luke 10:1), neither alone nor in large groups; allowing for an experience that is at once personal and shared. The pairs are not sent to a specific place, but to "every town and place where he himself intended to go" (Luke 10:1), hence to a multitude of places. Not only is the destination not specified, but the trajectory of the journey would also be determined by the reception experienced in the different locations (vv. 8–11). While they are not going to a specific place, their task is to announce a new reality to take place, the kingdom of God, whose nearness can be connected to the announced intention of Jesus to go there himself. They are sent as ambassadors. Jesus will even go further in his association with the apostles: he identifies himself with them by declaring, "Whoever listens to you listens to me, and whoever rejects you rejects me, and whoever rejects me rejects the one who sent me" (Luke 10:16). Hence, the apostle is not only not speaking of his own initiative but carries an identification with the one who sent him, he bears witness to him and shares his fate.

A sense of journey emanates from the instructions, since despite the absence of temporal markers regarding the length of the endeavor, it is suggested that more than one town would be visited by each pair. The time required for such ongoing visits by the pairs of disciples seems at odds with the unspecified—but potentially narrow—window offered in Jesus's ascent to Jerusalem. The nonspecification of the timeframe could suggest a *kairos* type of time, a favorable time not well captured by chronology, and it could also point at the future mission of the apostles, in time opened after the ascension of Jesus. The apostles are not to move from house to house (Luke 10:7), but from village to village. Their aim is not to settle forever in any place; they are itinerants and will come back to Jesus. The disciples leave with a clear purpose in mind: a mission of proclamation of the coming kingdom of God and of healing of the sick (v. 9) as eschatological signs of the coming of the kingdom. The journey of the disciples is not leisurely; they are expected to show zeal and focus by not greeting people "on the road" (v. 4), keeping their gaze upon the mission entrusted to them.

The conditions in which the disciples would journey are typical of a pilgrimage. Their luggage should be minimal. They are to carry "no purse, no bag, no sandals" (Luke 10:4). Such austerity in the living conditions opens a space for vulnerability and trust. They would need to rely on the hospitality of others to carry on their journey, obtaining lodging and food (vv. 7–8). Doing so, they must develop a trust in the value of their mission and a trust in the one who sent them, in addition to a culture of exchange and dependency with the people who welcome them. The dimension of exchange is underlined already in the initial offering of peace, a traditional Jewish greeting, as a gift presented to the household by the disciples—a gift to unfold in the proclamation of the good news. But such a gift can also be refused. Hence, Jesus clearly lays down the potential pain and risks presenting themselves in the journey. Metaphorically, he warns the disciples that he is sending them out "like lambs into the midst of wolves" (v. 3). Their efforts would not always be welcomed, and the image suggests a hostility that could even become life-threatening—a foreshadowing of things to come.[85] Rejection is the most obvious potential pitfall, deserving a lengthy treatment in Jesus's discourse of commission (vv. 10–16). The words of Jesus are harsh for the towns that would reject the disciples and their message.

Upon the return of the disciples, the most striking feature of the narrative is the mutual joy (Luke 10:17, 20, 21) of the disciples and of Jesus for what had been accomplished. The joy "in the Holy Spirit" (10:21) expressed by Jesus erupts in a prayer praising the Father for the simplicity through which this revelation was made.

In this initial sending of the disciples in mission, a shape similar to that of the pilgrimage phenomenon is used to convey the mission: a sense of purpose and destination, minimalist material conditions, vulnerability allied with trust, effort and pain, potential for hospitality or rejection. The mission is carried in the name of another, in the Spirit, by preaching a reality beyond themselves, with a return marked by unbounded joy! This shape of mission-pilgrimage would then be experienced in the early Church, as expressed especially in the Acts of the Apostles, but would also instigate various returns to an apostolic life throughout history, especially through religious orders.

A Dynamic Diffusion: Apostolic Labors in the Acts of the Apostles and Beyond

The Acts of the Apostles describe the Christian life as "the way" (*hē hodos*).[86] Such a dynamic image suggests an embodied journey of faith to be traveled by oneself and with others. Despite this unique Way, the early Christian community was historically led to dispersion in many different geographical ways. Persecution struck in Jerusalem after the death of Stephen, scattering the community of believers throughout Judea, Samaria, and beyond (Acts 8:1; 11:19). Missionary zeal also provided an impulse for the journeying in multiple ways. In Acts, the missionary experience of Paul is certainly the paradigmatic example of a pilgrimage-like mission, but the story of Philip and the eunuch returning from pilgrimage is also very compelling in that regard.[87] This is where we will start before moving to Paul's experience.

The Encounter Between the Ethiopian Eunuch and Philip

The encounter between the Ethiopian eunuch and Philip (Acts 8:26–39) offers an interesting parallel with the story of the disciples on the road to Emmaus. It is also a story about a return pilgrimage. The unnamed Ethiopian eunuch was on his way home from a pilgrimage to Jerusalem to worship (8:27–28), but his quest was not fulfilled by his worship in the holy place of Jerusalem. It was either unresolved or ongoing. Hence, he was reading the Word of God (8:28) and showed his eagerness to understand its meaning (v. 34).

Philip, on the other hand, was coming from a place of exile, as he found himself in Samaria because of the dispersion from Jerusalem. While in this dislocated place, though active apostolically, an angel of the Lord invited him to go on the road (Acts 8:26). After encountering the Ethiopian in his chariot, Philip was impelled by the Spirit to engage the traveler (8:27–30). By discussing the Scriptures, he came to share the good news about Jesus (8:35), naming the personal divine destination of the pilgrimage.

The response of the Ethiopian to that encounter with Philip was swift: he asked to be baptized on the spot, and so he was (Acts 8:36, 38). A radical encounter and transformation happened for that individual. Returning from a long-distance pilgrimage to worship in Jerusalem, he enfleshed in baptism the answer he found to his quest through Scripture. The encounter on the road with the apostle Philip provides the key to his pilgrimage, paradoxically reaching his deeper destination on the return road.

For his part, Philip is "snatched away" by the Spirit as soon as the Ethiopian's quest is brought to a resolution through baptism (Acts 8:39), very much like Jesus disappearing from the disciples' view as they recognized him at the breaking of the bread. Philip then continued his itinerant preaching in various towns, while the Ethiopian continued on his journey home "rejoicing" (8:39–40) and certainly transformed.

Like the encounter of Jesus with the Emmaus disciples on their anti-pilgrimage, the encounter on the road of the Ethiopian eunuch with Philip showcases a pilgrim mission. In each instance, the pilgrims were on their return journey, away from Jerusalem. Somehow, an encounter happened, and through the scrutinizing of Scripture, a proclamation. The apex is reached in a life-transforming sacrament that highlights the absolute transcendental value of the encounter, revealed at once as an embodied encounter with the divine. Then follows the abrupt disappearance of the one encountered, but the joy remains, along with a transformation of the pilgrims.

Paul, the Missionary Pilgrim

Beyond the crisp story of Philip and the Ethiopian eunuch, the larger narrative of Paul's encounter with the Lord and his life of ministry offers invaluable insights into pilgrimage as mission.[88] From the moment of his conversion on the road to Damascus, Paul was on the move, on a quest, and later on a mission up to his martyrdom in Rome. His was a pilgrim style of mission, in line with the commissioning of Luke 10.

The quest, then ministry, of Paul entailed an embodied commitment. It unfolded in a series of travels. From the short trek between the place of encounter with the Lord to Damascus, where Ananias met him (Acts 9:17), to many apostolic endeavors of foundations, Paul's life put him on the road. His travels were mostly forward-looking. His trips to Jerusalem were outliers because he mostly desired to go to places where he had not been before, and where the gospel had not yet been preached.[89] In that geographical dimension, Paul runs counter to the ethos of pilgrimage; albeit there is movement aplenty, it is not one of return, but of constant moving forward. Paul races.[90] Such embodied commitment had consequences in his personal life. It led to a life of total following through celibacy, a state he even advocates for others (1 Cor 7:7).

A clear departure affects Paul's pilgrimage. First, the encounter on the road to Damascus, which was a life-shattering event for him. But then there is the departure for missionary work in a manifold way: to Arabia, with the Church of Antioch, then as apostle of Jesus Christ.[91] Paul discovered progressively his vocation as "apostle to the Gentiles,"[92] which became the leitmotif of his existence and the intention of his pilgrimage.

In the manner of the disciples sent in a pilgrim fashion by Jesus, Paul experienced the efforts and the vulnerability of itinerant ministry. He experienced innumerable hardships from beatings to shipwrecks, and boasted of them:

> Five times I have received from the Jews the forty lashes minus one. Three times I was beaten with rods. Once I received a stoning. Three times I was shipwrecked; for a night and a day I was adrift at sea; on frequent journeys, in danger from rivers, danger from bandits, danger from my own people, danger from Gentiles, danger in the city, danger in the wilderness, danger at sea, danger from false brothers and sisters; in toil and hardship, through many a sleepless night, hungry and thirsty, often without food, cold and naked. (2 Cor 11:24–27)

In a more prosaic way, Paul refused to receive money for his ministry (1 Cor 9:18; 2 Cor 11:17), except from his beloved Philippians (Phil 4:15–18),[93] emphasizing the simplicity of his life and his radical freedom.

A remarkable feature of Paul's missionary pilgrimages is the experience of companionship along the road. Companions in mission constantly surround Paul. Barnabas had been a long-time partner; Priscilla and Aquila, fellow tentmakers, were also great supports.[94] The endearment of companions shown in his letters is quite striking;[95] despite being revered as a towering figure and claiming an authority from the Lord, Paul was a team worker, and spoke highly of many of his coworkers.

One paradigmatic aspect of Paul's pilgrim experience is the clear orientation that molded his destinations. Paul is driven. Geographically, he moves forward, up to Rome, his destination—in hope of even reaching Spain! Regarding the aim, his vocation is to proclaim the gospel with zeal and freedom. At the heart of all lies Christ. He is the one encountered. He is the one proclaimed. He is the one sought. Christ is the source and the telos, the destination of the race. And this preaching of Christ is all-encompassing; Paul preaches with bluntness Christ crucified (1 Cor 2:2), no less. As an apostle of Christ, Paul is already living a reality of intimacy with God but hopes also to reap the reward of an everlasting presence to the Lord. His gaze is eschatological.

Although the status of Paul as a Jerusalem pilgrim is debated, Paul's missionary work can be read through the lens of pilgrimage, as seen in this brief sketch. While drawing on many regular pilgrim tropes, it also highlights some exceptional elements: the lifelong nature of the commitment, the centrality of Christ, and the forward-looking destination—up to the *eschaton*—of his mission.

Mission and Pilgrimage: Being Led by the Spirit in Acts

A key player of the narrative about pilgrimage-like mission in the New Testament is the Holy Spirit. The best scriptural *locus* to examine the Spirit's role in that regard is in the Acts of the Apostles. Through the story of Philip and the Ethiopian eunuch, some instances of explicit agency of the Spirit were already highlighted, but the Spirit's role is pervasive in the whole of the book. The Spirit is mentioned more than fifty times in Acts. This association is not fortuitous. In the Bible, the Spirit is associated with images of movement and fluidity,[96] inspiration—in the prophets—and change.[97] The Spirit escapes control, brings newness.[98] The Spirit is also intimately related to Christ, both in his lifetime, from the incarnation to the death and resurrection, and in the continued mission of the proclamation of the gospel.[99] The missionary way of the disciples, modeled after Christ, is guided by the Spirit, as Acts illustrates. The missionary role of the Spirit in Acts can be delineated along three main lines: presence, discourse, and action.

First, the overarching role of the Spirit in the mission and life of the early Christian community is revealed most eloquently in its affirmed presence. This presence is marked by two characteristics: the suddenness of its coming[100] and its enduring aspect.[101] The recognition of the presence of the Spirit—being "filled with" the Spirit—punctuates the narrative of Acts, from the event of Pentecost (Acts 2:4) to the eschatological promise of an outpouring of the Spirit on all people (Acts 2:17).

Second, the guidance of the Spirit becomes more evident in the Spirit's incitement to discourse. In many instances, the momentously affirmed in-filling of the Spirit is accompanied by speech: for Peter (Acts 2:4; 4:8), Stephen (Acts 7:55), or the assembled community (Acts 4:31). The discourse that follows in each instance gains an added weight through this direct inspiration. In some instances, the agency of the Spirit is expressed even more directly; it is the Spirit who speaks to or through the individual. It happens to Philip (Acts 8:29), Simon (Acts 10:19; 11:12), to the various individuals who set aside Barnabas and Paul for mission (Acts 13:2), or through Agabus the prophet (Acts 21:11). The agency of the Holy Spirit in discourse is also presented as an inspiring and confirming force in the decisions of the leadership of the community (e.g., Acts 15:28).

Finally, the role of the Holy Spirit entails action. The Spirit warns about risks (Acts 20:23), or even attempts to prevent them—through the voice of those speaking "in the Spirit" (Acts 21:4). At times, however, the action is presented in a forceful way. The Spirit *took* Philip *away*—suddenly—after he had baptized the Ethiopian eunuch (Acts 8:39),[102] *prevented* Paul and Timothy from preaching either in Asia or in Bithynia (Acts 16:6–7), and *bound* Paul to go to Jerusalem (Acts 20:22).

Through these numerous explicit mentions of the role of the Spirit in Acts, a portrayal is sketched of individuals and a community on a mission under the guidance of the Spirit.[103] Hence, the Spirit emerges as the divine dispatcher for a community on the move, in its pilgrim-like mission of spreading the gospel of Jesus Christ, in a style that is consonant with the very being of the Spirit.

The Spirit is not only the initial catalyst for mission by sending, but profoundly shapes its style.

From the Sending of the Apostles to the Vita Apostolica

The sending of the disciples in the Gospels and the Acts of the Apostles in a pilgrim style is not simply a one-time event; it became in Christianity a paradigm for apostolic mission under the guidance of the Holy Spirit. The connection between mission and pilgrim-like conditions has been instrumental in the reinvigoration of Christian life throughout history, and most emblematically through the following of Christ seen as *vita apostolica*. The periodic resurgence of the apostolic ideal is often understood as a contribution of the Spirit that brings newness to the Church.

Although poverty and chastity had been standard vows for religious men and women, the monks' vow of stability in the Western Church came to be part of the core definition of religious life. Gyrovague monks were regarded with suspicion, while missionary monks—who even traveled to foreign lands—abounded, as their aim was to settle and establish stable communities in proclaiming the gospel.[104] In the Middle Ages, the evangelical sending in mission of the disciples, as *vita apostolica*, became a blueprint to reenvision religious life. Shying away from the more stable *ethos* of monastic life, the mendicant orders of the thirteenth century, most prominently the Dominicans and the Franciscans, espoused the model of a *vita apostolica*, a more mobile, and often also more materially poor, type of religious life.[105] This way of Christian living was intended for religious, usually as part of a lifelong commitment to mission. The movement toward a recovery of the pilgrim-like way of life of the apostles became anew a way of life.

The (second) *Rule of St. Francis* offers both a direct reference to the sending of the disciples in Luke's Gospel, and to the pilgrim existence. In its third chapter, dealing with the travels of the brothers, these are advised to offer peace to any house they enter, and to eat the food set before them,[106] advice taken directly from the sending of the disciples in Luke 10. Further along, the *Rule* stresses that the brothers are not to appropriate for themselves any house, place, or anything (*nec domum nec locum nec aliquam rem*).[107] They are to serve God in poverty and humility, "as pilgrims (*peregrini*) and strangers in this world."[108] This direct reference to the pilgrim life, tied with the *ethos* of material detachment advocated by St. Francis for his brethren, underlines the enduring value of the connection between pilgrimage and mission.

This rediscovery of the *vita apostolica* would also impact subsequent periods of reform in the Church,[109] not only for missions *ad gentes*, but also for interior missions. Hence, the first-century biblical narrative has been used throughout history as a blueprint for missionary style. As such, it ties the pilgrim style to the heart of the evangelical mission of the Church.

Conclusion: Mission as Pilgrimage

Mission is at once a style and an action, that of proclaiming the gospel. As testimony, it pertains to the whole person—as exemplified by the testimony of martyrdom—as well as to what is said. To summarize this incursion into mission as pilgrimage, we can look at pilgrimage through the perspective of mission and the lens of the pilgrimage characteristics.

In mission as pilgrimage, the conditions "on the road" strike the right chords: embodiment, vulnerability, effort, alterity. Furthermore, the self is transformed, as we have seen with Paul, and it aims at transforming others. Movement is necessary, but it is not only geographical. A clear sense of transcendence emerges since missionaries are sent by the Spirit to carry Christ's work. The memory carried is not linked to the physical destination of the pilgrimage, but tied to its source, Christ, through Word and sacraments. The "intention" of pilgrimage as mission displays a more concrete content, as missionary activity, but is also more open-ended since the destination is evanescent.

Two important additions to our understanding of pilgrimage were made. First, a sense of destination that is no longer geographical, even when it traverses various spaces, as Paul did. The destination is at once Christ, in an intimate key, but also the *eschaton*. Second, the role of the Holy Spirit has been highlighted in a way that it was not in the phenomenology of pilgrimage. This is an invaluable component.

Other Pilgrim *Theologoumena* in the New Testament

The approach adopted thus far in our exploration of pilgrimage in the New Testament consisted in looking at the pilgrim structure expressed in various moments, especially in narrative form, through journeys in the Gospels and the Acts of the Apostles. It left aside a number of references to *pilgrimage* vocabulary, particularly in the epistles, which would be drawn upon in later theological reflections on pilgrimage, and especially the pilgrim status of the Church.[110] There is no single Greek word in the New Testament that corresponds to our contemporary definition of *pilgrim*, therefore words translated as "pilgrim" are also translated as "foreigner," "stranger," "alien," or "exile."[111] The history of translations plays a great part here. Some New Testament translations, such as the New Revised Standard Version, do not contain any cognate of *pilgrim*, whereas the Latin Vulgate has nine cognates of *peregrinari*,[112] and the King James Bible, two.[113] Hence, emblematic sayings on "strangers and pilgrims" from the King James Bible, with reference to Hebrews 11:13 or 1 Peter 2:11, appear or disappear depending on the translation, inviting caution. The difficulty lies not with the translators, but with the nonspecificity of the "pilgrim" content of words such as *parepidēmos*, translated in a more straightforward way by "foreigner." Consequently, it is difficult to chisel an etymological understanding of pilgrimage in the epistles. Taken in the context of pilgrimage, the core meaning of this diverse vocabulary certainly tends to promote the *foreignness* of Christians—in line with the etymology of the Latin *peregrinus*—more than to present pilgrimage as an idyllic state. Four passages in the New Testament epistles, in Ephesians, Hebrews, 1 Peter, and 2 Corinthians, represent the most important instances of pilgrim vocabulary. We will look at each in turn.

In his letter to the Ephesians, Paul emphasizes that Christians are no longer "strangers [*xenoi*] and aliens [*paroikoi*]," but that they are "citizens [*sympolitai*] with the saints and also members of the household [*oikeioi*] of God" (Eph 2:19). The vocabulary of pilgrimage is used as a comforting idea for a struggling community. The foreignness of the Christian (pilgrim) is overcome in Christ, who is the cornerstone of the new holy temple (Eph 2:20–21) comprising both Jews and Gentiles. This idea of belonging is carried in the true citizenship, that of God's household, which is the reverse of the foreignness that some Christians could have experienced. This change of status is presented as reconciliation (Eph 2:16), establishing a new unity. The house of God is no longer only Israel. Christians are no longer pilgrims, but citizens in God's dwelling place.[114] The accent is therefore placed on the unity of the people, and its inscription in a dwelling—not on movement and foreignness.

The Letter to the Hebrews speaks powerfully about the faith of Abraham, expressed in deeds. He lived as a foreigner in the promised land, under a tent (Heb 11:9). Abraham, Isaac, Jacob, and their heirs

> died in faith without having received the promises, but from a distance they saw and greeted them. They confessed that they were strangers [*xenoi*] and foreigners [*parepidēmoi*] on the earth, for people who speak in this way make it clear that they are seeking a homeland. If they had been thinking of the land that they had left behind, they would have had opportunity to return. But as it is, they desire a better country, that is, a heavenly one. Therefore God is not ashamed to be called their God; indeed, he has prepared a city for them. (Heb 11:13–16)

The passage is built on the distinctions between what *is* (faith, the seeing and embracing of the promise) and what is not *yet* (the homeland/city), which is applied to the state of the Christian, who while on earth is constantly seeking a different country (a heavenly one). The constancy of the desire is highlighted by the precision that they would have had enough time to return, to cease to desire the heavenly country and become anew citizens of the earth. But they did not. Consequently, the pilgrim state is here characterized by a *faithful* desire for a divine destination. This destination would be the new land of the promise, though on a different realm from Abraham's promised land, for the Abrahamic migrant differs from the Christian pilgrim, whose land is heavenly. Hebrews displays an eschatological perspective for pilgrimage; the horizon of the pilgrim is none other than heaven. The pilgrim condition is thus a passage to be traveled in faith. These verses are especially important because of their translation as "strangers and pilgrims on the earth," which underlines the transient nature of the pilgrimage on earth, less embodied than desirous to be completed in a heavenly destination.

The First Letter of Peter also uses *parepidēmos* (1 Pet 1:1; 2:11), translated as "aliens and exiles," but also at times as "pilgrims," to show the distance that the addressees should keep from "desires of the flesh" (1 Pet 2:11), hence from the world that they should not be a part of. They were told that they were "a chosen race, a royal priesthood, a holy nation, God's own people" (1 Pet 2:9). Consequently, the pilgrim state is one of radically *not* belonging to a world presented as decadent, but of displaying an honorable conduct in it (1 Pet 2:12). The emphasis lies in the *distance* from what the world represents, more than on the orientation toward any destination. Being a pilgrim in that regard means to stay away from the world.

A slightly different view emerges in Paul's second letter to the Corinthians. Paul contrasts the tent (*skēnos*) and the divine dwelling (*oikia*—2 Cor 5:1). The tent is provisory, mortal, bodily, whereas the heavenly dwelling prepared by God is eternal. We groan in the tent, longing for the heavenly dwelling (2 Cor 5:4). The nexus is the *oikia*, the house, and the *movement of being at home* (*endēmeō*) in the Lord and *being away from* (*ekdēmeō*) the body (2 Cor 5:6, 8, 9). Paul advocates leaving what is provisional—the tent, the body—to journey in faith toward the house of the Lord (2 Cor 5:6–8). A negative light is thus cast on the body. The pilgrimage is therefore not on earth, but the moving away from where and what we are to be in God. However, at the heart of both realities—being in the body or already at home with the Lord—stands the invitation to please the Lord (2 Cor 5:9).

These occurrences of pilgrim vocabulary in the New Testament underline the uneasiness of the being-pilgrim. What emerges from these texts is a depiction in which the being-pilgrim is not highly valued in itself. Comfort is reached when one is no longer a pilgrim, when the *telos* is attained. The goal is always to belong, to be citizen, to arrive, to be home, but the pilgrim is foreign. In addition, there is no romanticizing of pilgrimage here; the pilgrim is moving *away from*, even if the Lord is accompanying the pilgrim. But the yearning for the divine destination is also strong, and the eschatological dimension emphasized. Being pilgrim is the necessary means to reach the final destination of a stable state in God.

3. CONCLUSION

What is gained from such biblical journeys? First, the richness of potential approaches to pilgrimage is tantalizing. Individual journeys and figures are inspiring: Adam and Eve, Abraham, Moses, Jesus, the disciples, Paul. A collective dimension in exodus that molded a people through experience and birthed rituals and moral commitment. A portrayal of God as on the move, at first "nonfigurable," and always non-"graspable." Through the pilgrimages of Jesus and those of his disciples, pilgrimage is transformed. By the incarnation, holiness itself is embodied, diffused through saints and memorials, and sacramentalized most clearly in the Eucharist. In the mission of the apostles, pilgrimage becomes a style, potentially *the* style of Christianity. Throughout, a certain tension surfaces between the world and heaven, between now and the *eschaton*, between the "pilgrimaging" and the stable remaining (usually in God), between the road and the dwelling, between the inner disposition and the exterior praxis. Pilgrimage is not romanticized in the New Testament. The "road" is not idealized, and its uneasiness not swept away. The Bible has a lot to say that inspires pilgrimage.

There is no streamlined biblical theology of pilgrimage, and certainly no explicit obligation of pilgrimage in the New Testament, but also no condemnation. There are seeds and grounds for pilgrimage, which explain why Christian pilgrimage sprouted up centuries ago and is still flourishing. A space is open for theological inquiry and Christian living.

The next chapter opens a new dimension: an exploration of the depth of pilgrimage from a historical figure who lived out pilgrimage(s), reflected upon it, and adopted it as a formational tool for further disciples. Let us now turn our gaze to the pilgrim Ignatius of Loyola.

CHAPTER 3

The Modern Pilgrim

Identity and Formation in the Testament *of Ignatius of Loyola*

Ignatius of Loyola (1491–1556) not only lived pilgrimage, but also restated his own identity through it and used it as a formational tool. Born at the dawn of a new era, at the end of the Spanish Reconquista, the discovery of the Americas, and on the eve of the Reformation, by the end of his life, Ignatius had become a central figure on the religious scene. He was at the helm of a new but fast-growing religious order, the Society of Jesus, and had seen his influential guide to spiritual life, the *Spiritual Exercises*, approved by the Holy See. He was canonized in 1622 alongside his fellow Jesuit, Francis Xavier, crystallizing his status in the Church.

Ignatius offers a unique ground for pilgrimage studies. In our book, he opens up a single individual perspective, after our consideration of broader phenomenological and biblical dimensions. Ignatius had not only been a pilgrim himself, journeying most notably to Jerusalem, but he also used pilgrimage as a formation tool. Furthermore, in an account of his life, he used the word *pilgrim* to encapsulate his journey.

Born into a noble family in Loyola, in Spanish Basque country, Íñigo de Loyola was educated at home. In his teens he was to be a page in the court of Juan Velásquez de Cuéllar, a senior official of king Fernando of Aragon, to further his socialization into circles of power.[1] As an aspiring *caballero* (knight), he dreamt of honor and conquest—from women's hearts to military prowess. During a long recovery at the family castle following wounds suffered in military action (1521), he decided to change paths radically and undertook a pilgrimage to Jerusalem (1523–24), including a long stay in Manresa (1522–23), not far from the Abbey of Montserrat. Upon his return from Jerusalem, he set his sights on studying, first in Barcelona (1524–26), then in the prestigious universities of Alcalá (1526–27), Salamanca (1527–28), and Paris (1528–35). Gathering like-minded young men, he formed a group of companions who shared a desire to serve God as priests of reformed life. After completing their studies in Paris, Ignatius and his new companions regrouped in Venice, hoping to achieve their desired pilgrimage to Jerusalem only to be impeded by the war raging in 1537 between Venice and the Ottoman Empire, which prevented any ship from Venice to reach the Holy Land. Ignatius and his companions instead offered themselves to the pope to be missioned by him wherever he saw fit. Since the group of first companions decided to stay united through a formal structure in 1539, Ignatius was eventually elected to be in charge of them and would spend the rest of his life in Rome, guiding the growth of the newly formed Society of Jesus. He would do so while also giving the Spiritual Exercises and writing the *Constitutions* of the new order as well as innumerable letters.[2] At the same time, he was establishing a rehabilitation house for former prostitutes, called Santa Marta, a house for Jewish catechumens, as well as the Roman college, the ancestor of the Gregorian University. He died in Rome in 1556, after having presided for more than fifteen years over the rapid growth of his religious community.

Ignatius's own experience of pilgrimage was quite intensive. In the early months of his conversion experience, he undertook a pilgrimage to Jerusalem, desiring to live where Christ lived, hoping to stay there for his whole life (*T* 8, 45).[3] On his journey toward the Holy Land, he stopped at other pilgrimage sites. Early on, he visited the local Marian sanctuary of Aránzazu (*T* 13). Soon afterward, after having stopped at the house of a nobleman who had debts toward him, he donated some money to restore an image of the Virgin Mary (*T* 13). Then, at the Abbey of Montserrat he confessed his sins, gave up his sword in a vigil of arms, and traded his fancy clothes for the rough garb of a pilgrim. By then he was ready to undertake the journey to Jerusalem. Although Ignatius reached

Jerusalem as a young man, he had to return to Europe. The Franciscans who oversaw the Christian shrines of the Holy Land forced him to go back under threat of excommunication! However, this pilgrimage of the young Ignatius was the most influential he ever made.

The importance of the pilgrimage to Jerusalem for Ignatius is evident in its influence on his Parisian companions. After most of them had completed the month-long retreat of the Spiritual Exercises, and all had decided to commit themselves to a life of ministry, they gathered on August 15, 1534, at the Martyrium of St. Denys in Montmartre, just outside Paris, to vow poverty and chastity,[4] as well as to travel to Jerusalem after being ordained.[5] Ignatius's strong personal desire to follow in the very footsteps of Christ had spread to these other men. Although this collective pilgrimage never materialized, Ignatius kept the prospect of Jerusalem on the horizon. In lieu of Jerusalem, Ignatius would eventually journey to the Roman basilica of Santa Maria Maggiore, believed to contain relics from the crib of Jesus, to celebrate his first Mass, more than a year after his priestly ordination.

In addition to the instances of physical pilgrimage destinations Ignatius also regularly journeyed in the *manner* of a pilgrim—with little money, staying in "hospitals"[6] (almshouses), and journeying by foot.[7] Ignatius's companions in Venice would also adopt this way of life in their months of waiting for passage to Jerusalem. The way the companions later sent on mission journeyed was also analogous to that of pilgrims.[8] In his practice of pilgrimage, Ignatius remained faithful to medieval forms. His adoption of some material characteristics of pilgrimage for the sake of itinerant missions was inspired by the mendicant religious orders. Such pilgrim form was understood to be the proper way of being and ministering of the disciples of Jesus, as witnessed in the scene of the sending of the disciples.[9] From a phenomenological viewpoint, Ignatius was heir to a well-established tradition of pilgrimage practice, and it remained a leitmotif throughout his life either as a concrete experience or as an inner desire. The originality of the contribution of Ignatius to the study of the theology of pilgrimage does not lie on the account of his main pilgrimage to the Holy Land. Unlike other famous pilgrims to Jerusalem, Ignatius did not offer a detailed account of his personal journey there nor of the many sites that were accessible to sixteenth-century travelers, although some of his fellow pilgrims did.

What distinguishes Ignatius even more is the use of the notion of pilgrim as the key to the retelling of his own life experience. The "pilgrim" is presented as his identity, not only because of his personal practice of pilgrimage as a younger man but also because of his ongoing existential practice of what pilgrimage stands for. Ignatius represents a *total embodiment* of pilgrimage.[10] In the narrative of his life, Ignatius presents himself as "the pilgrim" as he unfolds three layers of pilgrimage.[11] The interest in that regard is not, first, Ignatius's own experience of pilgrimage, but his use of the concept of pilgrimage in the retelling of his life journey. The first layer is his medieval-type pilgrimage to Jerusalem in imitation of Christ. This dimension of pilgrimage has strong ascetical overtones. The second layer of pilgrimage is that of the discovery of his identity before God, his vocation.[12] This pilgrimage was concluded upon reaching Rome and stresses the early modern quest for identity. The third and final layer of pilgrimage is the mystical pilgrimage to God, which was still unfolding as Ignatius was narrating his journey. These three layers of pilgrimage illustrate the concurrent existence of medieval and early modern dimensions of pilgrimage in Ignatius's writing alongside a timeless, mystical one. Moreover, Ignatius transformed pilgrimage into a formational tool that would initiate others into a core religious experience.

1. THE "PILGRIM" AS IDENTITY IN THE *TESTAMENT*

The Text of Ignatius's Narrative of His Life

For centuries, the standard biography of Ignatius of Loyola was a book written by Pedro de Ribadeneira—or Ribadeneyra—(1526–1611), who, as a young Jesuit, had personally known Ignatius.[13] Ribadeneira's *Vita Ignatii Loyolae* was commissioned by Francisco Borja, third general superior of the Society of Jesus, to provide a comprehensive biography of Ignatius befitting a saint-to-be.[14] The *Vita* was meant to complete and supersede a narrative prepared by Ignatius toward the end of his life.[15] In previous years Ignatius had been pestered by some of his first companions to leave a "testament" of his spiritual journey,[16] for some feared that he might soon die, since the main tasks he had set forth as superior general were almost all accomplished: the *Spiritual Exercises* had been approved by the pope and published, and the redaction of the *Constitutions* was well under way.[17] Although Ignatius resisted at first, he decided in 1553 to grant his companions' wish and narrate his journey.

Despite his prolific literary output and his early love of calligraphy (*T* 11) Ignatius did not literally write the narrative that was asked of him. Over a period of several months between 1553 and 1555, he shared orally what would eventually become his narrative with Luís Gonçalves da Câmara, an important member of his Roman community.[18] Câmara confesses that he jotted down notes as bullet points right after their encounters and then wrote down progressively the full text whenever a scribe was available.[19] The current original text is written mostly in Spanish, but the last twenty-three paragraphs are in Italian. At the time, Câmara was in Genoa on his way to Portugal and did not have a Spanish-speaking amanuensis at hand. Such an unconventional arrangement raises the question of authorship, since, technically speaking, Ignatius did not write his own narrative. It is likely not a perfect verbatim of what Ignatius shared with Câmara. However, one could clearly assert Ignatius's rights as the "intellectual author" of the text. Câmara was known to have a good memory,[20] and his reverence for the founder of his community[21] likely fostered a desire to be as faithful as possible in conveying the words of Ignatius. Ignatius can most likely be credited with the overall narrative structure and the main content, though Câmara was the one who entrusted the work to paper—not an insignificant task. Had Câmara desired to smooth Ignatius's narrative, he would likely have removed the hesitations, the digressions, the abrupt changes of pace (especially the galloping beginning and the hasty end), and the embarrassing moments. Moreover, important members of the Jesuit order read Câmara's text,[22] and some knew of the different events recounted;[23] Câmara was accountable to them. It is also possible that Ignatius himself saw Câmara's text.[24] Hence, one can reasonably consider that the text now at hand is the one wished by Ignatius.[25]

Despite its importance as the final words about his life by the very founder of the Society of Jesus and its circulation in manuscript form, Câmara's text was never printed and practically disappeared,[26] buried in archives, until the end of the nineteenth century.

Although the Bollandists published the Latin version of the text in 1731,[27] the first modern edition of the original manuscript appeared in 1904 in the series *Monumenta Historica Societatis Iesu* (MHSI).[28] It accompanied a wave of translations in many important European languages, starting in the early twentieth century with two different English-language editions.[29] The title of this opus is subject to an ongoing debate. Many contemporary translations emphasize the "pilgrim" dimension in the title, *Pilgrim's Journey*,[30] which is the most descriptive. The more straightforward *Autobiography* also has many adherents.[31] The latter nevertheless obscures the fact that the text does not offer a complete narrative of Ignatius's life. The MHSI chose the noncommittal Latin *Acta*—a choice followed by some even today[32]—instead of the more common *Vita*, which usually refers to Ribadeneira's biography. A recent English translation gave it the title of *Reminiscences*, thrusting onto it an informal light that does not reflect the thoughtful perspective of the work.[33]

The most insightful way to describe this text is with the title given to the first English translation, *Testament*, a term borrowed from the preface by one of the original protagonists, Jerónimo Nadal.[34] A testament is an intimate document for one's heirs that draws on the wisdom learned from the past but opens up to the future in the form of advices. It testifies to what has been most important and thus what is worth bringing back to light and carrying forward. As such, a testament is both a testimony and a gift extended to the next generations. The *Testament* did not yet constitute the last words, since Ignatius was not on his deathbed, but by then he was already an old man nearing the end of his life. In his narrative, Ignatius confides in a person who symbolized the whole Society. Câmara is the active recipient of these words shared and entrusted in confidence, to one for the benefit of many. Anecdotally, the text itself would later be finalized by Câmara in a different language, while he was on the road, in an act of translation and transmission. The oral nature of the *Testament* is essential. Ignatius's *Testament* is not written in stone; his sharing is mediated by the fluidity of a conversation, showing that the fine point of his testimony is not entirely encompassed by the words in which it is preserved—though some words do stand out. The nature of the testament shared is experiential. The importance of receiving orally what Ignatius deemed essential is also exemplified by the final scene of the *Testament*, where Câmara relates his ultimate request to look at the papers that Ignatius was pointing at, which contained his spiritual notes. The response of Ignatius was unequivocal: *lui non volse*—he did not agree (*T* 101).[35] The testament was meant to be orally crafted directly by Ignatius in a conversation with Câmara, not to be deciphered or constructed by Câmara through reading. Ignatius, very much alive despite this testament, was sharing something that was still giving him life and had to be entrusted as a live document, with all its ensuing fluidity.

The apparent fragmentary nature of the *Testament* raised early questions about the completeness of the text. In terms of a comprehensive timeline, the *Testament* is lacking; this is precisely what prompted the redaction of the broader *Vita* by those who wanted a complete biography. The *Testament* condenses the first twenty-six years of Ignatius's life into a single sentence: "Until the twenty-sixth year of his life, he was a man dedicated to the vanities of the world and he took most delight in the exercise of arms with a large and vain desire to gain honor" (*T* 1). Likewise, the last fifteen years are summarized in a few paragraphs, and Ignatius concludes by saying that someone else, namely Jerónimo Nadal, could talk about the other things (*altre cose*) that happened in Rome (*T* 98). Thus, the narrative focuses on the years from his wounding in Pamplona and convalescence in Loyola—that signaled the beginning of his conversion journey—to his arrival in Rome, where he would settle as the founder and superior of the new Society of Jesus. The abrupt beginning, in particular, raised suspicions that Câmara, out of a sense of decency and respect for the figure of the founder, might have removed lurid details about Ignatius's sins.[36] However, if he had, he would not have mentioned in his preface that Ignatius shared some of his experiences from his preconversion life.[37] Since embarrassing moments were not censored elsewhere in the text, one might suppose that Ignatius did not consider the details of those early years, even in contrast to his conversion experience, to be relevant to his *Testament*, only stating emphatically his acknowledgment that he had been a thoroughly vain man. The abruptness of both the beginning and the end also serve as clear bookends that emphasize through their brevity the core narrative that is at stake, which makes no claim of being a comprehensive biography.

The text of the *Testament* is traditionally divided into 101 paragraphs.[38] After a sweeping dismissal of the first twenty-six years of his life, Ignatius describes his contribution to the unsuccessful defense of the city of Pamplona, and his subsequent lengthy recovery at the family castle of Azpeitia (*T* 1–12). During this time, he had the first inkling of personal religious experiences, which culminated in his decision to undergo a radical change of life, starting with a pilgrimage to Jerusalem. The following chapters narrate his journey to and residence at the famed Benedictine abbey of Montserrat, near Barcelona, where he made a general confession and changed his clothes, symbolic of his new life (*T* 13–18). Ignatius's stay in the nearby village of Manresa takes on a major part of the *Testament* (*T* 19–37). This period constituted the initiation of Ignatius into a deeper spiritual life through radical asceticism, spiritual conversations, and great spiritual experiences. His journey to Jerusalem through Spain and Italy is then narrated (*T* 38–48), emphasizing some of the encounters, as well as the delicate issue of poverty, followed by his return to Spain (*T* 49–53). At this point Ignatius had to search anew for God's will since he had to come back from the place where he thought God wanted him to be—Jerusalem.

The second half of the *Testament* follows Ignatius through his studies in Barcelona and Alcalá (*T* 54–63), Salamanca (*T* 64–72), and finally Paris (*T* 73–86). Throughout, Ignatius describes his run-ins with the Inquisition because of his apostolic zeal and the teaching he imparted, underlying the fact that the doctrine of his *Spiritual Exercises* was never condemned. His attempts at recruiting like-minded companions, at first unsuccessful, also loom large on these pages alongside Ignatius's apostolic activities, which had to be moderated to ensure the success of his studies. After the completion of his studies in Paris, he returned to his native Azpeitia to cure his faltering health, displaying his zeal for preaching and ministering to the townspeople (*T* 87–91). Reunited with his Parisian companions in Venice, Ignatius recounts their wait for passage, travel to Rome, local ministry, and decision to establish a religious community after their ordination (*T* 92–97). In the final paragraphs the activities of Ignatius in Rome are painted in broad strokes, from his giving of the Exercises to some of the early events and endeavors of the nascent Society of Jesus (*T* 98–101).

The limited temporal scope of the *Testament* enhances its cohesiveness. It draws attention to what Ignatius wanted to convey to his brothers about what could be called his core "pilgrim years," the seventeen-year period (1521–38) of journey to discover, deepen, and confirm God's call for him. Before the battle of Pamplona, the question was not raised, but after his arrival in Rome and subsequent election as the first superior of the new order, his vocation was settled. The years in between were spent on a journey in search of God's will.[39] In this regard, the text displays a strong unity insofar as it bears witness to Ignatius's journey of discovery of his vocation, which is embodied in the many places he traversed before reaching his final destination, not in Jerusalem, but in Rome. The emphasis on this period alone betrays the fact that the *Testament* is not simply a collection of nostalgic reminiscences, but that it brings to the fore the part of his life that informs best who he was even in the present—hence the importance of transmitting it. Still seeing himself as a pilgrim in his later years, Ignatius understood that these core pilgrim years most significantly shaped his identity. He thus prioritized the central components of the pilgrimage experience (e.g., desire, journey, destination) over a narrative of its background (prior to his wounding in Pamplona) or its lived-out accomplishment (after reaching Rome).

These "pilgrim years" of the core narrative cover the first two layers of pilgrimage in the *Testament*. The first layer corresponds to Ignatius's attempt to imitate Christ in a servile way, forcefully making his way up to Jerusalem, the very place where Christ trod, as the absolute destination. During this pilgrimage, Ignatius was able to fully live as a pilgrim, with only limited concessions to financial concerns. But this achievement proved to be short-lived. He was sent back to Europe and had to ask himself what to do next (*T* 50). The yearlong pilgrimage to Jerusalem gave way to a much longer pilgrimage of discovery of *God's* will for him—not simply of what *he* thought he should do. This tortuous and relentless journey started with a genuine question: "*Quid agendum?*," and a first inkling: to study. It would unfold over sixteen years of studies, companionship, ministry, and travels, and would find its response in the small chapel of La Storta, near Rome, where a vision would confirm Ignatius in his call as a companion of Jesus (*T* 98).

In Search of One's Identity

Although unmistakably personal, the text of the *Testament* never mentions the main character by name; he is always "he" (*él*). The question of name is not new for Ignatius, since he was christened as "Íñigo," a Basque name, yet later adopted the Latin "Ignatius" while in Paris. But the issue at stake here is different; his identity is revealed more progressively and on Ignatius's own terms, never to be encapsulated in a baptismal or chosen name. By contrast, the very first lines of Ribadeneira's *Vita* spell out unequivocally a certain posture for Ignatius, beginning with the following sentence:

> Ignatius Loyola, founder and father of the Society of Jesus, was born of a noble lineage in that part of Spain that is called the province of Guipúzcoa in the year of the Lord 1491, presiding in the chair of St. Peter pope Innocent VIII, and being emperor Frederick III, and reigning in Spain the Catholic monarchs Fernand and Isabel, of glorious and famous memory.[40]

Ribadeneira begins with a name, then adds a function, an origin, a place, and a religious and political context. The reader is situated at once. Not so in the *Testament*, which zooms in from the beginning on Ignatius's view on his personal experience.

Although Ignatius's *Testament* is undeniably personal and unique, the absence of the name opens up for the reader the possibility to read one's own journey as mirroring that of Ignatius.[41] A space is built within the narrative to project oneself into the story and assess one's own journey. Beyond the singularity of events and places, such a device fosters the claim to a universal storyline, that of a quest for God as one of progressive discernment and knowledge, toward a greater certainty, through doubts, experiences, and confirmation. The "he"—or "she"—of the story transforms it into a palimpsest over which one is invited to fill in one's own story. The narrative itself invites the reader to join in on the journey.

The *Testament* progressively qualifies this "he," at first with two names: the "wounded" (*el herido—T* 2, 4), and the "sick" (*el infermo—T* 3). Both exemplify the initial portrayal of Ignatius as an unhealthy being, incapable of movement, either bound to sin in his "previous" life or bound to his bed because of his wound. These expressions are used as Ignatius lies in bed and experiences a time of rest and transformation. Later in the narrative, as Ignatius is on the road to Jerusalem, albeit still with a long way to go, a single label appears innocuously: *el peregrino* (the pilgrim—*T* 15). Ignatius was no longer bound; he was on the road. This designation would remain, unchallenged, well beyond the narrative core of his pilgrimage to Jerusalem. Even as the superior general in Rome, Ignatius was still "the pilgrim" (*T* 99). Because Ignatius had already used this title to sign a letter thirty years earlier,[42] the choice of the elderly Ignatius to style himself as "the pilgrim" fifteen years after his travels had ended is significant, and it reveals his lasting appropriation of this self-identification.[43] Ignatius's use of the title "pilgrim" stretching over decades suggests that it was not only a literary artifice but rather expressed something essential and firmly established about his identity.[44] For the thirty-something-year-old Ignatius back from Jerusalem to label himself as a pilgrim in a letter is straightforward. For the sexagenarian Ignatius who remained in Rome for more than a decade after his extensive travels to use the same title reveals something else, something deeper. The pilgrim was still who he was in the present. It was his name, the name that was revealed to him through his life journey.[45] It was his identity. In the *Testament*, once the stage of being sick or wounded had been overcome in the becoming pilgrim, there is no coming back, nor any other stance, and it would endure up to the present.

The self-description of Ignatius as the pilgrim can be contrasted with other potential images that were also taken up by later hagiography and iconography: the knight, the soldier, the sinner, the priest, the founder, or the would-be saint. The figure of the *caballero* (knight), with its chivalric sense of honor and nobility, is present in the *Testament* (e.g., *T* 1, 2, 6, 17–18), especially in the episode where Ignatius entertains the idea of killing a Moor whom he thought had insulted the Virgin Mary (*T* 15). It is also in that story that Ignatius qualifies himself as pilgrim for the first time. Ribadeneira, on the other hand, while reproducing the episode in the *Vita*, qualifies Ignatius instead as a "soldier of Christ,"[46] which stresses the chivalric nature of Ignatius's potential gesture over the display of his faulty sense of discernment. Depictions of Ignatius as soldier of Christ abound. But while he is not averse to the spiritualization of the chivalric image,[47] it is not the one he chose for his *Testament*, although he is once qualified as a *nuevo soldado de Cristo* (new soldier of Christ) in the narration of his encounter with a spiritual woman (*T* 21). Another powerful image for Ignatius is that of "Companion of Jesus." Ignatius fought adamantly to have the name *Compañía de Jesús* or *Societas Iesu* accepted by the Holy See for his new religious order, since through the vision at the chapel in La Storta he felt that it had been confirmed by God (*T* 96).[48] His desire to imitate and follow Christ in everything is also on full display at the time of his conversion, as he writes down the words of Christ (*T* 11) and then plans to live like him—or his followers, the saints—in great poverty, in his very city of Jerusalem (*T* 8, 9). Although this identity was crucial for Ignatius, this was not the label that he settled on for his *Testament*. Ignatius himself also suggested the image of the *sinner* (*T* 32) and was not shy in talking about his sins (*T* 14, 25). About the *priestly figure*, the importance of priesthood for Ignatius could be missed by the reader of the *Testament*, since he does not even mention his long-awaited first Mass, but the reading of his *Spiritual Diary* highlights that reality.[49] Moreover, in the *Testament*, Ignatius does not claim explicitly his place as *founder* of the Society of Jesus, though he is clearly the central figure of the narrative and of the initial group of companions, and summarizes his Roman activities as head of the order in the final paragraphs. Finally, the figure of the *would-be saint* would evidently be inappropriate for Ignatius to claim since it would display a lack of humility. However, his biographers would subsequently call upon this latter image regularly.[50] The last three images were used abundantly in the early iconography of Ignatius of Loyola, even more than that of the pilgrim.[51] However, Ignatius settled on the figure of the pilgrim—a figure of movement, of the constant seeking of God, and of receiving oneself from God.

The adoption of the pilgrim label by the elderly Ignatius raises interesting questions about its continuous embodiment. Was the recounting of his pilgrim years mere nostalgia? How did he remain a pilgrim? What elements of the pilgrim's being continued to animate him? If pilgrimage is part of Ignatius's self-identity, how does it still hold sway in his sedentary life in Rome? By holding to the pilgrim dimension, does Ignatius diminish the importance of arriving and living out the fruits of pilgrimage, which are also essential components of the journey? In a further step, a closer analysis of key features of Ignatius's *Testament* will highlight the essential characteristics of the pilgrim *ethos*.

Features of the Journey

Various features of pilgrimage emerge from the text of the *Testament*. Some clearly exemplify the paradigmatic features of Christian pilgrimage developed in chapter 1 while some touch upon implicit or novel dimensions of pilgrimage. The intent is not to contrast the *Testament* with a model, but to bring them in dialogue, also acknowledging the singularity of the narrative journey of Ignatius. Hence, we will proceed with two sets of features revolving around movement, transformation, destination, then vulnerability and alterity, before finally moving to a third set highlighting the inner journey of the *Testament* through discernment and the Spiritual Exercises.

A Journey of Movement, Transformation, and Destination

A Movement Set by Desire

There is a gentle humor in the fact that Ignatius dictated his *Testament* while *ambulando*[52] (walking) and that Câmara completed the text while traveling, for the narrative is one that crisscrosses Europe and the Mediterranean Sea. Not every journey narrated by Ignatius qualifies as pilgrimage,[53] but the regular changes of location sketched in the work pace the rhythm of the development of the narrative. The description of physical movement is reinforced with instances of literary movement, thus entrusting the whole narrative with a sense of lively fluidity. From a lexicographic perspective, the *Testament* abounds with expressions pertaining to movement: *dejar/dexar* (to leave) occurs 39 times; *camino/caminar* (the road or to journey), 41 times; *pelegrino/peregrino*, 83 times; and in the Italian paragraphs (*T* 79–101), *andare* (to go or walk), 50 times![54] Such kinetic literary characterization is clearly in line with movement as an essential phenomenological component of pilgrimage.

Movement is set by desire. It anchors pilgrimage in a category that is close to that of "intention" described in chapter 1. Ruiz Pérez observes that "Ignatius seems to become a *pilgrim* exactly when he echoes the dynamic presence of desire."[55] Desire is what puts Ignatius on the path of a relentless quest, in perpetual movement. Desire will also propel the spiritual movement, just as in the Spiritual Exercises.[56]

Throughout the *Testament*, movement is depicted as carefully decided but also constantly threatened. The early stage of the *Testament* portrays Ignatius immobilized in bed, at times fighting for his life (*T* 3). In these moments he was, quintessentially, not moving as the *herido* or *infermo*. Ignatius escapes death suddenly, recovers progressively, and later stands up in order to write down the words of Christ (*T* 11).[57] As he convalesces, he toys with various dreams and fantasies while finally deciding to follow Christ's footsteps *en camino* (on the road—*T* 11). Two options of localization emerge. The first was the epitome of a stable place for the journey, a Carthusian monastery in which Ignatius would live and die unbeknownst to others (*T* 12). The journey would have been totally interior since it would have been realized in one place with limited contact with other people (Carthusians are hermits). Ignatius even had a servant inquire into this option, and he was pleased with the report he received, but he decided to take the second option: being on the road by going where Christ lived, Jerusalem.[58] This initial decision was fundamental and irrevocable for Ignatius. In a telling scene, his brother, Martín, tries to dissuade him while moving him from room to room (*T* 12), a movement that was closed onto itself, but Ignatius did not waver. Other occurrences would surface of a *grande insistancia* (emphatic insistence) of some people, along the way, to stop his journey, or to mitigate his way of journeying, for example, by accepting money or a horse (*T* 72, 87). However, as he journeyed with Jerusalem in mind, Ignatius would model decisively that only the attainment of the destination would make the genuine pilgrim stop. After the setback of his return from Jerusalem and his unenthusiastic choice of studies, only the divine confirmation of Rome as a propitious place for him would end the physical journey he had chosen to undertake. According to Diego Laínez's description of the event—alluded to in the *Testament*—Ignatius would have had these words sealed in the heart, *Ego vobis Romae propitius* (I will be favorable to you in Rome),[59] securing his commitment in a given place, Rome, through a divine injunction. A movement that was inaugurated as a quest for the place willed for him by God would conclude only by divine confirmation, fulfilling the desire.

Transformation

The displacement in space in the *Testament* is also accompanied by transformation, both exterior and interior, in a dialectical way. As part of his process of taking on the *persona* of the pilgrim, Ignatius marked a radical rupture at the Abbey of Montserrat by confessing his sins, leaving his sword, and donning sackcloth (*T* 17–18). By abandoning his noble clothes,[60] putting on humble garments, and taking up a staff, Ignatius was marking a clear rupture from his previous life and embracing that of a pilgrim. This humbling of himself, accompanied by a vigil ceremony to the Virgin Mary, and joined with a general confession, gave a ceremonial quality to his actions. Ignatius marked in his body his new religious identity.[61] This initial rupture marks the liminal character of pilgrimage; something was changed by his embarking on that journey. Ignatius was never to return to his old ways. Even as he journeyed back to Loyola many years later after his studies in Paris, he would not stay in the family castle but instead cast his lot with the poor of the local hospital (*T* 87).

This rupture only marked the beginning of his pilgrim's journey of transformation, even though a first glimpse of inner transformation (*mudança*) had already appeared to his relatives during his convalescence (*T* 10). His exterior appearance ran to extremes, at first, in forceful opposition to his previous vanity befitting a new convert. In Manresa, he let his hair and nails grow to such a length that he would frighten people (*T* 19). When his health faltered because of his extreme penances, he was urged to take better care of his body (*T* 34); he also saw the apostolic fitness of not looking unkempt (*T* 29). A later episode in Alcalá, in which some companions of his were asked to dye their clothes a different color, shows that this sense of an outer transformation endured for some time (*T* 58). However, the penitential concern for his exterior appearance marks mostly the early years of the narrative.[62] With time, such concerns vanished. Nevertheless, the transformation continued at a deeper level.

The inner transformation of Ignatius mirrored that of the external aspect. The journey achieved can be read back from the perspective of the actions described at both ends of the narrative. At first were the actions of vanity and battle, of a noble *caballero* (*T* 1–2, 4–6). At the end of the journey, the actions of a priest and founder: spiritual retreats and pious foundations (*T* 98). The end of a journey to seek one's orientation in life had concluded. The transformation would also result in a greater ability to discern God's voice, as we will see later.

Destination

The clear tension in the quest of the *Testament* can be read through the evanescent destination. Ignatius was a man of great desires, and his conversion did not change that anthropological reality. As a pilgrim, Ignatius was walking in a clear direction toward a destination. The first destination was a sacred place, Jerusalem. The meaningfulness of this place was given through its association with Jesus, who became central in Ignatius's mind by the time of his convalescence (*T* 8–11). Ignatius's quest was completely focused on reaching Jerusalem, from the convalescence in Loyola to the wait with the first companions in Venice (*T* 8, 9, 12, 16, 34, 85, 93).

However, a subtler course of action is also unfolding in the narrative as the second layer of pilgrimage starts. A clear breaking point intervenes in the middle of the *Testament*, after Ignatius had momentarily accomplished his desire to be in Jerusalem but had been sent back to Spain. He questions himself, in Latin in the text, *quid agendum?* ("What shall I do?"—*T* 50) The final answer to that question would be years in the making, but the subsequent step at that time was a mere inclination (*se inclinaba más*) to study (*T* 50), which denotes a low degree of spiritual insight.[63] Although the quest for Jerusalem would be transmitted to the group of the first companions, it was no longer the genuine *telos* of the endeavor, but became the expression, or symptom, of a more profound desire.

The inner transformation of the destination through the actual "pilgrimaging" is also noteworthy. Here, the experience of Ignatius echoes an emphasis—encountered earlier in this book, for example, by Protestant commentators—on the interiority of the genuine pilgrimage. Hence, the first impulse of Ignatius as pilgrim was to seek to do like Christ in a literal way: Jerusalem, the journey by foot in poverty, and the care of souls. It was the first *telos* of Ignatius's pilgrimage. For him, returning to Europe was a failure. He was forced to refine his understanding of the destination, and to embark on a journey of discernment. It is worth noting that after Jerusalem, Ignatius never made another major pilgrimage despite his many travels as a student. The orientation of the pilgrimage itself moved from a *where*, in this case Jerusalem, to a *what* and *how*.[64] Leaving aside his attempt to act like Christ, Ignatius was led to seek God's will, espousing in that regard the very *attitude* of Christ and not simply his *location*. The pilgrimage then became less about a place than a destination (it could be anywhere) and more about inner listening and transformation. From an exterior pilgrimage as imitation of Christ in his place, the pilgrimage became interior.[65] This radical and subtle change is best expressed in the distinction between the destination *sought* and the destination *attained*. Ignatius sought Jerusalem, and fiercely so. His destination was reached by being placed (*mettere*) with Christ by God the Father—through the vision of La Storta.[66] The preeminent location was not an earthly one, but a way of being existentially in relation to the Son and the Father, to be located in a divine space. The vision happened as he neared the gates of Rome and thus ushered Ignatius also into a new physical location that would be his for the rest of his life.[67] The distance is not far from the *place of* Christ, to being *placed with* Christ, but it was a journey that took seventeen years for Ignatius to complete and expressed God's full response to Ignatius's quest.

The transformation of the destination is already prefigured in the *Testament* by the description of the arrival in Jerusalem. While Ignatius is clear about the "great consolation" (*grande consolación*) and supernatural joy that accompanied the view of the city, he also mentions that he (later) felt the same devotion in visiting holy places (*lugares santos*—*T* 45). Thus, although the achievement of his quest seemed to be confirmed through spiritual consolation, Ignatius acknowledges that he experienced the same consolation in other holy places. Hence, in hindsight, he could decipher that the consolation was less about the place than about the holiness and proximity to God that it symbolizes.

Vulnerability and Alterity

Vulnerability

The act of going on a pilgrimage entails a certain form of vulnerability. For Ignatius, vulnerability took especially the shape of poverty—or the desire for it. In a very embodied way, Ignatius let go of his money while traveling from Loyola to Montserrat, even settling a debt owed to him to cut his financial ties, even symbolically (*T* 13). At the abbey he let go of his wealthy clothes and took the garments of a poor pilgrim beggar. In the *Testament*, the pilgrim's desired vulnerability was especially present in the constant discernment of the relationship to money, which could not easily be settled, as Ignatius would still see later in life.[68] Money is necessary on the journey, but too much care for money denotes a lack of trust. For Ignatius, dealings with money act as a litmus test. The many instances where he mentions this issue show how difficult it was for him to strike the right balance between the security of moving forward and the confidence that God would provide, thus remaining in that space of vulnerability.

In general, Ignatius wished to journey *solo y a pie*[69] (alone and by foot), without any human support. He wanted to refuse the ease of transportation of a donkey supplied by his family but did not want to shame his brother, so he rode it only while in their province.[70] His social capital as a member of the nobility was not something that he could dispense with as easily. Thus, he had to hide his identity or even take detours to avoid the familiar faces of those who could lavish praise and financial help on him (*T* 18). At times, while he did not want to accept any money, he was told that he could not book passage on a ship without it, which led him to scruples and to looking for help in his discernment (*T* 36, 40). Later, finding that it was not conducive to his educational formation to beg daily or live in an almshouse far from his classes, he accepted larger donations that allowed him to concentrate on his studies (*T* 73, 76). However, once, not wanting to keep a large amount of money himself, he entrusted it to a fellow Spaniard who spent it, leaving Ignatius penniless (*T* 73). The right equilibrium between receiving what is necessary while not hoarding money was a balancing act requiring discernment. The vow of poverty that Ignatius and the first companions took at Montserrat—and endured as the group of friends morphed into a religious community—bears the traces of such a balancing act between a desire for strict poverty and an obligation toward apostolic efficiency.[71]

Although the issue of the right use of money is emblematic for keeping open a healthy vulnerability, Ignatius encountered more direct threats. Nature was a source of vulnerability, especially in travels by sea (*T* 33, 49, 53). Dangerous roads were also a threat, either because one could get lost and take a difficult path, or because of armed conflicts.[72] Ignatius also witnessed, and fought against, gender-based aggression, as some men tried to impose themselves at night on a female pilgrim who traveled unconvincingly disguised as a young man.[73] Finally, he was put in jail for a few weeks, as some individuals grew suspicious of this itinerant student-preacher (*T* 60–62, 67–69). Hence, the vulnerability experienced by the pilgrim is not limited to a chosen attitude of dependence upon Providence but is also tied to situations that could literally be life-threatening.

Alterity

Pilgrimage entails encounters, and there is no lack of them in the *Testament*. Prima facie, the journey of Ignatius is a highly singular experience. As a pilgrim to Jerusalem, he insisted to go *solo*, alone[74] without guide[75] or companion. He mentions that having a companion to travel with could offer him a crutch in times of difficulty, but that he wanted to rely only on God himself and not on any other human being. Ignatius even kept his confessor of Azpeitia in the dark regarding his project of pilgrimage (*T* 17)!

Fellow travelers, good or bad, would fortuitously appear along the way (e.g., *T* 15, 32, 38–39, 41). Benefactors would help (e.g., *T* 42, 43, 49), and partners in spiritual conversations would manifest themselves and offer or receive guidance (e.g., *T* 21, 22, 37). Family members would also play their part (e.g., *T* 13), along with ecclesiastical authorities (e.g., *T* 17, 22, 23, 25, 40). A fleeting community of fellow travelers, both actual pilgrims and inner pilgrims, would take shape. In a way, the very populated narrative of the *Testament* demonstrates that, despite the "single" aspect that Ignatius emphasized, his pilgrimage was one of countless encounters, but also countless collaborations. Every individual mentioned played a part in his journey, whether they realized it or not!

Moreover, what started as a single-minded, individual pursuit of Christ was progressively transformed into a collective enterprise through a desire to gather other like-minded young men. Such groups, as well as other individuals in their orbit, female and male, would take root in Alcalá, then Salamanca and Paris, gathered around Ignatius through spiritual conversations. But the Spanish groups fell apart after Ignatius's departure, with some members taking laudable roads, others not (*T* 78, 80). A stable community that would withstand time came only during the years of studies in Paris, and even increased during Ignatius's absence.[76] The closeness that the companions gained along the road is shown when Ignatius declares that Diego Laínez and Jerónimo Nadal could fill in the details on his account (*T* 96, 98). The formation of such companionship marks a shift to a discipleship that not only looks vertically at God, but also horizontally at other disciples and at the good they can collectively produce.[77] This transformation is exemplified in an episode of the *Testament* in which Ignatius mentally assigns the status of apostle to those around him in a desire to obey them as fellow followers of Christ (*T* 75). The divine pursuit of the pilgrim was not finally hindered by the presence of others. On the contrary, Ignatius gradually realized that they became coagents of the pursuit. The fact that the Parisian group reunited with more strength in Venice—the group had expanded—also validated the journey, which will culminate beyond the narrative of the *Testament* in the unanimous election of Ignatius as the first general of the Society of Jesus.

The beginning of Ignatius's journey also portrays others as holy models, healers, and instigators. The models are the saints whose lives Ignatius explored in the *Golden Legend* during his convalescence,[78] pushing him to desire to emulate their ascetic practices (*T* 7–8). Facing death early in his convalescence, on the vigil of the Feast of Sts. Peter and Paul, he suddenly improved against all odds, an event he associated with his lasting devotion to St. Peter (*T* 3). Finally, the apparition of the Virgin Mary with the Child Jesus confirmed the change that he was starting to experience (*T* 10). Nevertheless, even as this broad celestial presence would take a back seat in the unfolding of the journey, which became more centered on the figure of Christ himself, it offered Ignatius the initial impetus to start his journey.

Hence, the presence of others, which at first seemed precluded by Ignatius himself, is shown to be mightily active both through the actual collaborators and companions on the journey, and also through a cloud of holy witnesses who pointed Ignatius on the way of following Christ.

Inner Journey, Discernment, and the Spiritual Exercises

The analysis of the phenomenon of pilgrimage in chapter 1 gave priority to its embodied version over a purely interior one. But the *Testament* of Ignatius is an eloquent example of a conjunction between both dimensions as the inner journey accompanies the physical movement and eventually extends beyond it.

The subtle change in the destination revealed *in fine* to Ignatius the *location* in which his vocation would blossom as a fruit of his inner journey. His vocation is expressed in his deeds as companion, priest, writer, spiritual director, and religious founder. It entailed a constant quest both in its orientation and its depth. His *identity* as pilgrim meant—through an interior turn—constant discernment. Ignatius's peregrination in his *Testament*, moving from one place to another, constitutes the visible face of an inner pilgrimage, which is an existential quest, asking, what am I *called* to do with my life? Despite many steps, trials, failures, and detours, Ignatius the pilgrim would eventually find confirmation through his final destination, but the journey was one of discernment.

Ignatius received little guidance in the way of discernment. His first attraction was to an image to imitate—Christ in Jerusalem—which he pursued relentlessly. He certainly was inspired by the lives of the saints he read in the *Golden Legend* in Loyola, but he also had to learn to appropriate this new life for himself. The episode of the encounter with the Moor—whom he could not decide whether to spare or kill, ultimately leaving the decision to his donkey—showed early on that he needed to refine his skills in that regard (*T* 15). He had to learn how to be an inner pilgrim, to know how to move forward one step at a time. Ignatius certainly received some guidance from his extended general confession at the Abbey of Montserrat (*T* 17),[79] and he also sought for a long time the advice of "spiritual people" (*hombres espirituales*).[80] The *Testament* witnesses his progress in gaining a more acute sense of discernment, from taking better care of his health and appearance in Manresa (*T* 29) to returning (unenthusiastically) to study in Barcelona (*T* 54) or focusing more seriously on his studies rather than on apostolic work in Paris (*T* 82). More than the role of experience or advice, however, the *Testament* puts forth a different driving force for Ignatius's growth in discernment: He was taught by God like a schoolboy (*T* 27).

The table was already set regarding the importance of discernment in the narrative of Ignatius's long recovery in Loyola, during which he discovered his alternating spiritual states: dryness after some thoughts entertained for a long time, joy and peace after others (*T* 8). This was Ignatius's own discovery of an inner world. It was a new continent for him. Ignatius acknowledges that he was blind (*ánima...ciega*) at first, since he was looking at large, visible deeds, desiring to do more penances than anyone else, even more than St. Francis or St. Dominic (*T* 14).[81] At that initial stage, in which he was also looking only at Jerusalem, his sight, though well-meaning, was turned onto himself and not yet onto God's will per se. It is only midway in the *Testament* that the issue of God's will (*voluntad de Dios/nuestro Señor*) was voiced explicitly—beyond what Ignatius thought that God wanted from or for him—and it occurred in the negative. Having reached Jerusalem he realized, through his forced return, that it was not God's will that he should stay there (*T* 47–50). This was the realization that prompted the question of what to do, and he had to ask what God's will really was for him. A long process of learning to discern God's will ensued for Ignatius. From the initial discovery of the movements of consolation and desolation,[82] the year-long stay in Manresa, and later experiences, a grammar and pedagogy of spiritual growth would eventually emerge as the *Spiritual Exercises*.

The Spiritual Exercises grew and were fine-tuned in the period covered by the *Testament*. In its final form the booklet of the *Spiritual Exercises* consists of a guide for a spiritual director. It offers a month-long retreat structured in four parts, called "weeks." During each week, various times of prayer are suggested, most of them contemplations based on gospel narratives, but some are distinct meditations or contemplations elaborated on by Ignatius.

Supplemental materials, like rules of discernment, complement the architectonic component. The *Exercises* were developed by Ignatius over time and likely gained their final shape during his time in Paris; they were approved by the Holy See in 1548 and printed soon afterward. As a retreat the *Exercises* were meant to be done once in a lifetime and were clearly aimed at discovering God's call within the person and having them decide to answer it. This is called the "election."[83]

From Ignatius's first intuition of the existence of a rich inner spiritual life in Loyola to the giving of the 30-day retreat to Dr. Ortiz at Monte Cassino (*T* 98), the *Spiritual Exercises* in their evolving form figure prominently in the *Testament*. The central experience in that regard, the stay in Manresa, was first envisioned as a short rest stop on the way to Jerusalem. Although it was static, it became the cradle of another journey that would come to be the journey of the inner pilgrimage. Time and again, in the *Testament*, Ignatius mentions his papers (*papeles/scritti*; *T* 67, 86), his giving the *Exercises* (*T* 57, 60, 67, 77, 82, 92, 98), and his run-ins with the Inquisition because of them.[84] Ignatius was adamant about having his booklet declared free of any error, or even lauded![85] Because the *Testament* gives ample space to the skirmishes related to the *Spiritual Exercises*, they are revealed as a sensitive issue for Ignatius. The *Exercises* were the fruit of Ignatius's own encounter and dealings with God, as well as a blueprint for others to do the same, based on what Ignatius found useful for himself and for others he directed (*T* 99). When they were examined by the Inquisition in Salamanca (*T* 64–70), they were still a work-in-progress, but they were presented as a single work for the first time (*T* 67), and they bore the mark of Ignatius's inner journey with God. In seeking the approval of the *Exercises*, Ignatius was also seeking the validation of his inner journey. The approval by ecclesial authorities of his text, despite the restrictions placed on his activity in Alcalá and Salamanca, was the warrant of the validity of his own pilgrim journey. The narration of his patient, and tortuous, discernment of God's will as he was working on the *Spiritual Exercises* also promotes them implicitly as a tool for others to enter into that inner pilgrimage, notwithstanding the physical pilgrimaging that Ignatius first intended. As we will see later, the experiences of pilgrimage and of the Spiritual Exercises are connected in Ignatius's program for future companions of Jesus.

Through the lens of the task of discernment, which is never accomplished once and for all, the meaning of Ignatius's use of the word *pilgrim* well into his settled time in Rome acquires obvious relevance. The inner pilgrimage journey revealed that the quest is more one of God Himself than of God's place. Such a question is always ongoing, hence the importance of discernment. The *ethos* of the pilgrim is not limited to the timeframe of raising the vocational question and then finding the answer but extends to his present life and unfolds as a quest.

Enlightening Digressions to the Present

Beyond the characteristics of pilgrimage that can be uncovered in the narrative of the *Testament,* some important literary devices offer heuristic tools. Although the *Testament* generally follows a strict chronological order, some digressions happen that are all the more significant, especially as they occur in the midst of the narrative.[86] In many cases, Ignatius highlights the importance of a narrative element by showing its impact on the present.[87] In some instances, however, Ignatius interrupts more firmly the temporal flow in order to fast-forward some subsequent elements. By doing so he draws attention to his essential concerns. Two occurrences of such device stand out: the fate of the early companions and his changing attitude toward death.

The clearest instance in which Ignatius uses such an excursus is the exposition of the fate of various early companions. By doing so Ignatius brings to completion each of their vocational stories, whether positive or negative. This presentation underlines the importance even of those early attempts as well as the role of fidelity. Such fidelity is exemplified by the exemplary, although short, Jesuit life of Diego Hoces, a companion added to the group in Venice whom Ignatius saw entering heaven in a vision (*T* 98). In contrast, the destiny of the early companions, prior to the Parisian group, was diverse.[88] The first digression pertains to informal members of the Parisian group, whose later religious commitment was edifying, though not through the Society of Jesus (*T* 78). One companion, Juan Castro, returned to Spain and became a Carthusian monk, while the other, Pedro de Peralta, undertook a pilgrimage to Jerusalem by foot, only to be stopped by a member of his family in Italy and sent back to Spain with the help of the pope. These events happened, as Ignatius mentioned, "many years later" (*T* 78). A second digression tackles the destiny of the companions Ignatius had in Spain, with whom he was hoping to regroup eventually in Paris. The reality was not so inspiring. Ignatius describes with precision what happened to them. Calisto, after eventful travels to America, returned to Spain a wealthy man. Caceres returned to Segovia "where he lived in such a way that he seemed to have forgotten his initial purpose" (*T* 80), while Artiaga eventually became a bishop and died under strange circumstances (*T* 80).

Just as he was reading his own story from the perspective of its end, Ignatius could look at the journeys of these companions and assess who remained faithful to the inner journey once undertaken, and who faltered along the way. Such digression into the future of the narrated story extends its consequences to the present. It underlines the status of the pilgrimage narrative as a story of the discernment of a vocation. It was the case for Ignatius, but also here for his early companions. The digressions to the final vocational outcome of various characters in the *Testament* implicitly prompt readers to question themselves regarding the discernment, faithfulness, and potential outcome of their own vocational path.

The second excursus is both insightful and fundamental because it offers a succinct reading of the road traveled from the inner perspective of Ignatius's own take on death.[89] The whole journey of Ignatius is condensed powerfully in three moments through this lens. This major and unexpected rupture of the narrative intervenes after Ignatius recounts a serious death scare that he had while at Manresa in 1522–23 (*T* 32). In his narration, more than death itself, he feared his inability to silence the thought—which he sees as a temptation—that he was righteous. He later asked the women who were taking care of him to shout at him, *pecador* (sinner), if he ever were to find himself again in a life-threatening situation, lest he forget that he is a sinner. A poignant consciousness of his sinfulness thus characterizes this first stage of his journey. Instead of continuing the narrative thread, however, Ignatius interrupts it and follows suit with two other instances of near-death, each introduced by an *otra vez* (another time; *T* 33).

The second vignette details a shipwreck that occurred in 1535.[90] At that time, as Ignatius was examining himself to prepare for his imminent death, he "could not fear his sins, nor being condemned, but he felt a great turmoil and pain, judging that he had not used well the gifts and graces that God our Lord has given him" (*T* 33). Sin is acknowledged but Ignatius does not fear it, nor is he focused on it. He is at peace about himself, his only disturbance being that he had lacked time to let God's graces bear fruit. This reveals an intermediate step in his journey. The third and final vignette of this excursus pertains to an illness in 1550—ten years after the foundation of the Society of Jesus—which was expected to be fatal. As he prepared himself for death, Ignatius recalls that "he had such joy and spiritual consolation at the thought of death, that he would melt in tears, and it came to be so constant, that many times he stopped thinking about death to avoid having too much of that consolation" (*T* 33). At this final stage, no regret surfaces, and much less concern for his sinfulness, but only an overwhelming joy at the idea of finally being completely united with God. In three stages over thirty years, through an initial concern for sinfulness, then a desire for service, and finally complete union, Ignatius maps in a nutshell the extent of his inner pilgrimage and the dislocation it entailed of his interior horizon. The three steps of this digression illustrate the threefold pilgrimage of Ignatius in the *Testament*. The initial ascetic pilgrimage, the long pilgrimage to discern a way in which to serve, and the final dimension of a pilgrimage whose destination is Godself.

The Heart of the Journey: Essentially an Experience of God

The pilgrimage narrated by Ignatius has a clear transcendental quality. The exterior movement is doubled down on by an inner pilgrimage: Ignatius's sights were set first on Jerusalem, but he discovered that the discernment of God's will was the key part of his journey. Moreover, the *Testament* presents God as both a protagonist and magnet of Ignatius's pilgrimage. God played a major role at the alpha and the omega of the journey. During his convalescence in Loyola, Ignatius recognized a diversity of spirits within him. Upon further reflection, he identified the prodding of the "good spirit," the Spirit of God, and was set on his journey. Although God is not portrayed as a meddling presence since Ignatius does not constantly mention God's hand at work in his pilgrimage, he nonetheless gives hints of divine intervention in his narrative (e.g., *T* 3, 5, 7, 25). The overall narrative of God's agency shows that the movement initiated at Loyola, which found its temporary fulfillment in Jerusalem, could only be brought to its complete fulfillment—despite the many attempts to interrupt by well-meaning individuals—through a confirmation of the place by God himself. But this narrative arc is constituted of countless elements, as we will see. Although highly christocentric, especially in its imitation—then following—of Christ, Ignatius's dealing with God is *in fine* inserted into a trinitarian framework that starts with the Spirit[91] and ends with the placement by the Father with the Son (*T* 96).

Images and Consolations

An interesting dialectic unfolds around the literary expressions of the encounters between God and Ignatius through images and consolations. Such occurrences highlight the crucial moments of Ignatius's pilgrim journey and show its trajectory toward greater interiority. Periods in which spiritual images and consolations occur are usually correlated in the *Testament*, although they can serve a distinct purpose.

The first visual interaction occurs in Loyola while Ignatius is confirmed in his plans to change his life and undertake a pilgrimage to Jerusalem through a *visitación* (visitation) of Our Lady with the Child Jesus (*T* 10).[92] Ignatius chose a word expressing the movement of this encounter—*visitation*—thus asserting that the image is not simply one originating from his mind, but it is a representation of God coming to him. Neither Mary nor Jesus speak, but the divine image definitively displaces the images that were there in his soul, painted (*pintadas*) of his former life, especially concerning sexual temptations. This visitation was also accompanied by a great spiritual consolation (*T* 10).[93]

Ignatius's time in Manresa provides us with two further instances of images. In both cases, Ignatius mentions that the visions are seen through the *ojos interiores* (the inner eyes; *T* 29), as opposed to external vision. These visions were christological in nature.[94] In the first, Ignatius perceived white rays coming from above the consecrated host at Mass, and "saw" (*vió*), this time through his understanding, that Christ was present in this sacrament (*T* 29). The second vision was one of Christ's humanity in the shape of a white body, neither tall nor short, without perceiving the body parts (*T* 29).[95] Ignatius mentions that he had this vision while in Manresa maybe between twenty and forty times, and he adds that he saw it also on the way to Padua, and another time in Jerusalem (*T* 29). Ignatius also learned in Manresa that a seductive image that can give consolation (*T* 19) must be carefully discerned. After he had a great spiritual experience, traditionally called the "Vision of the Cardoner" (*T* 30), as he prayed at the foot of a cross, the same image appeared, but unmasked, since Ignatius had recognized it as a demon (*T* 31).[96]

The way to Jerusalem and the time there represent the climax in terms of consolation, underlining from a spiritual perspective the importance of journeying toward—and reaching—the soil on which Christ dwelled. Ignatius mentions various instances of Christ appearing "in his usual way," which brought him consolation (*T* 41, 44), as well as other instances of consolation. During his time in Jerusalem, not only is consolation ever-present but it is described with adjectives of magnification. As he sees the city, Ignatius experienced a "great consolation" (*grande consolación*) with a "joy that appeared supernatural" (*con una alegría que no parescía natural*; *T* 45). At the Mount of Olives, he prayed "with great consolation" (*con harta consolación*; *T* 47). As he is forcibly brought back from the Mount of Olives, Ignatius narrates that he received again from the Lord a great consolation, and he seemed to see Christ over him at all times (*T* 48), an event that continued in great abundance until he and his fellow pilgrims reached the monastery. These are the last words in the *Testament* about his time in Jerusalem. The imprint of the Jerusalem experience on Ignatius, as revealed by his narrative, was tremendous, and cemented his association with Christ.

It is interesting to notice that despite the spiritual culmination in terms of consolation that the Jerusalem pilgrimage represents, it was not meant to be the destination for Ignatius. On his way there, he was nonetheless moved by a sense of "certitude" (*certidumbre*) more than once (e.g., *T* 42). In a sense, all indicators were pointing toward Jerusalem as the place for him to go and stay. However, by the time of his writing of the *Testament*, Ignatius had learned that even spiritual consolations and inner certitudes should be carefully discerned,[97] that their meanings take place not as isolated events but as parts of a larger journey. This is evidently more easily achieved as the journey nears completion than amid its unfolding.

The *Testament* remains silent about Ignatius's experience of consolation in his time of studies, which nonetheless corresponds to the longest time span. Even the decision to undertake studies was made not from a consolation, but from an "inclination"—rational and good for sure, but not supernatural. But as he was in the Venetian region after his studies and neared Rome, consolations and spiritual visions returned:

> During the time that he was in Vicenza, he had many spiritual visions, and many—almost daily—consolations, contrary to when he was in Paris, and all the more when he started to prepare himself to be ordained a priest in Venice, and when he was preparing himself to say mass. In all those travels, he had great supernatural visitations, of the kind that he used to have in Manresa. (*T* 95)

In this final part of his account, Ignatius links the intensity of his experience on the way to Rome explicitly to what had happened in the Manresa days as he was preparing to sail to Jerusalem. Both periods are foundational.

The crowning event of Ignatius's journey to Rome is his vision in the chapel of La Storta, a few miles away from the Eternal City. Ignatius sets the stage by mentioning that on the journey to Rome, he was "visited by God" in a special way (*T* 96). He had prayed to Our Lady, in his time of preparation for his first Mass, to join him to her Son. Hence, as he was praying in that chapel "he felt such change [*tal mutatione*] in his soul, and saw so clearly that God the Father was putting him [*lo mettava*] with Christ, his Son, that he would not dare even to doubt it, but that God the Father was putting him with his Son" (*T* 96). This vision builds up an *inclusio*, since the first "visitation" of the *Testament* was one of the Virgin Mary with the Child Jesus. But the travails of the journey between these two moments shed a distinct light on the vision of La Storta. The image is no longer static, looking upon Ignatius, but a vision of a movement that brings him in since he is *placed with* the Son. The Child

Jesus of the first visitation gives way to Christ carrying his cross in the labors of his work of salvation. In Manresa and Jerusalem, the divine visions that were personalized were also christological, but now the Father himself makes his appearance. This vision presents the culmination of a certain journey of quest for Ignatius. In it, the destination he had reached was divinely confirmed.[98] Hence, there is a double locational anchoring of the confirmation of the vision: the spiritual place in God with the Son carrying the cross and the geographical place of life in Rome.

Finding: The Culmination of the Third Pilgrimage

With the vision of La Storta there is a clear sense, both logically and narratively, that the pilgrimage of Ignatius has reached its destination. His vocation is settled, confirmed by God, and further validated by the passing of time; it had been more than fifteen years ago. The reader could also see that the text was coming to an end, as only a few paragraphs are to follow, but it was not the end of the journey for Ignatius. The third layer of pilgrimage was still unfolding since the final mention of Ignatius as "the pilgrim" (*T* 99) appears in the text after the vision of La Storta.

The epilogue of the *Testament* reverts to the present of the action of narrating and provides the reader with a further extension of that experience of God. Whereas the first mention of an apparition of God makes it clear through the expression of visitation that it was realized at *God's* sole initiative, in this final part God is presented as "found." Ignatius shares with Câmara the ease with which he would find God: "And any time and hour that he wanted to find God, he was finding him" (*T* 99). What started and was narrated as a quest on which Ignatius looked for God's will, as expressed by the place of incarnation he sought, ends with a genuine encounter in reciprocity: being visited by God and in return, finding him any time. As such, the space of an encounter is sketched that the relationship may inhabit at any time. What was sought and visited is now found and inhabited.

Through the language of "finding" (*trovare*) at any time, the *Testament* signals that what—or who—lies at the final destination, beyond the confines of the core narrative, is identical to the initial impetus, now seen more clearly. It is no longer seen at a distance, as something or someone to imitate, nor as a God to serve by following one's vocation. It is now a near presence, always to be found. This third understanding of pilgrimage opens a horizon that is not one of a particular response but of a space of infinite intimacy. It did not start after La Storta, for it had begun with the very start of Ignatius's quest and overlaps with the pilgrimage to Jerusalem and the quest for his vocation. As a mystical development this pilgrimage is not unfolded narratively by Ignatius but is only alluded to with discretion.[99] Unlike the journey of vocational discernment, it is not offered as a normative pathway to God. A blank space is left open by Ignatius, who had refused to let Câmara see his spiritual papers. The path of Ignatius was meant to be his alone.[100]

Such a new destination nonetheless invites the reader to reread the whole journey as one guided by the quest for God and the discernment of God's signs—the very process that Ignatius went through in dictating the *Testament*—and summons the reader to reflect on his or her own journey.

2. A JOURNEY TO BE TRAVELED BY OTHERS: PILGRIMAGE AS A FORMATIONAL TOOL

Pilgrimage had been an important individual experience, and it led to a literary journey of testimony for Ignatius. Since the narrative acted as a testament, it implies that the pilgrim *ethos* would also have an impact on followers. Pilgrimage was to become, in the hands of Ignatius, a tool of religious formation, a journey to be traveled by others. Since Ignatius himself did not reproduce his pilgrimage, and since the goal of Jerusalem morphed into a lifelong quest for God's presence and will, his formative use of pilgrimage did not imply a formal replication of his own experience. Ignatius instead moved from the external pursuit of an image to an attempt at incarnation.

Pilgrimage in the Novitiate

In 1539, as Ignatius and the first companions were deliberating on the foundation of the Society of Jesus, they devised a potential program of formation for men—initially priests—who wanted to join their group. They settled on three experiments that embody the core of their life, to be realized over a three-month period: the Spiritual Exercises, service to the poor in the hospital, and pilgrimage.[101] As the Society grew rapidly in its early years, forcing a stronger formative framework, a two-year novitiate including six main experiments would eventually emerge in the *Constitutions* of 1558, with pilgrimage still one of the main ones.[102] Thus, every single Jesuit novice would have to experience the life of a pilgrim as part of his formation for religious life, a reality unique among Roman Catholic religious communities. By securing a place for the experience of pilgrimage at the heart of the formation of future Jesuits right from the start, Ignatius highlighted the centrality of this reality for his understanding of the identity he wanted to mold in his followers. The core experience that shaped his identity was now meant to be embodied by others in order to help them vigorously enter into their journey with God.

When asked in February 1555 by Câmara about the reason (*motivo*) behind the pilgrimage experiment, Ignatius replied that he himself appreciated the experience and how much it helped.[103] In the *Constitutions* he presents the rationale for the pilgrimage in these words:

> The third experience is to spend another month in making a pilgrimage without money and even in begging from door to door, at appropriate times, for the love of God our Lord, in order to grow accustomed to discomfort in food and lodging. Thus too the candidate, through abandoning all the reliance which he could have in money or other created things, may with genuine faith and intense love place his reliance entirely in his Creator and Lord.[104]

The experience, seen in this light, becomes one of radical trust in God, and caution against placing one's trust in any created thing.[105] The single-mindedness of purpose that pilgrimage gained in the *Constitutions* highlights the core aspect of fostering one's relationship with God, which was uncovered in the *Testament*, but this aspect is set at the basic level of an ascetic practice and early trust-building. Such trust in God would be useful for the later journey of ongoing discerned refinement of one's vocation, but the experiment of pilgrimage itself does not reach that point.

The novitiate pilgrimage is of a different kind than Ignatius's own experience. The novice is sent, usually with another novice, and they know the length of their endeavor. Ignatius's initial pilgrimage to Jerusalem was longer, at first done in secret, and strictly individual despite some chance encounters. Ignatius also envisioned the destination of his initial pilgrimage to be his final destination, something not envisioned in the novitiate pilgrimage, since the pilgrims are expected to come back and move on with other experiments. Ignatius also knew that not everybody could endure the radical pilgrim experience he had, which entailed desired, extreme poverty. In the legislative texts, provisions were made to adapt the experiments, potentially leaving the Jesuit-to-be in one of the experiments for a longer time, to the detriment of another. In the case of the pilgrimage in particular, Ignatius mentioned to Câmara that, having seen that some pilgrims got sick, he had to moderate it and leave it to the discretion of the local superiors.[106] Throughout the history of the Jesuit order, this experiment has probably been the one most adapted to specific circumstances, or even at times left aside.[107]

Pilgrimage as Petition, Penance, Discernment Tool, or Dismissal

The novitiate experiment of pilgrimage is not the only instance in which Ignatius employed pilgrimage in formation or governance. He also used it for petitionary purposes, as penance, as a discernment tool, and as a way to dismiss people from the Society of Jesus.[108] Ignatius once sent some Jesuit priests two by two from Rome to Loreto to pray for the recovery of Pope Marcel in April 1555.[109] The pope nevertheless died after a very short pontificate.[110] Ignatius also imposed pilgrimages as a penance after a serious offense.[111]

The most common uses of pilgrimage for Ignatius, outside the novitiate, were either as a discernment tool or for dismissal. Regarding discernment, the best example is that of Micer Andrea, a Flemish priest who, while in the Jesuit house in Rome, was ambivalent about his vocation and thinking about going back to his native land.[112] Ignatius's advisors suggested that he send Andrea on pilgrimage to Loreto alone, with little money and only the clothes he had on his back. If, once he arrived, he wanted to be released from his vows, it would be done *ipso facto*.[113] First, however, he would be advised to present himself before the statue of Our Lady to decide whether he wanted to remain in the order; he could stay there to ponder his decision for eight days. Ignatius added two things to this suggestion. First, that every mark of affection should be given Andrea, but not money since he thought it better for him to endure some hardships. Second, that he should make his decision while in Loreto, since God is usually more present in a place where he is venerated.[114] The time of pilgrimage, which takes place outside the confines of ordinary life, offers the space to assess one's life and commitment and make a more peaceful choice. Moreover, for Ignatius, the fact that the destination is a sacred place, where the divine is present in a special way, had an intrinsic value, crowning the pilgrimage experience.[115]

The final use, as a method of dismissal, is the most intriguing. Câmara writes of it briefly: "The way to dismiss, is usually the Father [Ignatius] sending one on a pilgrimage; and he prefers to dismiss someone who has to leave, instead of letting him go, and this, in order that he [the dismissed] would leave with love."[116] Ignatius's care for individuals, even as one was dismissed from the Society or leaving of his own initiative, is patent in the desire that they would go *con amor* (lovingly), without rancor or disappointment. The act of sending someone on a final pilgrimage also encapsulates the reality that the former novice or Jesuit now must find anew the place where God calls him. By sending one on a concluding pilgrimage, Ignatius was reminding the dismissed that the road continued for them, albeit in a different way. According to Câmara's account, that genuine sense of care bore fruit, as many former Jesuits remained on friendly terms with the Society.[117]

Pilgrimage for Others: Asceticism versus Discernment

In hindsight, Ignatius's uses of pilgrimage as a discernment tool, for dismissal, and for novitiate experiments are all tied together in an effort to unleash an inner journey. The unifying purpose was to remove the men from a known space to let them enter—or not—into a discovery of themselves and, potentially, into a new relationship with God. For the novitiate experiment of pilgrimage, the main element appears to be an ascetic experience that can be linked to another main novitiate experiment, the month-long service in the hospital, a time of humble service of the poor. The uses of pilgrimage as penance, petition, or even devotion are clearly related to ascetic practice.

On the other hand, the trust developed in the Lord through the novitiate pilgrimage is essential as a foundation for the discernment formalized in the other main experiment, that of the thirty-day Spiritual Exercises. Ignatius clearly tied discernment to pilgrimage through the whole framework of the *Testament*. When used outside of the novitiate as a tool of discernment or employed to dismiss someone, pilgrimage acts as either a confirmation moment or as the starting point for further discernment of God's call on one's life.

What does Ignatius call forth from his own use of pilgrimage as a formational tool? The imitative component of Christ is furthered by an imitation of the disciples of Christ, both in an evangelical way and in the concrete example of the early companions of Jesus. The novices on pilgrimage are called to enter into the way of proceeding of professed members of the Society of Jesus, who were, according to Ignatius's ideal, to live simply as men sent from one place to another to accomplish brief missions. Connected to the more spiritual approach of the month-long Spiritual Exercises, the pilgrimage could jumpstart an embodied discernment of one's vocation as a Jesuit—or not—or, even more specifically, one's call within the order. Ignatius could not expect full discernment to unfold within a scripted timeframe, at least not for a refined sense of God's call beyond a state of life (his own vocational discernment was a very long process), but the seed was meant to be sowed accordingly. As for Ignatius's third dimension of pilgrimage, the proper mystical one, its lofty and far-reaching destination is singular and could not be reproduced; hence, no hint of it is present in Ignatius's uses of pilgrimage for others. However, the very rootedness in God fostered by the practice of pilgrimage would allow for an inner journey in God to blossom in the novice.

3. CONCLUSION

The *Testament* of Ignatius reveals itself as a multilayered narrative that blends an experiential journey of pilgrimage with a narrative reflection on identity through the prism of pilgrimage. The dialectic between an inner and exterior pilgrimage is well-developed and demonstrates the intimate relationship between the two through the importance of discernment and a constant "unknowing" that accompanies every decision. By doing so, the *Testament* bears witness to the transition from a medieval conception of pilgrimage, emphasizing the ascetic dimension, to a modern one, linked more to interiority and identity, while still preserving the medieval aspects.

Pilgrimage, as expressed in the *Testament*, remains essentially a quest for God, who is both the impetus and the goal of the journey. Yet the end of the journey is not to touch holy relics or stand in a holy place, but a patient discernment of God's desire for one's place in the world, and ultimately, one's place in God. It is not predetermined. The quest entails a work of progressive proximity to the divine through prayer and physical journey. It is a vocational quest both in doing and in being.

The journey of the pilgrimage, understood as a quest for one's vocation in relationship with God, is thus at once ongoing and lifelong. Ignatius was "the pilgrim" until the end. Building upon this understanding, pilgrimage becomes not only a foundational experience but also a formative one. By thrusting the ascetic experience upon a would-be Jesuit, Ignatius fosters a pedagogy of radical trust in God and plants the seed for a potential journey of listening to God, even if the one sent was finally dismissed. In this regard, pilgrimage takes its place alongside the Spiritual Exercises, which contributes the spiritual framework, and the hospital experiment, which emphasizes the spirit of service, to fashion an evolving sense of the divine and of the embodied human journey with God.

Seen through the eyes of Ignatius, pilgrimage appears rooted first in a personal experience. While singular in its unfolding, it is also presented as having universal value, since it can be used broadly as a formative tool. Linked at first to the person of Christ and his imitation, it also unfolds as a way of following him, introducing the apostolic dimension described in the previous chapter. Nonetheless, the collective dimension witnessed in the constitution of the Hebrew people through the experience of the exodus would be tackled anew in a reflection on the Church as a "Pilgrim Church." This is the focus of the next chapter.

CHAPTER 4

The Pilgrim Church

To be pilgrims and strangers means that the growing, journeying, adventuring is never done. There is always more. Too many Christians, too many churches, grow for a while and take a rest, sometimes a very long rest. They cease to ask, "What is next? Where are we going?"

—Dee Dyas, "Medieval Patterns of Pilgrimage"[1]

In recent decades, the Church has eagerly embraced her identity as the "Pilgrim Church." This title came through the Second Vatican Council (1962–65), which defined her, among other images,[2] as *Ecclesia peregrinans*, a "*Pilgrimaging* Church."[3] The image struck the right chord and was taken up liturgically and theologically in the aftermath of the Council. Despite the apparent newness of the image, its roots run deep, since it draws on the biblical vision that portrays God's people as wanderers. It presents the image of a Church in movement, on a quest, opening its windows to the realities of the world surrounding her. In time, "Pilgrim Church" would become one of the most beloved ways to talk about the Church.

The prominence of this collective religious image was enhanced by the premier character of the Church documents that popularized it, the work of an ecumenical council. Despite the long history of the popular practice of pilgrimage among Christians, the elevation of the image of the Pilgrim Church cannot be credited to an eruption of popular piety into high-end doctrinal work. Was it an explicit reflection on our times? Not necessarily, but the theme of pilgrimage was consonant with our times, explaining at least in part the subsequent success of the expression.

The core of this chapter deals with the theme of the Pilgrim Church as self-definition for the Church before and after the Council. As we saw earlier, issues of translation require careful treatment. At times, we will indicate the original words used since the pilgrimage vocabulary can be notoriously elusive depending on translation.

The sources of the Council will be covered as they are called forth in the conciliar documents. The scope of biblical material is much narrower than what we analyzed in chapter 2, since the Council focused on the Exodus story and the epistles in its explicit references. Of the theological tradition on pilgrimage, only Augustine is brought forward, since his *City of God* alone is referenced regarding pilgrimage. This exploration of pilgrimage in Augustine will be our first step.

Pilgrimage is a multifaceted reality, and the idea of the Pilgrim Church does not escape this. Different vantage points contribute to a fuller understanding of the concept, its reception, and its experiential reality. Consequently, the second part of the chapter explores the features and context of the Pilgrim Church according to the various documents of the Second Vatican Council. The occurrences of pilgrim vocabulary will be the guiding light to decipher the changing attitude of the Council fathers toward the pilgrim dimension of the Church. In a third section, I analyze the reception of the dimension of pilgrimage in the liturgy through the Eucharistic Prayers, especially the only Eucharistic Prayer that originated from an episcopal conference in the aftermath of the Second Vatican Council and eventually gained universal status.[4] That prayer, the "Eucharistic Prayer for Various Needs" is built around pilgrimage, no less! Through it, the pilgrim theme reached the heart of Christian worship. In the fourth section, we see how the idea of a Pilgrim Church was not restricted only to conciliar theological documents or to the prayer of the Church but was also embodied in the pilgrimages of the post-Council popes. Pilgrim popes, especially Paul VI and John Paul II, are embodied symbols of the Pilgrim Church. I analyze their discourses and actions on pilgrimage as they modeled a pilgrim ethos as heads of the Church. Throughout, the guiding question is the search for the understanding of pilgrimage at work, in order to decipher the operative definition of *pilgrimage* in the many claims regarding the Pilgrim Church.

Finally, we bring into dialogue the experience of pilgrimage, as defined in chapter 1, with the Pilgrim Church, challenging the *peregrinitas* of the Church in light of the categories of the ideal type of pilgrimage. How deeply pilgrim is the Church? To take up the questions of Dee Dyas quoted at the beginning of this chapter: "What is next? Where are we going?" In other words, how does the Church's choice to name herself a "Pilgrim Church" still call her to move forward with becoming more pilgrim?

1. *PEREGRINATIO* IN AUGUSTINE'S *CITY OF GOD*

The place of the *City of God* as a backdrop and source for the Second Vatican Council's treatment of pilgrimage is secured through an explicit reference made to Augustine by the Constitution on the Church *Lumen Gentium*, the only reference to a theological author in regard to pilgrimage in this document.[5] The *City of God* is the product of a mature Augustine (354–430), bishop of Hippo. The immediate impulse for the oft-interrupted writing of this work[6] was the sack of Rome by the Visigoths in 410, the consequences of which led Augustine to ponder the history of humanity and the tension at work in it between the human city and the city of God.

The first line of the preface in book 1 of the *City of God* already alludes to pilgrimage by introducing the city of God that "*sojourns as a stranger* amidst the ungodly [*inter impios peregrinatur*]."[7] In this tale of two cities, pilgrimage (*peregrinatio*) is depicted as a necessary experience of the Church on earth on her way to her true home and heavenly destination. Hence, *peregrinatio* is more than a side theme;[8] it connects the two organizing principles of the entire opus.[9] According to Sarah Stewart-Kroeker, it even constitutes "Augustine's dominant image for the human life....The *peregrinatio* image pervades Augustine's writings. It is a defining image for his theology and a window into his central theological concerns."[10] *Peregrinatio* appears nearly a hundred times in the *City of God*,[11] gaining a more precise meaning there than in other Augustinian works.[12] Augustine's notion of pilgrimage is not based on the pilgrim-travelers of his day.[13] In fact, "Augustine himself mentions several pilgrims in *City of God*, although he usually does not name them *peregrini*."[14] The concrete *peregrini* that Augustine could identify were what we would call today refugees, since they had fled Rome for North Africa in the wake of the turmoil affecting the Eternal City.[15] Consequently, Augustine's concept of pilgrimage is anchored primarily not in experiential knowledge, but in its potential fruitfulness as a theological construct. Some important characteristics of the Augustinian *peregrinatio* stand out: the unpleasantness, the tension in faith, the teleological orientation, the foreignness, and the formative dimension.

The pilgrim dimension of the *City of God* strongly underlines the misery, toil, and mortality that this city of God experiences in the world.[16] The *peregrinatio* is an intrinsically painful experience for the Church, an ordeal, in line with the actual experience of travel; "*peregrinatio* is a singularly unpleasant business, one that must be gotten along with as best as possible."[17] The romantic mystique of travel plays no part in the Augustinian pilgrimage of the Church. The negative light cast on the reality of the world led many commentators of this great work to lament the devaluation of the earthly human experience that it presupposes.[18] Augustine's entire opus is based on the distinction, if not the opposition, between the two cities. The place of the city of God is ultimately not in this world, though God's Church journeys here, and has to partake in social life.[19]

Despite its hardship, the pilgrimage of the city of God is nonetheless done in faith.[20] The pilgrimage of the Church happens in the world, but her nature is not of this world. In a proleptic way, some of the fruits of the heavenly destination of the pilgrimage are already enjoyed,[21] but their fullness lies ahead. Unlike its modern-day experiential counterpart, *peregrinatio* is fundamentally, for Augustine, "a social, not an individual, event."[22] It is an event of a community, of the Church. In that regard, Augustine is in direct line with the exodus experience. The connection with the Church already in heaven is clear, since those pilgrims have already reached the destination that faith hopes for,[23] but Augustine struggles to reconcile the distinct Pauline views of Ephesians 2:19 and 2 Corinthians 5:6–8 regarding the relationship with the Lord during the pilgrimage.[24] On the one hand, Christians are portrayed as "no longer strangers and *peregrini*, but you are citizens with the saints and also members of the household of God" (Eph 2:19). On the other hand, their current pilgrimage keeps them away from the Lord (2 Cor 5:6–8). Pilgrimage entails a tension, even in faith.[25]

Another important component of the Augustinian pilgrimage of the Church is its strong teleological thrust.[26] Those of the city of God still on earth constantly seek and desire what is above. Earth is not home. It is not the destination. There is a clear destination, which is heaven, and a potent and relentless thrust toward it. Part of the Church has already arrived, and the journeying Church longs to be there. The orientation of the city of God is eschatological; the Church is in the world while not being of the world, striving for the heavenly city. The mature Augustine abandoned the consideration of pilgrimage through the Neoplatonic theme of a *reditus ad patriam*,[27] of a "return." While heaven is indeed the Christians' true *patria*, it is one toward which they strive, a new place, not one to which they simply return. The movement is forward-looking, not circular.

In his use of the adjective *peregrina* to qualify the Church or the city of God, Augustine relies on the classical legal definition of *peregrinus* as "stranger, foreigner," not the modern-day definition of *pilgrim* as "religious traveler."[28] Throughout the *City of God*, Augustine emphasizes the radical foreignness of the Church via-à-vis the world. The concept of *peregrinus* is rooted in Roman law, which stresses the difference in status of the foreigner (*peregrinus*) as contrasted with the citizen (*civis*).[29] Hence, the Church is not—and cannot be—at home in the world. This image of *Ecclesia peregrina* is essential to understand both the Church and pilgrimage: "Augustine, using this city imagery, consistently describes the *civitas Dei* on earth as *peregrina*, and this remains his most used, and his most useful, epithet for it."[30] Unlike the later *Ecclesia peregrinans*—"Pilgrimaging Church"—of the Second Vatican Council, the *peregrina* applied to the Church in the *City of God* emphasizes not her movement, but her radical foreignness.[31]

Finally, the status of *peregrini* shapes Christians and entails a formative dimension and ethical implications. Although pilgrimage is more an image[32] than a concrete experience—as exemplified linguistically in the Augustinian distinction between the metaphorical *peregrinari* and the physical *ambulare*[33]—it does nonetheless entail a "process of moral and aesthetic formation."[34]

The radical foreignness of the Christian *peregrinus* while on earth would lead to a particular understanding of the *utor/fruor* distinction, in which the *peregrinus* in the *City of God* would no longer be considered as having *dominium* over the goods of the earth, but only the *usufruct*, or perhaps even the *usus*.[35] This formative element is part of a larger *reformatio* called forth by Christian life.[36] Hence, in an interesting reversal, the *image* of *peregrinatio* ultimately leads to an experience of the whole person that would encompass even one's very body.[37] This would result, for example, in the willingness by the *peregrinus* to confront evil and endure persecution, and in their radical dependence on God, demonstrated by prayer and hope.[38]

The single reference to Augustine's *City of God* that appears in the conciliar documents originates from Book 18. In the first two sections of that book, the city of God is described as *peregrina*, in the sense of *stranger*.[39] However, in chapter 51 of the same book a more active depiction of the "pilgrimaging" of the city of God is offered in two instances using the present participle *peregrinans* and the gerund *peregrinandum*. In the first instance, the city of God is set against its adversaries—here, the devils—in a clear opposition between the two cities, emphasizing nonetheless God's protection of his city.[40] The second reference of the same section is the one carried over into the conciliar document: *inter persecutiones mundi et consolationes Dei peregrinando procurrit ecclesia*.[41] In these concluding words to that chapter in Book 18, Augustine nominally ascribes to the Church (*ecclesia*) the action of "pilgrimaging," and not simply to the city of God. The Church is depicted as caught between the persecutions of the world and the consolations of God, hence between her current localization on earth, in contrast to the human city, and the proleptic presence of God prefiguring her final achievement in heaven, where she is evidently not yet. Despite that tension, the Church pushes forward, pilgrimaging (*peregrinando*) in a journey that extends not only from the time of Christ and his apostles, but also from Abel, to the end of the world.[42] This passage encapsulates essential characteristics of the Augustinian *peregrinatio*: its harshness, the foreignness of one's location, the teleological thrust, the faith dimension, and the collective body that makes the pilgrimage. As such, this brief quote conveys the main tenets of Augustine's thought on the Church's pilgrimage, which informed the reflection of the Second Vatican Council.

At the end of his study on *peregrinatio* in Augustine, Claussen questions in a discrete footnote the influence of Augustine's notion of pilgrimage on subsequent generations, "I remain unsure of how 'historically important' Augustine's *peregrinatio* has been. While I am certain that it plays an important role in the proper understanding of *City of God*, it seems that later generations took the word, and took it quite eagerly, but left most of the concept behind."[43] A similar concern can be raised about the expression "Pilgrim Church" for the Second Vatican Council, as we will see. Nevertheless, in terms of textual evidence, it is from the Augustinian source that the conciliar fathers of the 1960s would draw for their reflection on the Church in her pilgrimage.

2. THE "PILGRIM CHURCH" IN THE DOCUMENTS OF THE SECOND VATICAN COUNCIL

A major area that the Second Vatican Council transformed is ecclesiology. The Council renewed the theological imagination around the depiction of the Church, releasing it from a neo-Scholastic definition to embrace a variety of images drawn from patristic theology or the lived experience of the Church.[44] Among those images, the "Pilgrim Church" (*Ecclesia peregrinans*) stands out, as it was chosen to head chapter 7 of the Dogmatic Constitution on the Church *Lumen Gentium*. The moniker "Pilgrim Church" endorsed by the Council was then incorporated into various Eucharistic Prayers, ensuring its diffusion throughout the Christian community. It was also echoed by many postconciliar theologians.[45]

Between Augustine and Vatican II, the theological depiction of the Church in pilgrimage significantly moved from *Ecclesia peregrina* to *Ecclesia peregrinans*, from a Church experiencing her foreignness in the world to a Church recognizing herself as engaged in the world while keeping her gaze on Christ. The distinction between the adjective *peregrina* and the present participle *peregrinans* also underscores the difference between a state of being and a verbal action, between a static image of foreignness and a dynamic image of movement. Despite the recourse to Augustine, the Second

Vatican Council relies on a more optimistic reading of the world, as expressed eloquently by the incipit of the Pastoral Constitution on the Church in the Modern World *Gaudium et Spes*: "The joys and the hopes, the griefs and the anxieties of the men of this age, especially those who are poor or in any way afflicted, these are the joys and hopes, the griefs and anxieties of the followers of Christ."[46] In keeping with the Council's stated methodology for theological reflection,[47] the consideration of the pilgrim nature of the Church is supported by a biblical meditation.[48] Surprisingly, however, the conciliar members do not draw a connection between the religious experience of pilgrimage practiced by countless Catholics, which they were aware of, and their reflection on the Church in pilgrimage. The discourses of the various participants at the Second Vatican Council contain many references to concrete pilgrimages,[49] but no connection appears, either directly or indirectly, in the text of *Lumen Gentium* to the practice of pilgrimage. It shows the disconnection between popular religiosity and theological reflection, since the participants knew about pilgrimage, but do not refer to it as a bone fide theological source, whereas inscriptions in catacombs are deemed worthy.[50] The conciliar fathers treated pilgrimage in the Augustinian mold of a theoretical reflection.

The concept of the Church as "pilgrimaging" marks an epochal shift from a consideration of the Church as a *societas*, which emphasizes stability and order, especially when the adjectives *perfecta* or *inaequalis* are thrown into the mix.[51] The "pilgrimaging" Church suggests a stronger connection to the world than the ethereal expression of the Church as the "Mystical Body of Christ" favored by Pope Pius XII.[52] It also leaves behind the more adversarial connotations of the "Church Militant," favored by many a catechism.[53]

The theme of pilgrimage was alluded to in the inaugural discourse of the Second Vatican Council by Pope John XXIII.[54] Exposing the duty of the Council to guard and teach more efficiently the Christian doctrine, he states that "this doctrine embraces the whole human person, composed of body and soul, and it also bids us, who are inhabitants [*incolae*] on this earth, to tend as pilgrims [*peregrinos*] toward the heavenly homeland [*ad caelestem patriam*]."[55] The pilgrim dimension of human life is portrayed in line with the body/soul dichotomy by the distinction between our being *incolae*, inhabitants of the earth—a statement of fact—and a command to be *peregrinos* (pilgrims) in our orientation toward heaven. Hence, the pope does not presuppose that all are pilgrims, unlike some translations of this passage,[56] but that while all are residents of this earth, we should also strive for the heavenly city. Because he previously expressed strongly his disagreement with doomsayers who see the contemporary world only through negative lenses,[57] the pope advocates for the performance of one's duties to both the earthly and the celestial cities.[58] Through his Augustinian reference to the two cities, his positive view of the world—not a place that the pilgrims flee but a place they inhabit—and his anchoring of the command to be pilgrims at the heart of the consideration of doctrine that the Council was called to achieve, John XXIII already planted the image of pilgrimage at the beginning of the conciliar gathering.

A reader of the documents of Vatican II in English would miss most references to the dimension of pilgrimage because of the semantic richness of the cognates of *peregrinor* and the absence of a commonly used English verb for the action of going on a pilgrimage.[59] Hence the translation of cognates of *peregrinor* (e.g., *peregrinatio, peregrinus*) results in "journey," "sojourn," "wander," "traveler," "wayfarer," as much as "pilgrimage" and "pilgrim."[60] To explore the breadth of the Second Vatican Council's understanding of pilgrimage, I will analyze all the occurrences of cognates of *peregrinor* in the conciliar texts, as well as the few mentions of *viator* (traveler), since it plays a similar semantic role—as in the expression *Ecclesia viatorum* (Church of travelers/pilgrims; *LG* 50).[61] This analysis of the various "pilgrim" occurrences illuminates the central expression of the *Ecclesia peregrinans* and reveals the unsettledness of the Council's understanding of the Church's pilgrimage. I will proceed in chronological order, moving from *Sacrosanctum Concilium* to *Lumen Gentium*—the central piece—then to *Dei Verbum*, and *Gaudium et Spes*, before concluding with some final thoughts on the *peregrinitas* of Vatican II.

Pilgrimage in *Sacrosanctum Concilium*

The Constitution on the Sacred Liturgy *Sacrosanctum Concilium* (December 4, 1963) is chronologically the first major document of the Council to use the vocabulary of pilgrimage in two instances. The first occurs in a description of the true nature of the Church, which contains four sets of two opposite qualifiers contrasted through a *tamen* (and yet). Hence, the Church is human and yet (*tamen*) divine, visible and invisible, active and contemplative, present (in the world) and yet pilgrim toward a future city (*in mundo praesentem et tamen peregrinam*).[62] The contrast between the presence in the world and the pilgrimage to the future city (of heaven) harks back to the primary Latin root of *peregrinus* as foreigner, alien, noncitizen who was coming *from* a foreign land—although here the movement is *toward* a different land/city. The pilgrim dimension of the Church is depicted in opposition to its current embodiment on earth, and its ethereal accent is reinforced by the other qualifications with which it lines up: divine, invisible, contemplative. Hence, the perspective is clearly eschatological. Furthermore, the image is here a collective one, in which the Church as a whole is described as pilgrim.

The other mention of pilgrimage in *Sacrosanctum Concilium* appears in the comparison between the earthly liturgy and the heavenly liturgy, "which is celebrated in the holy city of Jerusalem toward which we journey as pilgrims [*ad quam peregrini tendimus*]."[63] Here pilgrims are individuals who are collectively on their way to a place, Jerusalem, beyond their actual reach—since Jerusalem metaphorically depicts the ultimate divine *locus* of the heavenly liturgy. The tension toward a destination, albeit an inaccessible one, gives dynamism to the picture and highlights the teleological aspiration of the pilgrims.

Pilgrimage in *Lumen Gentium*

The Dogmatic Constitution on the Church *Lumen Gentium* (November 21, 1964) contains the main trove of expressions about pilgrimage regarding the Church among the documents of the Second Vatican Council.

In the first chapter of the document, pertaining to the mystery of the Church, the verb *peregrinor* appears three times. The most straightforward classical meaning of *peregrinor* is to journey or travel abroad or away from home.[64] Each occurrence brings subtle nuances and paves the way for the elucidation of the *Ecclesia peregrinans* of the third chapter of the document. The first mention underlines the estrangement of the Church from the Lord as she journeys on earth: "The Church, while on earth it journeys in a foreign land away from the Lord is like in exile [*Dum vero his in terris Ecclesia peregrinatur a Domino, tamquam exsulem se habet*]" (*LG* 6). The alienation expressed in its Latin etymology by the *peregrinor*, and clearly underlined by the translation of the journey "in a foreign land," is reemphasized both by the "like in exile" and the indication of a movement "away from" the Lord. For the latter, reference is given in the text to 2 Corinthians 5:6, in which Paul starkly underlines that our being in the body (human, perishable) entails separation from the Lord (*apo tou kyriou*). By that reference, the authors of the constitution suggest that the journey of the Church, which is earthly and embodied, is lived at a distance from the Lord, even "away from" him, since being at home with the Lord would come only after having left the body (2 Cor 5:8). The pilgrimage is not *with* the Lord. This accentuation is nonetheless mitigated in the last part of the sentence, since it states that the Church "seeks and experiences those things which are above [*ita ut quae sursum sunt quaerat et sapiat*]," holding in tension the teleological dimension of what is desired (*quaerat*) with the presence of what is already attained (*sapiat*). This initial depiction of the journey nonetheless emphasizes the distance from God experienced on the way.

The second instance of pilgrimage is voiced in a different context, which connects the earthly experience of Christians as pilgrims with their proximity and imitation of Christ: "On earth, still as pilgrims in a strange land [*in terris adhuc peregrinantes*], tracing in trial and in oppression the paths He trod, we are made one with His sufferings like the body is one with the Head, suffering with Him, that with Him we may be glorified" (*LG* 7). While the translation emphasizes the location in a "strange land," the overall thrust of the passage underscores the proximity to Christ achieved by those on a journey on earth.[65] The journeying is no longer presented as an instance of moving away from the Lord, but as the very *locus* of a becoming closer to him by sharing his experience. Another important feature is that the pilgrim experience is expressed in the present through trial and persecution (*in tribulatione et persecutione*), as well as union with the passion of the Lord (*Eius passionibus*), all markers of extreme hardship.[66] Hence, the dimension of effort, or even penance, of the pilgrimage is strongly underlined here. Furthermore, pilgrimage then acts as a formative movement of conformation to Christ through trials.

Lumen Gentium then calls on Augustine to evoke the Church who journeys (*peregrinando*; *LG* 8)[67] "amid the persecutions of the world and the consolations of God" (*LG* 8),[68] carrying her mission of proclaiming the cross and death of the Lord until he comes again. According to Augustine's words, this journey is affected by both the external attacks from the world and the inner consolations of God, devising a path of tension between alienation from the world and nearness to God in the realization of her mission. The path trodden is both one of hardship and fidelity, and that tension is further developed in the subsequent sentence, which locates the "sorrows and challenges" facing the Church not only "from without," but also "within itself" (*LG* 8). The moving character of the journey, its unsettledness, is also expressed through the images of the shadows (*sub umbris*) present in its ongoing revelation of the mystery of the Lord, while "in the end, it will be manifested in full light [*lumine pleno*]" (*LG* 8). This third mention of pilgrimage connects the journey of the Church through the earthly tensions (from outside, and from within) to her essential mission of proclaiming God's mystery. The journey is the inescapable *locus* of this proclamation, and as such, it plays an essential role for the accomplishment of the Church's mission.

The second chapter of *Lumen Gentium*, devoted to the topic of the people of God, features the dimension of pilgrimage in two instances. The first harks back to the historical experience of Israel, who "wandered as an exile in the desert [*in deserto peregrinabatur*]" (*LG* 9). Once again, the translation is heavy-handed, using *exile*, since the context is that of a journey in a foreign land, which, in the biblical narrative, is a journey of liberation from Egypt toward the promised land—hence, not an exile. The Council draws a parallel between the desert journey of Israel—already the Church of God (*Ecclesia Dei*)—and that of the new Israel, the Church of Christ (*Ecclesia Christi*), which is in search (*inquirit*) of a "future and abiding city [*futuram eamque manentem civitatem*]" (*LG* 9). The parallel between the two "churches" and their movement is presented in a positive light, emphasizing on the one side the "desert" component of the current pilgrimage and, on the other side, the teleological dimension of the future city sought—reached in the case of

Israel, hoped for in the case of the Church of Christ. Calling upon the experience of the people of Israel in the desert opens the richness of biblical narratives to think about the current experience of the Church.[69] The second mention of the journeying Church in that chapter of *Lumen Gentium* straightforwardly states that "the Church, now sojourning on earth as an exile, is necessary for salvation [*Ecclesiam hanc peregrinantem necessariam esse ad salutem*]" (*LG* 14). Once again, the translation emphasizes the "exile" dimension, while the immediate context does not necessarily call for it.

Before the chapter on the Pilgrim Church, a further mention of pilgrimage is found in the chapter on the hierarchical structure of the Church, which introduces a new teleological dimension to the Church's pilgrimage. Describing the role of bishops, the Council writes that through them, Christ "directs and guides the People of the New Testament in their pilgrimage toward eternal happiness [*ad aeternam beatitudinem peregrinatione*]" (*LG* 21). This first use of *peregrinatio* as a substantive in *Lumen Gentium*, as opposed to cognates in a verbal form, highlights two characteristics of pilgrimage. First, the ultimate *telos* of pilgrimage is "eternal happiness." Earlier, the end of the pilgrimage was presented under the guise of a future city, or even Jerusalem, in *Sacrosanctum Concilium*. Now, the image of a physical destination is left aside for that of the state of being of happiness or blessedness (*beatitudo*), no longer affected by the turmoil of time, since it is eternal. This teleological orientation shies away from the hardships of pilgrimage mentioned previously to focus on the state reached at the completion of the journey. The second noteworthy element is that Christ is presented markedly as the one who "directs and guides [*dirigit et ordinat*]" (*LG* 21) the pilgrimage of the people. The agency of Christ is immediate. The pilgrim people is no longer described as moving away from the Lord (*LG* 6), or as imitating and being united with his sufferings (*LG* 7), but as being guided through all things by Christ—who acts through the ministry of his servants. Hence, although the consummation of the potential union between the Lord and his people is not fully achieved, the relation between them is not one of mere distance, in longing and desire, but one in which the Lord is portrayed as being supremely active in the direction he imparts for the journey of his people.

The use of cognates of *peregrinatio* in the first six chapters of *Lumen Gentium* already sketches important features of pilgrimage in a multifaceted way, even before reaching the chapter that develops the expression *Ecclesia peregrinans*. Hence, even in those early occurrences, the tension between the individual dimension of pilgrimage and its collective understanding is present. There is a sense of physical and temporal journey. The alienation or foreignness of the journey appears, reinforced by the mention of exile. Various *teloi*, or destinations, are offered, from the image of the city to the *telos* of eternal happiness. The hardships and tensions inherent to the journey are evoked, just as the link with the Hebrews' experience of exodus and its desert. Finally, *Lumen Gentium* shows the place of the Lord as a desired model or actual guide. The table was set to explore the Church in depth through a novel, yet ancient, image: the Pilgrim Church.

Chapter 7 of *Lumen Gentium*, whose complete title is "The Eschatological Nature of the Pilgrim Church [*Ecclesiae peregrinantis*] and Its Union with the Church in Heaven [*Ecclesia coelesti*]," forcefully ushered in a new depiction of the Church. The *Ecclesia peregrinans* quickly became a preferred way to talk about the Church. The contrast already built in the title between the two understandings of the Church—pilgrim versus celestial—locates her in relation to space. The Church in heaven is literally depicted in a certain place, where it remains eternally, whereas the contrasting figure is not that of the Church simply on earth, but of the Church in movement, *peregrinans*, hence not "in" a place, but moving through space(s) with an embedded eschatological *telos* in heaven. The *Ecclesia peregrinans* is therefore not in a state, but *in* movement, a "pilgrimaging" Church.[70]

This chapter of *Lumen Gentium* was actually a latecomer, since it was not included in earlier drafts of the constitution, and it was incorporated in the discussion on the Church after the intervention of Pope Paul VI.[71] Its main purpose was to address the place of the Communion of Saints at the very core of the definition of the Church. It is ironic that what was first thought to pertain mostly to the heavenly Church through the development of the idea of the Communion of Saints came to define in its reception what the Church is (on earth) par excellence.

In this chapter, the couple *Ecclesia peregrinans/coelestis* functionally replaces that of *militans/triumphans*, which had been traditionally used to distinguish the Church while on earth, and that which is in heaven.[72] The overtone of the traditional dichotomy is more combative, since the roots of both verbs, *militare* and *triumphare*, harken back to fight, battle, war, and victory.[73] Both, however, were present participles emphasizing action, although for the former as ongoing process, and for the latter as celebratory result. The move to *peregrinans/coelestis* infuses a renewed sense of movement, in its fragility, dispossession, and yearning. This radical shift of emphasis operating in these images was not necessarily detected by early commentators of the conciliar documents.[74]

The image of the Pilgrim Church constitutes the backbone of the chapter, not only as *Ecclesia peregrinans*, but also as *Ecclesia viatorum* (*LG* 50), the Church of the travelers, of those who are on the way, on the move.[75] In addressing the relationship between the members of the Church on earth with those in heaven, *Lumen Gentium* contrasts the *viatores* (wayfarers; *LG* 49–50) who journey on earth (*peregrinantur*)[76] with the brethren who rest in the peace of Christ (*LG* 49), the saints (*LG* 50). The pilgrimage metaphor unfolding here underlines at once the movement of the Church and her members, but also her clear purposefulness in an eschatological orientation. While the groans and travails of the earthly stance of the Church are mentioned in the opening paragraph of chapter 7 (*LG* 48), the "pilgrimaging" of the Church and her members is mostly driven by the tension toward the heavenly realization of the Church. The world, as the *locus* of the pilgrimaging Church, is portrayed in an ambiguous light. On the one hand, it is meant to partake in the eschatological "restoration of all things," alongside humanity (*LG* 48). It is also the place where human beings are called to perform the work entrusted to them by the Father (*LG* 48). On the other hand, the world is also the place of "vicissitudes," depicted in stark contrast with the "City that is to come" (*LG* 50). Therefore, the world is not a neutral place, but it is not unambiguously either good or bad. It is a necessary place to be traversed, journeyed into by the pilgrimaging Church.

The main thrust of this chapter is to reinforce the connection between the Church already in glory, and the presently visible component of the Church. The nexus is achieved through the category of holiness (*sanctitas*). Holiness is a divine attribute, and the saints in heaven, the holy ones, are especially invested of it through their proximity without limit with Christ (*LG* 49). The Church on earth is already "signed with a sanctity which is real although imperfect" (*LG* 48), already through the sanctification of daily life and work by the laity (*LG* 34). The connection between saints and would-be saints is exemplified in two ways. The first way is through the memorial dimension, since the Church has a long history of remembering her deceased members, and of honoring especially her martyrs (*LG* 50). Second is through exemplarity. The way the saints lived their lives on earth is at once an inspiration to keep the ultimate goal in mind, and also shows "a most safe path...[to] be able to arrive at perfect union with Christ, that is, perfect holiness" (*LG* 50). Hence the communion with God, which could be personal, extends to the communion with the fellow travelers of the Pilgrim Church, and includes those who traveled before us. This communion is never interrupted; on the contrary, it brings the pilgrims closer to Christ (*LG* 50).

Although the central divine person in this consideration of the Church is Christ, and despite a mention of the Father, a special accent is put on the Holy Spirit. It is noticeable that evocations of pilgrimage, or growth, are often accompanied by mentions of the Spirit.[77] This central chapter of *Lumen Gentium* is an excellent point in case. The "mission of the Spirit" is to carry forward the work of restoration started in Christ, by teaching through faith the meaning of earthly life (*LG* 48). The Spirit already bestowed upon Christians is at work in the groaning of believers to be with Christ, following Paul's words.[78] The Spirit is also the principle of union with Christ, and in the Church, between the saints in heaven, and the members of the Pilgrim Church (*LG* 49–50). The Spirit is finally at the center of the liturgical and sacramental signs of that communion.

The connection between pilgrimage and the Spirit is not simply a secondary theological reflection. There is a convergence, a fittingness for the Spirit to be closely linked to the pilgrim dimension of the Church. As pilgrim, the Church must discern, move ahead in an ambiguous world, not lose sight of the horizon, and keep steadfast hope. The Holy Spirit is the divine Person who is most difficult to pinpoint, the most fluid, the one called upon for discernment, growth, and guidance. Thus, the new emphasis on the pilgrim nature of the Church espouses the contours of a renewed interest for the figure of the Spirit in the life of the Church and her members.[79]

The eighth and final chapter of *Lumen Gentium*, on the Blessed Virgin Mary, Mother of God, further develops the theme of pilgrimage. The first instance introduces a new dimension, that of the "pilgrimage of faith" (*peregrinatione fidei*) of Mary (*LG* 58). Pilgrimage is presented in an individual key, as opposed to the collective dimension underlined earlier in the *Ecclesia peregrinans* or the (plural) *viatores*. *Lumen Gentium* presents Mary's pilgrimage of faith as a response to the progressive revelation of the Word of God in the preaching of her son, Jesus. This pilgrimage was accompanied by a faithful perseverance "in her union with her Son unto the cross" (*LG* 58). Hence, the movement of Mary's pilgrimage was one of greater understanding of her son's mission, which drew her into a greater union with him. For Mary, pilgrimage and union go together; the union was achieved *through* the pilgrimage of faith, not despite or at a distance from that pilgrimage. Since this use of the image of pilgrimage is the only one that is exclusively individual in the documents of the Second Vatican Council, this passage could play a central role in a contemporary interpretation of pilgrimage for individual Christians in light of the Council and set Mary as a model pilgrim.[80]

The second occurrence brings us back to a more familiar terrain in the context of the exaltation of Mary's maternity and her care for "the brethren of her Son, who still journey on earth (*peregrinantibus*) surrounded by dangers and difficulties,[81] until they are led into the happiness of their true home (*ad felicem patriam*)" (*LG* 62). Here, the pilgrimage of believers is located in the midst of challenging circumstances (dangers and difficulties) and presented as a time of passage, or even exile, toward a happy homeland.[82] *Lumen Gentium* 21 had earlier presented such happiness, in that case as *beatitudo*, as the eschatological horizon of the earthly pilgrimage. Despite the hopeful *telos*, the document falls back on a more negative outlook of a pilgrimage surrounded by dangers, and in hope of a final heavenly remedy.

Mary is then presented in a final occurrence as the "sign of created hope and solace to the wandering people of God [*peregrinanti Populo Dei*]."[83] As glorified in body and soul in heaven, Mary shines forth on those who are yet to be perfected, since they journey on earth, as a "sure hope and solace" of the state they should set to reach (see *LG* 68). By portraying Mary as a model, an embodied *telos* of pilgrimage is proposed.

Overall, the final chapter of *Lumen Gentium* shows the ambivalence of the notion of pilgrimage. On the one hand, it relies on a conception of pilgrimage as earthly journey among hardships. On the other hand, by its novel application to the pilgrimage of Mary herself, qualified as a pilgrimage of faith, a positive value of growth over time, accompanied by fidelity and union with Christ, is introduced. Hence, the end goal is not set away as separated from the pilgrimage itself, as is the case when the pilgrimage is depicted as a temporary time of trial, but is clearly lived out already through the pilgrimage.

Pilgrimage in *Dei Verbum* and *Gaudium et Spes*

The theme of pilgrimage also appears in conciliar documents posterior to *Lumen Gentium*, most notably in *Dei Verbum*[84] and *Gaudium et Spes*.[85] In *Dei Verbum*, a passing mention is made of the "pilgrim Church on earth" (*Ecclesia in terris peregrinans*; *DV* 7). Tradition and Scripture—the subject of that constitution—are portrayed as a mirror through which the Pilgrim Church can contemplate God on earth, before finally seeing God face-to-face (in heaven).[86] The earthly pilgrimage of the Church is paralleled with her temporal and incomplete knowledge of God accessible through Scripture. Because *Dei Verbum* is devoted to the importance of divine revelation—and Scripture's inescapable role in it—the value emphasized is not altogether negative, but underlines the incompleteness at the heart of pilgrimage, as well as its teleological orientation toward the hoped-for face-to-face with God.

The role of pilgrimage in *Gaudium et Spes* is more marked, and it starts with the famous opening paragraph of the document:

> The joys and the hopes, the griefs and the anxieties of the people[87] of this age, especially those who are poor or in any way afflicted, these are the joys and hopes, the griefs and anxieties of the followers of Christ. Indeed, nothing genuinely human fails to raise an echo in their hearts. For theirs is a community composed of people. United

> in Christ, they are led by the Holy Spirit in their journey [*peregrinatione*] to the Kingdom of their Father and they have welcomed the news of salvation which is meant for every person. That is why this community realizes that it is truly linked with humankind and its history by the deepest of bonds. (*GS* 1)

Two elements stand out in this use of *peregrinatio*. The first is the strong trinitarian setting: Christians are depicted as united *in* Christ (*in Christo coadunati*), led *by* the Holy Spirit (*a Spiritu Sancto diriguntur*) *to* (the kingdom of) the Father (*ad Regnum Patris*). The *telos* is clear—the kingdom of the Father—as well as the agency of the Spirit and the presence of Christ. This trinitarian dimension is further emphasized by the plural of the subject and the insistence that the good news welcomed by Christians is meant for all (*omnibus*). This is the only instance of a crystal-clear trinitarian setting of pilgrimage in the conciliar documents. It also highlights in a special way the agency of the Holy Spirit. The second outstanding element is the positive value ascribed to the human experience. This theme runs through the whole constitution and colors the understanding of the journey of Christians in this world filled with joys, hopes, griefs, and anxieties. The location of the pilgrimage at the heart of the human experience is portrayed as an opportunity rather than a threat. As *Gaudium et Spes* states, the community of believers is "truly linked with humankind and its history by the deepest of bonds" (*GS* 1).

In its fourth chapter, on the role of the Church in the modern world, *Gaudium et Spes* weaves anew the pilgrimage of Christians with humanity as a whole.[88] At first, it signals that "the People of God during its earthly pilgrimage [*peregrinationis terrestris*]" can benefit the human family through the manifestation and exercise of the mystery of God's love (*GS* 45). Hence, the pilgrimage of the Church in the world is presented as the means through which she can accomplish her mission. The relationship with the world is not one of estrangement, but of involvement; the Pilgrim Church has something to offer to the world. This connection is given a new light a few lines later in the same paragraph. After having evoked the centrality of the Lord as the goal of human history, and the role of the Father in his elevation, it states that "enlivened and united in

His Spirit, we journey [*peregrinamur*] toward the consummation of human history" in which all things will be reestablished in Christ, "both those in the heavens and those on the earth."[89] The pilgrim journey is then not one of separation or flight from the world, but a journey guided by the Spirit, and whose aim is a reconciliation between heaven and earth. Such reconciliation would constitute the consummation of human history, no less. The fact that the pilgrimage is realized in the world is confluent with its bringing to fullness humanity as such. Once again, a positive value is ascribed to pilgrimage: its anchoring in the world, guidance by the Spirit, connection with Christ, and teleological dimension.

The final mention of pilgrimage in *Gaudium et Spes* at once reaffirms the traditional teleological dimension of pilgrimage, while strengthening the call for Christian involvement in the world, "Christians, on pilgrimage toward the heavenly city [*Christifideles, ad civitatem caelestem peregrinantes*], should seek and think of these things which are above. This duty in no way decreases, rather it increases, the importance of their obligation to work with all people in the building of a more human world" (*GS* 57). The legitimate orientation of pilgrimaging Christians toward heaven is explicitly coupled with an *increased* involvement in the very place of the pilgrimage, namely, in this human world. Hence, not only is there no flight away from the world, nor simply an acknowledgment of the presence of Christians in the world, but there is an obligation to collaborate with other women and men to make the world a better and more human place.

As the latest conciliar document we consider, *Gaudium et Spes* is the one whose semantic field around pilgrimage is the most consistent and mature. The optimistic view of humanity exuding from its pages flows into its understanding of pilgrimage as both eminently teleological and rooted in a human experience that is larger than Christianity, while anchored in a strong trinitarian framework. The document reconciles the potential tension and distance between the earthly embodiment of pilgrimage, and the heavenly destination—including the persecutions in between! Engagement with both dimensions is entailed. And the divine guidance in pilgrimage is reinforced.

The Second Vatican Council and the *Peregrinitas* of the Church

The various occurrences of pilgrimage in the documents of the Second Vatican Council allow us to sketch the contours of the *peregrinitas*[90] of the Church. As a discourse, it is not connected with the multiple experiences of pilgrimage in the Church, never even alluding to them. As such, it is not explicitly historically informed. As a metaphor and a theological construct, it is rooted in a biblical imagination.

How does the *peregrinitas* deployed at Vatican II fare regarding Augustine? Several elements are kept: the fact that it does not rely on actual experiences of pilgrimage, the metaphorical nature, the teleological dimension, and some references to the negative character of the pilgrimage (e.g., tension, exile, turmoil). What differs is the greater engagement with the world (it is less about foreignness), and the positive view of the pilgrimage itself (which is worthy in itself and accompanied by God's presence).

The portrayal of the *peregrinitas* of the Church at Vatican II is complex, in evolution, and at times ambiguous. Nonetheless, it proved its fruitfulness by taking its place firmly into subsequent theological discourse. Let me highlight some important characteristics of this *peregrinitas*.

1. Pilgrimage expresses an existential uneasiness. Building on the original Latin meaning of *peregrinus* as foreigner, the *peregrinitas* of the Church unfolds under the guise of exile, or through the experiences of turmoil and struggles in the world—up to persecutions. Such unease entails that the pilgrimage is lived out in a context likely adversarial. Even the perspective of a final reconciliation, expressed in *Gaudium et Spes*, presupposes a latent discrepancy, if not adversity.
2. However, numerous passages highlight the importance of being on earth, of the contemporary commitment. The Church and her members are not just waiting for the heavenly city to arrive; the earth is the place in

which the Pilgrim Church accomplishes her mission. The commitment to the world is paradoxically an essential component, not a place to escape from, while knowing nonetheless that it is not the ultimate destination.

3. The eschatological dimension of the pilgrimage is present both as the tension toward its *telos*, but also as the link between earth and heaven, between the pilgrims and the saints. The pilgrimage of the Church is nonetheless strongly driven by a horizon that extends beyond the earth to reach the heavenly city.
4. The Council sketches a trinitarian framework, with an emphasis on the working of the Holy Spirit, which firmly roots pilgrimage in the very movement of God's being. It stresses the divine agency that propels the Church's pilgrimage. The presence of God is not postulated only in the *telos*, but also in the pilgrimage itself. The Council decided in the end against the 2 Corinthians 5 version of pilgrimage *away* from the Lord.
5. Finally, a certain turn toward a more personal interpretation can be discerned. Yes, it is the *Ecclesia* as a whole who is *peregrinans*, but personal moments also appear, as in the presentation of Mary and her pilgrimage of faith, her union with the Son, and the model she provides for others. The tension between the collective—the most common—and the individual elements in the *peregrinitas* of the Church opens a space for the inclusion of and dialogue with individual pilgrims.

At this point, the *peregrinitas* of the Church was still perceived mostly through a theological lens. The concept would find a broad diffusion through the Eucharistic Prayers, but also gain an embodied dimension through pilgrim popes. There was still space for growth in the Church's understanding of herself as pilgrim.

3. THE RECEPTION AND DIFFUSION OF THE *PEREGRINITAS* IN THE LITURGY: PILGRIMAGE IN THE EUCHARISTIC PRAYERS

The conciliar insight into the pilgrim nature of the Church benefitted in subsequent years from a magnificent megaphone in the Eucharistic Prayers. The affinity between pilgrimage and the Eucharist runs deep, going back in an explicit way to the Last Supper, the experience of the disciples on the road to Emmaus, to contemporary gatherings of pilgrims at shrines.

While for centuries the Roman Canon used a single Eucharistic Prayer in Latin, new prayers were introduced in the wake of the Council, opening up an opportunity to translate the legislative and theological work of conciliar documents into words of worship—in an inversion of the axiom *lex orandi lex credendi.* Prayed in the Church on a regular basis and in vernacular languages, Eucharistic Prayers spread widely the new understanding of the Church developed during the Second Vatican Council. Two main Eucharistic Prayers mention pilgrimage: Eucharistic Prayer III and the Eucharistic Prayer for Various Needs.

Eucharistic Prayer III

Eucharistic Prayer III, which is one of the three new Eucharistic Prayers introduced alongside the Roman Canon (Eucharistic Prayer I), was written for the first postconciliar *editio typica* of the Roman Missal of 1970, and further translated in various languages. As such, it benefitted from a place of honor. The mention of the Pilgrim Church appears in the following paragraph, after the epiclesis:

> May this Sacrifice of our reconciliation, we pray, O Lord, advance the peace and salvation of all the world. Be pleased to confirm in faith and charity your pilgrim Church on earth [*Ecclesiam tuam, peregrinantem in terra*], with your servant N. our Pope and N. our Bishop, the Order of Bishops, all the clergy, and the entire people you have gained for your own.[91]

The notion of pilgrimage is treated lightly here, simply qualifying the Church (of the Lord), as on her pilgrimage on earth. It specifies the location of the pilgrimage, but not its eschatological horizon. The Church is further defined by her hierarchical structure: pope, local bishop, order of bishops, clergy, and people. While there is no eschatological tension, there is also no tension with the world. The prayer for the peace and salvation "of all the world" directly precedes the mention of the earthly pilgrimage of the Church, juxtaposing its location between the world and the earth, the locus of the Church's pilgrimage. The pilgrimage is finally ascribed to the Church as a whole (it is the *Ecclesia* that is the subject of the *peregrinantem*), pushing to the fore a representation of a Church collectively on the move.

Eucharistic Prayer for Various Needs

The conditions for the creation of the Eucharistic Prayer for Various Needs (in its four variants) were remarkable. While three new Eucharistic Prayers were initially approved in 1968 in the aftermath of the Second Vatican Council, proposals for new Eucharistic Prayers flourished around the world.[92] In 1973, the Roman Congregation for Divine Worship decided to restrict the possibility of new Eucharistic Prayers only to "special circumstances," leaving the door open for potential Eucharistic Prayers submitted by episcopal conferences.[93] The bishops of Switzerland wrote a Eucharistic Prayer that was approved by the Holy See and caught the attention of other episcopal conferences, who asked permission to use it.[94]

The immediate impetus for the redaction of the prayer was "Synod 1972" of the Church in Switzerland.[95] Replying to further questions from the Congregation regarding the possibility of simply adding a few elements to existing prayers, the president of the Swiss Conference of Bishops put forward various reasons in favor of a new prayer, expressing in essence that "the Eucharistic prayer as a whole should be written in the language of our time."[96] This desire led the authors of the prayer to emphasize, in the judgment of Vincenzo Raffa, the theme of pilgrimage, since "all the variable parts were inspired, in a more or less obvious way, by the idea of pilgrimage."[97] Hence, the Church in Switzerland found in the theme of pilgrimage an inspiration "in the language of our time" for her worship.[98] Anton Hänggi confirms that *synod*, with its etymology of *syn* (together, with) and *hodos* (way, journey), was the leading metaphor for the prayer, rooted in the understanding of the people of God as a "pilgrim people."[99]

Given the polyglot nature of the country, and the fact that it was originally written in the vernacular and not in Latin, three versions of the prayer can be considered original: German, French, and Italian.[100] It was then translated in other languages, and eventually into Latin in 1991.[101] That triple origin means that each version has the authority of an original version,[102] and that the Latin is only a translation. The differences among the three original versions are not anodyne, warranting a close reading. However, in the wake of the establishment of the Latin text, the three original versions were revised in the 1990s to harmonize them, while respecting the originality of each language.[103] I will use the German, French, and Italian versions as they now stand.[104]

The pilgrim stage is set early when the prayer mentions the parallel between the experience of the pilgrims on the road to Emmaus and the experience of those partaking in the eucharistic celebration in the present. Jesus "opens the Scripture and breaks the bread" for the disciples,[105] just like he does for the assembled Pilgrim Church. Followed by the *epiclesis*—which calls upon the Holy Spirit—this introduction precedes the institution narrative at the heart of the Eucharistic Prayer, and grounds firmly the Eucharist into pilgrimage.

The main explicit mention of pilgrimage intervenes after a part devoted to the Church, the hierarchy, the people of God in the world, and finally, the faithful departed:

> Lord, renew your Church (which is in N.) by the light of the Gospel. Strengthen the bond of unity between the faithful and the pastors of your people, together with N. our Pope, N. our Bishop, and the whole Order of Bishops, that in a world torn by strife your people may shine forth as a prophetic sign of unity and concord.[106]
>
> Remember our brothers and sisters (N. and N.), who have fallen asleep in the peace of your Christ, and all the dead, whose faith you alone have known. Admit them

> to rejoice in the light of your face, and in the resurrection give them the fullness of life.
>
> **Grant also to us, when our earthly pilgrimage is done, that we may come to an eternal dwelling place and live with you for ever;** there, in communion with the Blessed Virgin Mary, Mother of God, with the Apostles and Martyrs, (with Saint N.) and with all the Saints, we shall praise and exalt you through Jesus Christ, your Son.[107]

The central pilgrim component can be read as follows in the different original versions, and the Latin translation:

GERMAN[108]	FRENCH[109]	ITALIAN[110]	LATIN[111]
"Wenn unser eigener Weg zu Ende geht, nimm auch uns auf in dein Reich, wo wir für immer die Fülle des Lebens und der Herrlichkeit erwarten...."	"Et lorsque prendra fin notre pèlerinage sur la terre, accueille-nous dans la demeure où nous vivrons près de Toi pour toujours...."	"Concedi anche a noi, al termine di questo pellegrinaggio, di giungere alla dimora eterna, dove tu ci attendi...."	"Concede nos quoque, terrena exacta peregrinatione, ad aeternam pervenire mansionem, ubi tecum semper vivemus...."

There are slight differences among the three vernacular versions[112] around the mention of pilgrimage. First, only the French and the Italian use the technical word ascribed to pilgrimage (*pèlerinage, pellegrinaggio*) whereas the German *Weg* (journey or way) is broader than *Pilgerfahrt,* which denotes pilgrimage in a religious sense. Second, only the French version specifies the *locus* of the pilgrimage, the earth (*sur la terre*), whereas the Italian emphasizes "this" pilgrimage (*questo pellegrinaggio*), and the German, the specificity, if not the individuality, of the pilgrimage by stating *unser eigener Weg* (our own journey/pilgrimage). The connection to the prayer for the deceased is made explicit only in the German and Italian by an "also" (*nimm auch uns*; *anche a noi*) that refers to the previous petition, something absent from the French version. The *telos* of the prayer is strikingly different; in the French—similar in that regard to the English translation—it is God's abode (*demeure*) where "we will live with you for ever" (*où nous vivrons près de Toi pour toujours*), whereas the Italian talks of the "eternal abode" (*dimora eterna*) where God is waiting for us. The German conveys here a different point: the destination is God's "Kingdom" (*dein Reich*), where the "fullness of life" (*die Fülle des Lebens*) and the glory (*Herrlichkeit*) await us. God's dwelling place and God's kingdom refer, however, to distinct biblical concepts.[113] In summary, the different original versions of this prayer bring interesting peculiarities to the fore.

The mention of the pilgrimage comes after a paragraph devoted to the Church, which highlights, in the first variant of the prayer, the "unity and concord" that the Church is called to embody in the world, first by the unity seen hierarchically between the faithful and its pastors. This unity is then heralded as a prophetic sign in "a world torn by strife," an emphasis on the conflictual nature of the world not seen, however, in opposition to the Church, but certainly in contrast with the Church. This unity is also emphasized through the term *people* applied to the Church twice, underlying her unified nature despite the distinction between the faithful and their pastors. Finally, the prayer for deceased brothers and sisters reveals the extent of the unity sought in the Church, even beyond the realm of earthly life, toward eternal life.

Having prayed for the Church and the deceased, the prayer switches to an "us" that defines the worshiping community more narrowly. The prayer pertains to the *telos* of "our earthly pilgrimage." This use of pilgrimage emphasizes at once its "earthly" character, but also the character of ownership over the pilgrimage; it is not simply a metaphorical qualification for a distant "Pilgrim Church," but an embodied experience of ours. The *telos* would then be an "eternal dwelling place" where the pray-ers could "live with [the Lord] for ever," in the company of the saints, that is, the Church already in heaven. Like in chapter 7 of *Lumen Gentium*, pilgrimage connects by the Communion of Saints the Church on earth and the Church in heaven.

In the second of the four prefaces of this Eucharistic Prayer, under the title "God Guides His Church along the Way of Salvation" (*Deus Ecclesiam suam in viam salutis conducens*), pilgrimage is set as the guiding principle. The titles of the prefaces also suggest movement, through the repetition of *via* (way) in two of them, and of *pertranseo* (to go or pass through) in one.[114] The second preface starts by praising God as the creator of the world and the source of all life, before moving to a consideration of God's care for his Pilgrim Church:

GERMAN	FRENCH	ITALIAN	LATIN
"Du läßt uns niemals allein auf unserm Weg und bist immer da für uns. Einst hast du Israel, dein Volk, mit starker Hand durch die weglose Wüste geleit. Heute führst du deine pilgernde Kirche in der Kraft des Heiligen Geistes. Du bahnst ihr den Weg durch diese Zeit in die ewige Freude deines Reiches durch unseren Herrn Jesus Christus."	"Car tu n'abandonnes jamais ce que tu crées dans ta sagesse, mais tu te montres bienveillant, toujours à l'oeuvre parmi nous. Dans les temps anciens, en déployant la force de ton bras, tu as guidé ton peuple Israël à travers le désert. Aujourd'hui encore, tu accompagnes ton Église dans sa marche au milieu du monde, tu la soutiens de ton Esprit et tu la conduis sur les routes de ce temps vers la joie éternelle de ton Royaume, par notre Seigneur, Jésus, le Christ."	"Tu non ci lasci soli nel cammino, ma sei vivo e operante in mezzo a noi. Con il tuo braccio potente guidasti il popolo errante nel deserto; oggi accompagni la tua chiesa, pellegrina nel mondo, con la luce e la forza del tuo Spirito; per mezzo del Cristo, tuo Figlio e nostre Signore, ci guidi, nei sentieri del tempo, alla goia perfetta del tuo regno."	"Qui opera sapientiae tuae numquam derelinquis, sed in medio mostri adhuc providus operaris. In manu potenti et brachio extento populum tuum Israel per desertum dixisti; nunc autem Ecclesiam tuam in mundo peregrinantem, Spiritus Sancti virtute semper comitaris, eamque per temporis semitas in gaudium aeternum regni tui conducis, per Christum Dominum nostrum."

For you never forsake the works of your wisdom, but by your providence are even now at work in our midst. With

> mighty hand and outstretched arm you led your people Israel through the desert. Now, as your Church makes her pilgrim journey in the world, you always accompany her by the power of the Holy Spirit and lead her along the paths of time to the eternal joy of your Kingdom, through Christ our Lord.[115]

The prayer stresses the continuity of God's care for his people, from the moment of creation to eschatological arrival in the kingdom. For the journey, a stark parallel is established between the Lord's forceful guidance of Israel through the desert—with its implied hardships, aridity, and lengthy time frame—and today's (*Heute*; *aujourd'hui*; *oggi*) guidance of the Church. By the appeal to the exodus experience, the outcome of protection, liberation, and successful completion is suggested for the current journey of the Church.

As the Pilgrim Church (*pilgernde Kirche*; *chiesa pellegrina*)[116] journeys amid this world (*au milieu de ce monde*; *nel mondo*), she is clearly led by God. The preface emphasizes in that regard the agency of the Spirit. While the French version presents plainly the contribution of God's Spirit, both the German and the Italian versions mention the strength or power (*Kraft*; *forza*) of the Spirit's support. The Italian adds the element of light (*luce*) provided by the Spirit, alongside the Spirit's strength, opening to a guidance that is not only sheer force, but also discernment through knowledge. The final evocation of Christ's agency (*durch*; *par*; *per mezzo*) renders this prayer eminently trinitarian, since as part of the Eucharistic Prayer, it is addressed to the Father, and commemorates the agency of both the Spirit and Christ for the Pilgrim Church. The Church is not left to her own devices on that journey but is depicted as firmly held by the Trinity on the paths of this world.

The final joy, either eternal (*ewige*; *éternelle*) or perfect (*perfetta*), that awaits the Pilgrim Church upon reaching the kingdom dominates the emotional color of the prayer. It is not the hardships, persecutions, or the separation from God that are emphasized, but the promise of profound joy at the collective *telos* of the pilgrimage.

Conclusion: The Pilgrim Church in the Eucharistic Prayers

The adoption of the theme of the Pilgrim Church in Eucharistic Prayers is both a tribute to the ecclesiology of the Second Vatican Council and a testimony to the relevance of that image in the contemporary world. It also allowed for a wide dissemination of that image among the faithful, who could hear it in the liturgy, more often than they would encounter it in conciliar documents.[117] In every eucharistic celebration, there is a chance that Catholics hear the Church described as a pilgrim. The analysis of the Eucharistic Prayer III and that for Various Needs shows that while both explicitly refer to the Church as pilgrim, the latter unpacked the image more thoroughly. Pilgrimage came to be rooted more deeply into the self-definition of the Church with emphases distinct from even the conciliar documents.

Pilgrimage is consistently depicted in the Eucharistic Prayers positively, unlike the mixed portrayal uncovered in the documents of Vatican II. The potential struggles of the pilgrimage of the Church give way to the eschatological hope expressed in the *telos* of an "eternal dwelling place," and the "eternal joy" of the kingdom. The strong eschatological thrust from *Lumen Gentium* also runs through the prayers.

The biblical roots of the Church's pilgrimage are laid bare in the second preface of the Eucharistic Prayer for Various Needs, where the connection with Israel's experience of journey through the desert is paralleled with that of the Pilgrim Church, under the same compassionate guidance from God. The trinitarian framework exposed in *Gaudium et Spes* is similarly deployed in that preface, with a special emphasis on the guidance of the Holy Spirit.

Finally, a sense of personal appropriation of the pilgrim experience is fostered through the "we" of the earthly pilgrimage. The pilgrimage is not only that of an all-encompassing Church—even as the "Pilgrim Church"—but "*our* (earthly) pilgrimage," the pilgrimage of the very faithful gathered around the eucharistic table. The pilgrimage of the Church is theirs.

4. THE PILGRIM POPES: EMBODIED SYMBOLS OF THE PILGRIM CHURCH

Beyond the theological and liturgical expressions of a Pilgrim Church, the *praxis* of pilgrimage by the post–Second Vatican Council popes and their own reflections on it, either before, during, or after a pilgrimage offer another way to look at the emergence of the embodied theme of the Pilgrim Church in the second half of the twentieth century. There is a long tradition of bishops coming to Rome to visit the successor of Peter and the tombs of the apostles Peter and Paul, formalized as visits *ad limina apostolorum* (to the threshold of the apostles).[118] There is also a long tradition of popes staying at the Vatican without traveling. Most conspicuously, during the period between the loss of the Papal States (1870) and the Lateran Treaty (1929), popes considered themselves "prisoners" of the Vatican. The contrast with internationally traveling popes is stark. That new era began with Paul VI.[119]

I noted earlier that the documents of the Second Vatican Council do not refer textually to actual experiences of pilgrimages as a foundational source to envision the Pilgrim Church. However, the close connection between the papal pilgrimages and the unfolding of the Council suggests that they function as "embodied symbols" of the Pilgrim Church. In a way, it is a reversal of the methodology of the Council. What was not rooted discursively in an experience was nonetheless lived out concomitantly with the Council. Pilgrim popes were making the Church pilgrim. In the Catholic imagination, the pope acts as the most visible representative of the Church; he can speak with authority in her name. Hence, one can rightly assume that his demeanor or style in his role offers a key to understand even textual statements.[120] As the visible head of the Church, his actions pertain to the whole of the Church, since he preaches not only by his words. The fact that the conciliar popes went on pilgrimage underlines the importance that they bestowed on physically undergoing a pilgrimage as the Church was journeying through the Council. They were leaving Rome to go to other centers, or the frontiers.

I will focus first on Pope John XXIII's pilgrimage just before the Council began, and those of Pope Paul VI during the Council.

As a measure of continuity and contrast, we will also look at the pilgrimage to the Holy Land by Pope John Paul II, a tireless traveler, during the Great Jubilee Year of 2000, thirty-six years after his predecessor. The latter was also accompanied by important pontifical documents that explored the meaning of pilgrimage for the Church today. The questions for us are, "What do those pilgrimages mean? What do they reveal about the *peregrinitas* of the Church?"

John XXIII and Paul VI as Pilgrims

On October 4, 1962, one week before the beginning of the first session of the Second Vatican Council, Pope John XXIII made a one-day "Apostolic Pilgrimage" to Loreto[121] and Assisi, the first papal trip outside of Rome in almost a century. In his discourse at the sanctuary on the day of his pilgrimage, John XXIII mentioned that this pilgrimage added to the supplications coming for all churches throughout the world for the good march of the Council, and that it wanted to "symbolize also the journey of the Church [*il cammino della Chiesa*] toward the attainment of this spiritual dominion... [of] service and fraternal love, sigh of peace, ordered and universal progress."[122] The pope connected his own act of pilgrimage of the day with the overall journey of the Church, and located that journey in light of the upcoming ecumenical council. His pilgrimage was then one of petition to the Lord for the Council, but also constituted a larger symbol. Reflecting on the theme of the incarnation—fittingly for a shrine holding the Santa Casa—John XXIII reminded his auditors that "we are all pilgrims [*pellegrini*] on earth, with an effusive prayer on our lips which, though its expressions are varied, is shared by all: let us go to the homeland [*patria*]."[123] This journey (*cammino*) of human beings is stated a few lines later as being rooted in the incarnation, and geared toward our *heavenly* homeland (*patria celeste*) and the elevation to the noble status of coheirs in heaven.[124]

Despite the simplicity of this papal discourse at a shrine, important features are highlighted here that would be echoed in the more formal inaugural address of the Council, *Gaudet Mater Ecclesia*, a text mentioned earlier in this chapter. Four elements are notable. First, the grammatical subject of pilgrimage alternates between the Church (as a collective institution whose journey is analogical) and the individual, either singular or plural. The plural dimension, including potentially everybody, is clear in the "we are all pilgrims," and includes the pope himself who had indeed made the journey to Loreto. By realizing this pilgrimage on the eve of the Council, and by linking it to his own personal pilgrimage there sixty-two years earlier, as a young seminarian, John XXIII was bridging the personal dimension of pilgrimage with the collective pilgrimage that he was seeing the Church doing in this world, and was envisioning for the Council to tackle courageously. A second feature is the strong eschatological thrust of the mentions of pilgrimage; the destination is clearly the heavenly city. The same thrust would be powerfully expressed in the constitution *Lumen Gentium*. A third feature is more subtle and potentially circumstantial: the configuration of the human pilgrimage to the incarnation of Christ.[125] The human journey shadows that of Christ onto heaven, with a qualitative distinction between the Son and the coheirs. This dimension would be stressed even more in Pope Paul VI's pilgrimage to the Holy Land. A final characteristic is the inherent dynamism of the pilgrimage image and praxis. Pilgrimage entails movement. John XXIII could have prayed for the upcoming Council in Rome, but he went to the shrine of Loreto, and from there, reminded all that pilgrimage requires movement toward a destination: heaven, or even the spiritual goods that the Church seeks for and in the world. The pope did not only proclaim that the Church is pilgrim; he went on a pilgrimage for the Church.

Pope Paul VI, who succeeded John XXIII as Bishop of Rome in 1963 after the first session of the Council, also positioned pilgrimages prominently in his ministry. At the conclusion of the second session of the Council, on December 4, 1963, he stunned the assembly and the world by announcing an upcoming pilgrimage to the Holy Land: "We are so convinced that to obtain the success of the council we ought to raise many fervent prayers, and multiply the [good] works, that, after careful reflection and many prayers addressed to God, we have decided to go as pilgrim to the region that is the homeland of our Lord Jesus Christ."[126] The trip took place one month later, from January 4 to 6, 1964. After a pilgrimage to Loreto by his predecessor centered on the incarnation and the domestic life at Nazareth, this pilgrimage would encompass the full breadth of the Christ event, and have ripple effects beyond the Catholic Church and the Christian world.

Paul VI assigned a purely spiritual aim to his pilgrimage to the Holy Land, an orientation he would reiterate as he journeyed through a region of the world rife with political and religious tensions.[127] His desire, in visiting the holy place "where Christ was born, lived, died, and, risen from the dead, ascended into heaven," was to "commemorate in person the main mysteries of our salvation, namely the Incarnation and the Redemption."[128] The spirit in which the pope planned this humble and short pilgrimage was threefold: prayer, penance, and spiritual renewal.[129] Such a perspective is consistent with the traditional depiction of pilgrimage. The penitential dimension was extolled especially during the prayer at the Holy Sepulchre.[130] The intentions brought to the pilgrimage were quite ambitious and extended beyond the business of the Council itself. The pope mentions four orientations: (1) to offer to Christ his Church; (2) to call back to the (Roman) Church her separated brethren; (3) to pray for peace; (4) to implore Christ for the salvation of the whole humanity.[131] These aims, reiterated in the many public interventions during the pilgrimage, represent a conscientious widening of horizon from the Loreto pilgrimage of Pope John XXIII. They also offer a clearer articulation of the purpose of that pilgrimage. Therefore, the pilgrimage of Pope Paul VI to the Holy Land, though humble and unexpected, was not meant to be only a personal spiritual experience; as head of the Church, the message of his pilgrim gesture was meant to echo powerfully throughout the world. At the intersection of the religious and the political front, Paul VI, a former diplomat, would even call himself a "pilgrim of peace" (*pèlerin de la paix*),[132] pointing at the hoped-for transformation brought by pilgrimage.

Upon his return from Jerusalem, Paul VI delivered some remarks to the College of Cardinals about his pilgrimage.[133] He described his trip as an "act of presence to a pilgrim journey (*viaggio di pellegrino*) that asks for nothing, and doesn't do more than pray, reflect, and bless."[134] The pilgrimage felt mysterious even to him, especially the "mysterious bond between that land, Jesus Christ, Peter, his successors, and Rome."[135] He then devotes most of his comments to the unexpected aspects of this pilgrimage, the "enthusiasm" and "marvelous spiritual explosions" experienced among

Orthodox, Jews, Muslims, and Catholics, and the fateful encounter with Athenagoras, the Ecumenical Patriarch of Constantinople.[136] Athenagoras invited Paul to embark on a journey of reconciliation, of peacemaking "to show the world that we are brothers again."[137] The other patriarchs came, but also the Anglicans, and the Protestants, to extend a hand and affirm their desire to be united in the Lord.[138] Paul VI highlighted the centrality of encounters in the pilgrimage experience; the change of location, the steps taken allow for the creation of a space in which new or renewed relationships can occur. Paul related those encounters among Christians to Christ as the *locus* in which union would be possible.

In line with the centeredness on Christ and the prayerfulness in which he conceived his pilgrimage, Paul VI shared the moment in which he felt himself "suffocate from emotion and tears": "the holy Mass at the Holy Sepulchre, while pronouncing the words of consecration, and in the adoration of the sacramental presence of Christ in the place where Christ consummated his sacrifice."[139] At this moment, the connection between Christ and his self-offering on the cross, Paul VI as priest celebrating the Eucharist at the very place of this historical event, and the eucharistic commemoration of the sacrifice reached its apex. The encounter with a present God in a place of memorial significance was achieved. Paul VI touches upon the inalienable core of his pilgrimage—to renew the encounter with the Lord himself—and highlights the fittingness of the Eucharist for that pilgrim encounter.

Both John XXIII and Paul VI had thus interwoven the praxis of pilgrimage into the theological encounter of the Council.[140] They both called attention to the supernatural dimension at work in the conciliar gathering, and to the necessary rootedness of the latter in fervent prayer. According to Henri de Lubac, the pilgrimage to the Holy Land in particular was a powerful reminder of the centeredness on Christ that Paul VI had advocated in his inaugural discourse for the second session of the Council.[141] Through that lens, the pilgrimage was not an event disconnected from the conciliar proceedings, but the very embodiment of their inner principle. The pilgrimage made manifest what was essential.

Paul VI undertook only one other trip qualified as a pilgrimage during the Council: a visit to India in December 1964 during the International Eucharistic Congress.[142] That pilgrimage was described by the pope as "strictly religious," following the "traces of the Apostle St. Thomas and the glorious St. Francis Xavier."[143] It was also an opportunity to "manifest the consideration, the respect, and the love that the Catholic Church has for the peoples of the Asian continent, their civilizations, and their deep religiosity."[144] At his arrival on December 2, 1964, the pope portrayed himself as "a pilgrim of peace, of joy, of serenity and love,"[145] casting anew this first pilgrimage of a pope to this part of the world as a benevolent encounter with a new people. The pilgrim pope brought his desire for peace, joy, and love in the world to the encounter. A few months later, in his speech at the United Nations in New York City, Paul VI mentioned pilgrimage, claiming that he felt that he had come to the "epilogue to a laborious pilgrimage in search of an opportunity to speak heart to heart with the whole world," which the assembly represented.[146] That pilgrimage had started two thousand years before with the missioning of the disciples by Jesus at his ascension to preach to all nations.[147] At the United Nations, and toward the end of the Second Vatican Council, Paul VI felt that this journey was entering a new phase.

The pilgrimages of Pope John XXIII and Paul VI emphasize the relationship with Christ, and connect not only with him as a person, but also with his mission to be pursued—through the Council and beyond. Pope Paul VI also highlighted de facto in his pilgrimages the importance of encounters, especially beyond the confines of the ecclesial realm. In particular, Paul VI was extending an olive branch, an embodied offer of peace.

The Pilgrimage of Pope John Paul II during the Great Jubilee Year of 2000

Successor to Paul VI after the brief pontificate of John Paul I, Pope John Paul II was a great traveler, reaching the count of 104 international apostolic visits.[148] One of his most significant pilgrimages was to the Holy Land at the heart of the Great Jubilee Year 2000, in the footsteps of Paul VI's landmark pilgrimage. This pilgrimage was preceded by important pontifical documents. The "Bull of Indiction of the Great Jubilee of the Year 2000 *Incarnationis Mysterium*" (November 29, 1998)[149] had already mentioned pilgrimage in generic terms, but three contemporary documents focused more directly on that notion. Two of these documents emanated from the Pontifical Council for the Pastoral Care of Migrants and Itinerant People: "The Pilgrimage in the Great Jubilee" (April 25, 1998)[150] and "The Shrine: Memory, Presence and Prophecy of the Living God" (May 8, 1999).[151] Finally, John Paul II released a "Letter Concerning Pilgrimage to the Places Linked to the History of Salvation" (June 29, 1999)[152] before his pilgrimage to the Holy Land. These three documents share many tropes. Together, they constitute the most important group of pontifical documents reflecting theologically on pilgrimage. I have already quoted some of their insights in previous chapters, but since they shaped John Paul II's pilgrimage to the Holy Land and offer a snapshot of the development of the theology of pilgrimage, I will briefly highlight some innovative features.

"The Pilgrimage in the Great Jubilee" (1998) offers a comprehensive presentation of the theological underpinnings of pilgrimage in the Christian tradition, starting with Israel's experience of pilgrimage (from Adam onward). The result is a nuanced and rich understanding of pilgrimage, since it even considers contemporary phenomena that could fall under the extended umbrella of pilgrimage, such as tourism,[153] visits to natural sites,[154] but even migration—depicted as "universal pilgrimages."[155] This expansion of the confines of pilgrimage is also visible in the biblical treatment, highlighting an analogical comprehension of pilgrimage, which, however, does not always uphold the genuine differences at work. Although the initial depiction of pilgrimage is very individual and potentially self-centered (through the threefold actions of conversion, intimacy with God, and plea for material needs),[156] the document opens up a horizon of social commitment by stressing the importance of the pilgrim's experience of peace—already mentioned strongly in the pilgrimage of Paul VI—as well as the conquest of the jubilee values of social justice.[157] The connection between pilgrimage and social justice is not obvious to most contemporaries, but it draws back on the shared biblical roots of migrants and pilgrims, as we saw in chapter 2, and on the ethical commitment that pilgrimage entails, as seen in the exodus and its aftermath. On a practical level, this emphasis on social justice most likely benefitted from the fact that the pontifical council that authored the document deals primarily with migrants and itinerant people, although pilgrims fall under its purview. The missionary dimension of pilgrimage is also highlighted through the work of evangelization—a primary reason for the Church to encourage pilgrimages[158]—and the fact (or the hope?) that a Pilgrim Church becomes *ipso facto* missionary.[159] Moreover, the document specifies the means to sustain the pilgrim journey of the Church, her *viaticum*: the Word of God and the Eucharist.[160] Finally, in its consideration of the pilgrimage of Christians today, the document uses the image of the "tent of meeting" as the thread, emphasizing the (manifold) encounters at the heart of the pilgrimage experience.[161]

Another document of the same pontifical council called "The Shrine: Memory, Presence and Prophecy of the Living God," which was issued a year later, focuses on the shrine as the destination of pilgrimage, or "milestones"[162] of one's journey, and highlights the importance of the living encounter with God in pilgrimage. As the title indicates, the text unfolds three temporal aspects of the shrine: memory, presence, and prophecy. The "memory" is not relegated to the past, since past events commemorated at the shrine or through the shrine call for consequences in Christian life, namely, awe and adoration, thanksgiving, sharing, and commitment.[163] This sense of commitment is rooted in "divine solidarity,"[164] in recognition of the shared love from God for all. The second dimension, the divine presence at the shrine, is seen mostly through the Word of God, the sacraments, and the Church,[165] elements that are emphasized in a Christian understanding of the shrine. The final dimension, prophecy, extends beyond the narrower frame of eschatology,[166] which was the lens of chapter 7 of *Lumen Gentium*, to include hope, joy, and conversion.[167] Hence, the prophetic dimension of the shrine is not simply future related, but aims at making ever more present what is signified by the shrine. Rooted in the "place" of the shrine, the document does not significantly engage either the seeking involved in the journey or the pilgrim's own bodily disposition in relation to the shrine.

Released a few weeks after the previous document and in preparation of his upcoming pilgrimage to the Holy Land, Pope John Paul II's "Letter Concerning Pilgrimage to the Places Linked to the History of Salvation" (June 29, 1999) continues the reflection on pilgrimage through spatiality, though in a more meditative and personal key. Following the dynamic biblical image of the "tent"[168]—that God pitched among us—instead of the temple, John Paul II sketches a history of the places of salvation, from the initial "concentration" in Jerusalem of the sacred space for Israel to its summit reached in "Christ, who is, in his person, the new 'temple' (cf. John 2:21)."[169] Casting his upcoming trip as an "exclusively religious pilgrimage,"[170] as Paul VI did before him, he singles out the "upper room," the traditional place of the institution of the Eucharist and of the event of Pentecost, as "a return to the very origins of the Church,"[171] emphasizing an ecclesial focus, whereas Paul VI had a christological one with the highlighting of incarnation and redemption. The final lines of the letter emphasize the eschatological outlook of the pilgrimage, both collectively, by the "imminent coming of God's kingdom," and individually, through the "summons to a new life."[172] Pilgrimage is thus intrinsically an interior journey as well.[173] The final wish expressed in the document highlights the desire that this journey be not simply a personal one for the pope, but "an image of the journey of the whole Church."[174]

The actual pilgrimage of John Paul II to the Holy Land, from March 20 to 26, 2000, unfolded as a multifaceted event. The pope presented himself as a pilgrim whose desire was "to come here and to pray in the most important places which, from ancient times, have seen God's interventions, the wonders he has done,"[175] and especially the place where Christ lived, died, and rose from the dead. As a pilgrim, the pope was moved by an emotional experience of transcendence, when he stated at the conclusion of his pilgrimage that "these have been days of intense emotion, a time when our soul has been stirred not only by the memory of what God has done but by his very presence, walking with us once again in the Land of Christ's Birth, Death and Resurrection."[176]

In the line of the pilgrimage of Paul VI, and amid a geopolitical situation that was still thorny, John Paul II advocated for peace and justice, and reiterated that theme as central to his pilgrimage.[177] This concern was especially emphasized in meetings with political authorities from both sides of the Israeli-Palestinian divide.[178] The papal pilgrimage was branded as nonpolitical and religious, but its aim was not devoid of consequential social justice hopes.

In keeping with pilgrimage's focus on encounter, John Paul II significantly expanded the outreach to other faith communities. While the encounter in Jerusalem between Pope Paul VI and Patriarch

Athenagoras led to a remarkable breakthrough for ecumenical relationships, John Paul's pilgrimage came at a time of maturity of this dialogue but included an extended hand to the Jewish and the Muslim communities.[179]

Since the pilgrimage to the Holy Land occurred during Lent and a few days after the great "Day of Pardon" (March 12, 2000) of the Great Jubilee Year, it is not surprising to find a penitential tone to the event. One of the most potent images of this pilgrimage was that of the pope, alone, leaving a message at the Western Wall, asking for forgiveness for the treatment of the people of the covenant, and stating a desire for brotherhood.[180] Paul VI's prayer at the Holy Sepulchre was also highly penitential, but it was cast in a more general mold. As such, both pilgrimages drew on the strong penitential roots of Christian pilgrimage.

A new aspect developed by John Paul's pilgrimage is the direct connection with refugees. The documents on pilgrimage by the Pontifical Council on Migrants and Itinerant Peoples were already putting forward the intrinsic connection between pilgrims and migrants, but this concrete pilgrimage put it into practice. After a visit to Bethlehem, the pope went to the nearby refugee camp of Dheisheh. With extreme subtlety, he drew a parallel between the place of Bethlehem, which for Christians recalls a moment when the Holy Family was not welcomed (Luke 2:7) but where God was present, and the plight of contemporary refugees. The pope himself did not spell out the connection, but just declared, "It is deeply significant that here, close to Bethlehem, I am meeting you, refugees and displaced persons."[181] The simple mention of the place sufficed. Later in the same speech, he advocated once again for justice and peace. By doing so, John Paul II was drawing attention to the social justice issues related to people's movement in the world; while some can afford to choose to be pilgrims, other are forced to be refugees, but all should recognize that they are a people on a journey toward God, and with one another, with the ethical commitment it entails.

A final element to highlight from John Paul II's pilgrimage to the Holy Land is not found in the discourses but was witnessed to without any words. The frailty of the body of the pilgrim pope was on display. The John Paul II who visited the Holy Land in 2000 was a man severely affected by health issues, especially the Parkinson's disease that would result in his death a few years later. Unlike Paul VI, who was not even one year into his pontificate when he traveled to Jerusalem, John Paul II had been pope for twenty-two years. The visible frailty of his body suggested the personal toll and effort that the visit of places entailed, the vulnerability that the pilgrim John Paul was willing to experience and let the whole world see. Pilgrimage was not an easy image.

Conclusion: Pilgrimage and the Popes

What do the pilgrimages of recent popes say about—or to—the Pilgrim Church? The pilgrimages of the popes, in theory and practice, confirm the polysemy of the notion of pilgrimage. They reaffirm the strong eschatological language found in *Lumen Gentium*. The tension identified in the evolution of the pilgrimage language in the documents of Vatican II, from a focus on the otherworldly homeland to a more robust engagement with the world, is sketched in a similar arc in the documents and events surrounding papal pilgrimages, from John XXIII to Paul VI and finally John Paul II. They also show in a practical way a Christ-centeredness, as exemplified by the choice of places to go on pilgrimage, almost all related directly to Christ himself, most evocatively in Jerusalem.

At the same time, papal pilgrimages fall back on the actual traditional practice of pilgrimage. The insistence on the traditional components of the pilgrimage (e.g., penance, memory), the link with the sacraments (especially the Eucharist and the sacrament of reconciliation), and the presence of the concrete shrines visited—and not simply the hoped-for heavenly Jerusalem—reinforce the depiction of pilgrimage as an individual's religious act. Consequently, despite references to the collective dimension of pilgrimage, papal pilgrimages risk being perceived as an individual's pilgrimage, not that of the collective Church. The pilgrim pope could then be simply an example to imitate rather than the initiator of a movement carrying through from the head the whole Body of the Church.

But the papal pilgrimages also open new horizons to understand the pilgrimaging of the Church. The pontifical documents leading up to the Great Jubilee Year of 2000, especially, aim at recovering more extensively the biblical roots of pilgrimage and at presenting the nucleus of a cogent theology of pilgrimage. They show the centrality of the encounter, not only with God through religious activities in shrines, but also through the contacts with different people, even non-Christians. They also strongly emphasize the outward-looking dimension of pilgrimage, evangelization, but also work for peace and justice. This care extended even to the encounter with and commitment to refugees, highlighting a recovered social justice dimension of pilgrimage.

Finally, these pilgrimages, around the Second Vatican Council and the Great Jubilee Year of 2000, showed that the pope himself is a pilgrim. He is moving, on the way. He is praying, making steps to come closer to God. He is recalling God's gifts in places. Hence, by showing himself to be a pilgrim in a very literal sense, the pope also invites the Church herself to be a Pilgrim Church.

5. EMBRACING PILGRIMAGE AND CHALLENGING THE *PEREGRINITAS* OF THE CHURCH

The Church uses various lenses to explore her pilgrim nature, her *peregrinitas*: the Augustinian take on the Church as a foreign element in the world, a city of God, not of this world; the Second Vatican Council embracing the image of a dynamic Church, grounded in Christ, led by the Spirit, orientated toward the *eschaton*, yet involved on earth while on her pilgrimage, with all the turmoil, difficulties, and joys that it entails; the image of a collective Body in movement adopted in the prayer of the Church, especially for the Eucharistic Prayer for Various Needs, with its unique history and status, and its pilgrimage framework. The Church of the second half of the twentieth century was also led by pilgrim popes, who, in their travels, discourses, and writings, brought forward a concrete embodiment of pilgrimage in deeds and words. Each of these perspectives contribute to a richer understanding of pilgrimage. Some of these aspects could challenge and stretch pilgrimage as it is most often experienced: the collective dimension—against a purely individual pilgrimage—the ethical component of social justice, the role of proclamation, or the eschatological thrust.

In return, the phenomenology of pilgrimage that we sketched in chapter 1 could also challenge the *peregrinitas* of the Church. The vantage point is no longer Augustinian or biblical, but the very experience of pilgrimaging. Pilgrimage is a lived religious experience located at the fringes of the institution. It is also a reality that appeals today beyond the confines of organized religion and constitutes a contemporary metaphor for life. What is pilgrimage telling the Church today? This is what we explore in the following pages. The underlying assumption is that her *peregrinitas* is not accidental for the Church, something that she simply must endure, but instead belongs to her very nature. A further assumption is that the pilgrim experience can sharpen the edges of our understanding of the pilgrim nature of the Church.[182] The Church can embrace the lived experience of pilgrimage, allowing a Church of pilgrims to become a Pilgrim Church.

Being a pilgrim requires the intention of being so. It requires knowing oneself *as* one pilgrimaging. The Church already uses in her communal prayer the image of the Pilgrim Church, but the consciousness of the pilgrimaging, with everything it entails, is still ahead of her. The dimensions of transcendence and memory in pilgrimage are well taken up by the Pilgrim Church. Regarding transcendence, her attention to God is central to her very being, and she is also well aware of the Tradition that constitutes her through a myriad of saints. The Church celebrates the sacrament of the Eucharist, born of pilgrimage, and which commemorates the central event of the faith, the self-offering of the Son. Sacramentally and historically, the Church memorializes.

The Church is challenged by the pilgrim embrace of movement, as opposed to stability. Traditionally, the Church has preferred stability (think of medieval monasteries or Tridentine-established parishes) over itinerant ministry, reserved to the *missio ad gentes* or sporadic local missionary endeavors. Centuries before the Pilgrim Church title, the *homo viator* had been a medieval trope with negative implications.[183] The pilgrim ethos calls for a change of paradigm from an emphasis on place to a celebration of movement, a shift from the monk to the pilgrim. Such embrace of movement is consonant with a postmodern posture in which institutional structures are looked at with suspicion, and where nimbleness is necessary to adapt to a fast-changing world. Movement entails embracing change and growth but also uncertainties and potential mistakes. The embrace by Pope Francis of discernment and synodality illustrates such openness to movement, not for its own sake, but in recognition of the fact that the Church is still pilgrim, under the guidance of the Spirit moving her and the world.[184] The Church has not yet reached the *parousia*.[185] The embrace of movement also entails an embrace of history in all its concreteness, with its detours, its accomplishments, its flaws, and dead ends. The Church is on a trajectory that is informed by history, but whose end is not found in the past.

Pilgrimage invites the Church to reflect on its destination. Is she herself the destination, in a self-referential and complacent way ("The journey is the destination")? Is the destination clearly and firmly beyond herself, beyond her grasp even? Does the destination still attract? The ultimate destination of the Church is heavenly, eschatological. But there is a healthy tension with the commitment to the world, in order to take the pilgrim embodiment seriously. The destination cannot be only of this world. In her self-definition, the Church includes her members who are already in glory, the *Ecclesia triumphans* or *coelestis*. They show where the fulfillment of the destination as God's presence lies for the Church. The destination of the Church is not even a place (heaven), but a person, Jesus-Christ, as the gate to the Trinity. The personhood of the destination eludes the potential grasp of the Pilgrim Church. Christ is before us, but Christ is also with us.

Since departure means at once starting and leaving things behind, what does the Church leave behind in her pilgrimage? The Church can easily be weighed down by what is hers. She can also be kept back by where she is already, what her center is, her footprint. Pope Francis's repeated mention of the frontiers, the peripheries where the Church should go and be present, reminds the Church of the importance of extirpating herself of spaces of comfort and quiet.[186] His choice at the beginning of his pontificate to make his first apostolic visit to Lampedusa to migrants and refugees was a stark symbol of that invitation to go outside of the sacristies. To leave is the beginning of the journey. It is fateful, but it can also be painful. By leaving, the Church reminds herself that she is not the destination.

Embodiment is paramount for pilgrimage. There is first the very concrete and personal body that is necessary for the journey.

It is a body that can suffer, that shows its flaws, its limitations, but also its strength and resilience. The body is inescapable. The destination is not reached without it or outside of it. The journey cannot move forward without it. An engagement with physicality, with inner-worldliness, is unavoidable. Embodiment requires to take leave of the pessimism or scorn toward the body. For the Pilgrim Church, the consequences are twofold. On the one hand, embodiment leads to the reaffirmation of the beauty and dignity of the body in all its forms. Individual bodies are necessary means for the journey. On the other hand, the Church's embrace of embodiment entails a renewed commitment to the social body of the world in its struggles. We saw in this chapter how commitment to social justice was integral to the personal witness of the pilgrim popes, even in their most religious endeavors. The Pilgrim Church should particularly see echoes of her *peregrinitas* in the migrants and refugees, the many millions of people who leave home and embark on a fateful and embodied journey. Their vulnerability in motion calls for a special ethical commitment on the part of the Pilgrim Church.

The thread of "embodied holiness" highlighted in chapter 2 stresses the importance of embodiment. It is through that lens that the very destination—God and his holiness—is made present to the world, but also throughout the world in the multitude of saints, their relics, and in all the pilgrims who journey in and toward holiness. Pilgrimage is enfleshment of holiness. Through the incarnation, God showed the world that the way to God in response was one of enfleshment.

A Pilgrim Church embraces her own vulnerability. Calling on the strength and power of the almighty God, the Church often relishes her own power and authority. For centuries, the Roman pontiff was the sovereign of the Papal States, but the Church also endured—and still endures—persecutions, plundering, and martyrdom. The desire to overcome vulnerability is natural, but pilgrimage calls for an embrace of vulnerability, poverty, need, and brokenness, since they crack open the possibility of encounter, beyond the (false) self-sufficiency that power, money, prestige, self-assurance, and tradition breed. Pope Paul VI's claim to go to Jerusalem as a simple pilgrim showed a disposition toward dispossession that was anchored deeply in his pontifical style.[187] The Pilgrim Church embracing vulnerability carries with her, like a pilgrim, only what is essential.[188] She sheds the superfluous. She also allows her vulnerability to be known. As part of the journey toward the Great Jubilee Year of 2000, John Paul II led the Church to a path of repentance, acknowledging sins and mistakes of the Church throughout her history.[189] This recognition allowed the Church to move toward genuine encounters with a lighter baggage, restoring relationships through reconciliation and humility.

The intrinsic alterity encountered in pilgrimage challenges the Church. Modern-day pilgrims overemphasize the individual dimension of their endeavor, but they soon realize that the encounter of others is a strong component of pilgrimage, even an inescapable one. The Church has a clear understanding of herself as a collective Body; a Body united around Christ in the Spirit and made visibly present in a paradigmatic way in the eucharistic action. But the value of encountering those beyond herself has been only more recently affirmed—beyond the context of the work of evangelization. In the 1960s, observers from other Christian churches were invited to attend the Second Vatican Council. In 1986, Pope John Paul II gathered representatives from different faith communities to prayer for peace in Assisi. Papal visits to synagogues or mosques are common, and in the pilgrimages to Jerusalem of both Paul VI and John Paul II the desire of encounters ran high. Dialogue and action across religious boundaries are encouraged, but tensions remain regarding the *de iure* place of the religious other in God's plan.[190] Can, or should, a Pilgrim Church embrace alterity and diversity not only within herself, but also beyond herself as part and parcel of her pilgrimaging?

Finally, is the Church transformed by her pilgrimage, or is it simply a nice image? Does she allow herself to be transformed? Does the enfleshment of holiness take place? Pilgrimage ends with an open question about transformation. The Pilgrim Church should also nurture that same question. The Church should let herself be questioned in her *peregrinitas* through the experience of pilgrims.

Epilogue

Pilgrimage and the Holy Spirit

> May the journey that I intend to make in the Jubilee Year be an image of the journey of the whole Church in her desire to be ever more ready to respond to the voice of the Spirit, in order to go more quickly to meet Christ, the Bridegroom: "The Spirit and the Bride say, 'Come!'" (Rev 22:17).[1]

These final words of the letter of Pope John Paul II, written in preparation of his pilgrimage to the Holy Land, resonate with the clear voice of the Spirit. Pilgrimage is depicted as a journey in response to an invitation. The invitation is made in the Spirit to come at the encounter of the Bridegroom, Christ. The journey is not only a travel, but a call to conversion, a call to follow Christ in the Spirit.

The Holy Spirit has been a recurring theme of our research. It was found in unusual detours at times. Why does the Spirit constantly surface as we look for pilgrimage? Both the Holy Spirit and pilgrimage have been the subject of increased interest in recent decades.[2] The connection is more than fortuitous. The very being of the Spirit, as revealed through the Church's tradition, shows an innate affinity between pilgrimage and Spirit. The Spirit breeds movement. As *nexus amoris* in the Trinity, she connects Father and Son. She is part of the divine *perichoresis*, the divine dance at the heart of the Trinity. She also binds the faithful with God, crying in us, "Abba, Father" (Rom 8:15–16). Her biblical images suggest evanescence and power associated with primal elements of nature: fire, wind, breath. The Spirit is most often prayed to "come," not simply adored for her standing being.[3] But movement is often at risk of being overlooked, as opposed to the (obvious) stability of a place or a fixed image. The Spirit, being movement, is ungraspable. The action of the Spirit can be invisible as movement but is not fruitless.

In addition to movement, other characteristics of pilgrimage elucidated in chapter 1 speak to the Spirit. Movement is outgoing but leads to someplace, or more exactly, to someone. The destination of the pilgrimage is ultimately God, more than a place. This was also Ignatius's realization toward the end of his life's pilgrimage. The vulnerability mentioned of the experience of pilgrimage echoes the obliviousness to the Spirit. Such obliviousness in the theological discourse is symptomatic of the difficulty of pinpointing the person of the Spirit. In the creedal statement of the early fourth century, it led to the affirmation of the common worship of the Spirit along with the Father and the Son, but without further content.[4] The vulnerability of the Spirit might have led to the stern warning by Jesus about the importance of not misjudging her agency (Matt 12:31–32). Regarding memory, another essential component of pilgrimage, the Spirit is a continuous thread of God's self-communication expressed in creation, through the prophets, up to Christ and the Church.[5] The Spirit is one and the same, uniting all of history and unceasingly making God present. The role of remembrance attributed to the Spirit is highlighted in the promise made by Jesus that the Spirit as the Advocate would help the disciples to remember everything he has told them (John 14:26). At the eucharistic commemoration of the Last Supper, the Spirit is also called upon as the agent of transformation of the memory into the present of the participants.

Our biblical chapter let the Spirit shine in an explicit way in its New Testament component. The main feature here is the guidance of the Holy Spirit for mission. The Spirit guided Jesus the pilgrim in his earthly ministry. The Spirit also guided the apostles both explicitly in Acts and implicitly in the sending of the disciples in Luke 10—through the sign of joy, sign of the Spirit, that accompanied their return.

The pilgrim journey of Ignatius of Loyola indirectly highlighted the work of the Spirit. The journey of Ignatius was one of discernment, a role that he assigns to the Spirit in his *Spiritual*

Exercises. The discernment is initially that of one's identity before God, first through the imitation, and then through the following of Christ. Ignatius's quest reached its resolution in "finding" a God that was immediate. Such state denotes Trinitarian inhabitation, effected by the Spirit. The receptive desire of Ignatius to shape his life according to God's will is analogous to Mary's disposition at the Annunciation. She allowed herself to be transformed radically by the Spirit, receiving wholeheartedly a vocation that changed her life. Similarly, but over a much larger period, Ignatius was molded into discovering and receiving his vocation and was transformed along the way. In addition, his experience of the pilgrimage of discernment that started with a concrete pilgrimage to Jerusalem led him to make use of pilgrimage, alongside the month-long retreat of the Spiritual Exercises, as a main formation tool to prepare young people to become companions of Jesus themselves. By breaking up the familiarity of the quotidian, pilgrimage fosters encounters and hopefully, first, that of the Spirit of God.

By leading to a discernment of God's will in one's life, under the guidance of the Spirit, pilgrimage fosters the embodiment of holiness. Pilgrimage is paradigmatic on both counts. It is all about embodiment—even for an armchair pilgrimage. It is also all about holiness, which constitutes the ultimate destination. Ignatius detailed his lifelong pilgrimage as a way to holiness, both as Godself and also as holiness achieved in him.[6] In the context of the pilgrimage's embodiment of holiness, the Spirit could then be properly called the "embody-er" of the Holy.[7] The transformation hoped for in pilgrimage resulted in Ignatius, to use the words of Paul, being transformed into a divine temple, "a temple of the Holy Spirit" (1 Cor 6:19; see also 2 Cor 6:16). The Spirit, then, really appears as "the Giver of Life,"[8] a life-giving, life-transforming force.

Our final chapter, on the Pilgrim Church, lets the coextensivity of the Spirit and pilgrimage shine through the newness brought in the wake of the Second Vatican Council. The renewed engagement with the world, where the Spirit is active, led many to seek pilgrimage in this world—despite the many obstacles—with faith, under the guidance of the Holy Spirit. Such guidance was mentioned most forcefully in *Gaudium et Spes*, which deals with the Church in the world.[9] After Pope John XXIII famously "opened the window" by calling the council, the Pilgrim Spirit came and was coopted in the new emphasis on pilgrimage in the liturgy of the Church and in the symbolic actions of pilgrim popes. The Spirit leads the Church on her pilgrimage. The pilgrim paradigm befits a Spirit-filled Church.

Pilgrimage is in itself an open-ended endeavor beyond the destination. It leads to the Holy, and to transformation. There is an unfinished aspect to it. The lifelong pilgrimage of Ignatius continued even as he was dictating the *Testament*; he was grappling with his being-pilgrim at an advanced age and while stable in Rome. The pilgrimage of the Church is at once embodied and eschatological. It is rich, at times confusing and challenging. Its horizon is infinite. Likewise, this research was a journey, gathering insights along the way. A certain destination is reached but fullness is still ahead. Pilgrimage means that we accept that we will walk, discern, hesitate, encounter, make mistakes, sometimes pause, but—we hope—move forward.

Notes

INTRODUCTION

1. The title "Pilgrim Church" appears most prominently in the title of chap. 7 of the Dogmatic Constitution on the Church *Lumen Gentium* (November 21, 1964).

2. Craig Bartholomew and Fred Hughes, eds., "Introduction," in *Explorations in a Christian Theology of Pilgrimage* (Hants: Ashgate, 2004), xiii.

3. Bernard Lambert, "Le pèlerinage et l'histoire," *La Documentation catholique*, no. 1835 (1–15 août 1982), 768–69.

4. On the progressive constitution of a pilgrim identity crystalizing in the fourth century, see Pierre Maraval, "Comment s'est constituée une 'identité pèlerine' chez les chrétiens des premiers siècles?" in *Identités pèlerines: Actes du colloque de Rouen, 15–16 mai 2002*, ed. Catherine Vincent (Rouen: Publications de l'Université de Rouen, 2004), 19–29.

5. Walker gives the names of a "small number of the Christian visitors to Aelia/Jerusalem in the pre-Constantinian period" (Peter W. L. Walker, "Pilgrimage in the Early Church," in *Explorations in a Christian Theology of Pilgrimage*, ed. Craig Bartholomew and Fred Hughes [Hants, England: Ashgate, 2004], 80).

6. Earlier markers had been leveled in 135 during the reign of Emperor Hadrian, who built Roman (pagan) shrines over the major sites revered by Christians or Jews. See Christof May, *Pilgern: Menschsein auf dem Weg* (Würzburg: Echter, 2004), 28.

7. Walker, "Pilgrimage in the Early Church," 85.

8. Walker, "Pilgrimage in the Early Church," 82.

9. *The Pilgrimage of Egeria: A New Translation of the* Itinerarium Egeriae *with Introduction and Commentary*, trans. Anne McGowan and Paul F. Bradshaw (Collegeville, MN: Liturgical Press Academic, 2018).

10. John Wilkinson, *Jerusalem Pilgrims before the Crusades* (Warminster, England: Aris & Phillips, 2002).

11. Grégoire de Nysse, *Lettre* 2, in *Lettres*, trans. Pierre Maraval, Sources chrétiennes 363 (Paris: Cerf, 1990), 106–23.

12. Jerome, *Against Vigilantius* [excerpts], in *Pilgrimage in the Middle Ages: A Reader*, ed. Brett Edward Whalen (Toronto: University of Toronto Press, 2011), 30–33.

13. Victor Turner and Edith Turner, *Image and Pilgrimage in Christian Culture: Anthropological Perspectives* (New York: Columbia University Press, 1978), 175.

14. Karin Vélez, *The Miraculous Flying House of Loreto: Spreading Catholicism in the Early Modern World* (Princeton, NJ: Princeton University Press, 2019).

15. Dominique Julia, "Identité pèlerine, identité du passage," in Catherine Vincent, ed., *Identités pèlerines*, 235.

16. J. G. Davies, *Pilgrimage Yesterday, and Today: Why? When? How?* (London: SCM, 1988), 80–108. See also Graham Tomlin, "Protestants and Pilgrimage," in Bartholomew and Hughes, eds., *Explorations in a Christian Theology of Pilgrimage*, 110–20.

17. Tomlin, "Protestants and Pilgrimage," 111–12. For Martin Luther's early reflection on the right (or wrong) motives for pilgrimage, see Whalen, ed. *Pilgrimage in the Middle Ages*, 368–70 (the text is that of the *Explanations of the Ninety-Five Theses*, since the *Ninety-Five Theses* themselves do not mention pilgrimage).

18. Council of Trent, Decree "On Invocation, Veneration and Relics of the Saints, and on Sacred Images" (Session 25, December 3–4, 1563), in *Decrees of the Ecumenical Councils*, ed. Norman P. Tanner, SJ, vol. 2: Trent to Vatican II (London: Sheed and Ward; Washington: Georgetown University Press, 1990), 774–76.

19. Alphonse Dupront, *Du sacré: Croisades et pèlerinages, images et langages* (Paris: Gallimard, 2012), 408. These bishops were condemning abuses that were taking place during pilgrimages.

20. A low point was reached in 1800, when no Roman Jubilee was declared, contrary to custom. The year before, Pope Pius VI

had died in exile, and the conclave to elect Cardinal Barnaba Niccolò Maria Luigi Chiaramonti (Pope Pius VII) could not meet in Rome.

21. See Davies, *Pilgrimage Yesterday and Today*, 140–67; Stephanie Stidham Rogers, *Inventing the Holy Land: American Protestant Pilgrimage to Palestine, 1895–1941* (Lanham, MD: Lexington Books, 2011). The relative uneasiness with the word *pilgrimage*—making use instead of "study tours" or "visits"—has nonetheless endured to our day (see Andrew T. Lincoln, "Pilgrimage and the New Testament," in Bartholomew and Hughes, eds., *Explorations in a Christian Theology of Pilgrimage*, 43).

22. Because of the popularity of the *camino francés* (the main pilgrim road that starts in France), roads to Santiago have diversified (Camino portugués, del Norte, primitivo, etc.). Many ancient pilgrimage roads have been revived in other parts of Europe, e.g., the Via Francigena, from England to Italy, through France and Switzerland, while other routes have been created, inspired by the Camino.

23. Of the 327,378 pilgrims of the Camino who registered to get the official certificate, 9.35 percent report motives that were purely nonreligious, 47.87 percent report "religious and other" motives, while 42.78 percent report only religious motivations (Oficina del Peregrino, "Informe estadístico Año 2018," 2, accessed July 18, 2019, http://oficinadelperegrino.com/wp-content/uploads/2016/02/peregrinaciones2018.pdf.

24. The World Youth Days were held in Buenos Aires (1987), Santiago de Compostela (1989), Czestochowa (1991), Denver (1993), Manila (1995), Paris (1997), Rome (2000), Toronto (2002), Cologne (2005), Sydney (2008), Madrid (2011), Rio (2013), Krakow (2016), Panama City (2019). Lisbon is next in 2022.

25. Distinctions abound within each of these perspectives (e.g., between Anglicans and Pentecostals), but this general categorization is useful to delineate some general trends. Walton presents these three Christian perspectives in a parallel way, acknowledging their distinct take on the phenomenon of pilgrimage (Heather Walton, "Theological Perspectives on Christian Pilgrimage," in Avril Maddrell, Veronica della Dora, Alessandro Scafi, and Heather Walton, *Christian Pilgrimage, Landscape and Heritage: Journeying to the Sacred* [New York: Routledge, 2015], 22–40). For an anthropological example of the different take on pilgrimage according to various

Christian denominations, see Glenn Bowman, "Christian Ideology and the Image of a Holy Land: The Place of Jerusalem Pilgrimage in the Various Christianities," in *Contesting the Sacred: The Anthropology of Christian Pilgrimage*, ed. John Eade and Michael J. Sallnow (London: Routledge, 1991), 98–121.

26. Such inversion of perspective is clear in Lincoln's chapter on pilgrimage in the New Testament: "Christians could then be clear that journeys to Jerusalem, Canterbury, Oberammergau or Rome are not literal pilgrimages but can, and often do, play some significant part in the pilgrimage that is Christian existence." Andrew T. Lincoln, "Pilgrimage and the New Testament," in Bartholomew and Hughes, eds., *Explorations in a Christian Theology of Pilgrimage*, 43. Taking aim at N. T. Wright's *The Way of the Lord*, Lincoln vehemently defends the primacy of pilgrimage as the Christian's journey, and tries to undermine any value granted to the physical place.

27. Zygmunt Bauman, "From Pilgrim to Tourist—or a Short History of Identity," in *Questions of Cultural Identity*, ed. Stuart Hall and Paul du Gay (London: Sage Publications, 2011), 21. Bauman ties this understanding of pilgrimage to the necessity to leave the desert-like world.

28. Walton, "Theological Perspectives," 32.

29. Tomlin, "Protestants and Pilgrimage," 110.

30. Many of the chapters of the edited volume by Craig Bartholomew and Fred Hughes exemplify that trend (Bartholomew and Hughes, eds., *Explorations in a Christian Theology of Pilgrimage*). The genealogy of pilgrimage is addressed in chap. 2.

31. As mentioned in the introduction, however, criticism started with the beginning of pilgrimages themselves, as in the early example of Gregory of Nyssa in the fourth century. For example, contemporary critics of World Youth Day abound.

32. See, e.g., Dupront, *Du sacré*, 411.

33. John Paul II, *Incarnationis Mysterium: Bull of Indiction of the Great Jubilee of the Year 2000* (November 29, 1998), §7. Similarly, Turner called to attention the link between pilgrimage and mysticism, since both are faith journeys; "pilgrimage may be thought of as extroverted mysticism, just as mysticism is introverted pilgrimage" (Turner and Turner, *Image and Pilgrimage*, 33).

34. Aleksei Pentkovsky, ed., *The Pilgrim's Tale* (New York: Paulist Press, 1999).

35. As a polyglot French-speaking Quebecker, who has lived and studied in Europe, North America, and the Caribbean, and is now working in an academic setting in the United States, my cultural location undeniably influences how I envision pilgrimage. In addition, I am a Roman Catholic priest and a member of the Society of Jesus (Jesuits), another element that colors my perspective on pilgrimage.

36. James Martin, *Jesus: A Pilgrimage* (New York: HarperOne, 2014).

37. For example, Dupront, *Du sacré*, or Dominique Julia, *Le voyage aux saints: les pèlerinages dans l'Occident moderne: XVe–XVIIIe siècle* (Paris: Seuil/EHESS/Gallimard, 2016).

38. See the seminal work of Victor Turner and Edith Turner, *Image and Pilgrimage in Christian Culture: Anthropological Perspectives* (New York: Columbia University Press, 1978). More recently, see, e.g., John Eade and Michael J. Sallnow, eds., *Contesting the Sacred: The Anthropology of Christian Pilgrimage* (London: Routledge, 1991); Ellen Badone and Sharon R. Roseman, eds., *Intersecting Journeys: The Anthropology of Pilgrimage and Tourism* (Urbana: University of Illinois Press, 2004); Willy Jansen and Catrien Notermans, eds., *Gender, Nation and Religion in European Pilgrimage: Old Routes, New Journeys* (Burlington, VT: Ashgate, 2012).

39. See, e.g., Danièle Hervieu-Léger, *Le pèlerin et le converti: La religion en mouvement* (Paris: Flammarion, 1999).

40. See e.g., Peter Felkai, "Medical Problems of Way of St. James Pilgrimage," *Journal of Religion and Health* 58 (2019):566–71. The author mentions that the medical literature about the Camino is very limited, compared to that pertaining to the Hajj (566).

41. See Simon Coleman and J. Elsner, *Pilgrimage Past and Present: Sacred Travel and Sacred Space in the World Religions* (Cambridge, MA: Harvard University Press, 1995); Simon Coleman and J. Eade, *Reframing Pilgrimage: Cultures in Motion* (London: Routledge, 2004); Dionigi Albera and John Eade, eds., *International Perspectives on Pilgrimage Studies: Itineraries, Gaps and Obstacles* (New York: Routledge, 2015); and *New Pathways in Pilgrimage Studies* (New York: Routledge, 2017). The first chapter of *International Perspectives on Pilgrimage Studies*, titled "International Perspectives

on Pilgrimage Studies: Putting the Anglophone Contribution in Its Place" (1–22) and authored by the co-editors, offers a succinct presentation of the evolution of the field of pilgrimage studies from an integrated international perspective.

42. Furthermore, May developed some of his insights on the opportunity that pilgrimage offers with regard to evangelization (Christof May, "'Mal weg' sein—ob das ausreicht? Pilgern als Chance christlicher Verkündigung," *Geist und Leben* 81, no. 3 [2008]: 174–85). An insightful German book came to my attention as I was doing the final revision of my manuscript: Michael Rosenberger, *Wege, die bewegen: Eine kleine Theologie der Wallfahrt* (Würzburg: Echter, 2005), which unwraps sequentially more than a dozen dimensions of pilgrimage (e.g., change, adventure, prayer, community) through the lens of anthropology, theology (and sometimes spirituality), and the praxis of pilgrimage.

43. See esp. Pontifical Council for the Pastoral Care of Migrants and Itinerant People, "The Pilgrimage in the Great Jubilee" (April 25, 1998); "The Shrine: Memory, Presence and Prophecy of the Living God" (May 8, 1999); and Pope John Paul II, "Letter Concerning Pilgrimage to the Places Linked to the History of Salvation" (June 29, 1999).

44. Contemporary studies on pilgrimage usually do not address recent pontifical pronouncements about pilgrimage.

45. Further comparisons of the fruits of this research with other types of pilgrimages would be welcome but go beyond the intended scope of this book.

CHAPTER 1: WHAT IS CHRISTIAN PILGRIMAGE?

1. In French, I focused on the dictionaries *Le Nouveau Petit Robert* (Paris: Dictionnaires Le Robert, 1993) and *Larousse* (http://www.larousse.fr/dictionnaires/francais). In English, I looked at *Merriam-Webster* (https://www.merriam-webster.com/dictionary), Oxford University Press's *Lexico.com* (www.lexico.com), *Dictionary.com* (www.dictionary.com), *Cambridge Dictionary* (https://dictionary.cambridge.org/dictionary/english), *American Heritage Dictionary of the English Language* (https://ahdictionary.com), *Collins English Dictionary* (https://www.collinsdictionary

.com/dictionary/english), and *Random House Kernerman Webster's College Dictionary* (http://www.thefreedictionary.com/pilgrimage). For Spanish, I relied on the *Diccionario de la lengua española* of the Real Academia Española (https://dle.rae.es).

2. "Le lieu qui est le but de ce voyage" (*Le Nouveau Petit Robert*). This meaning was used from the eighteenth century onward. Could it be linked to the weakening of the actual practice of pilgrimage in the post-Enlightenment Church, insofar as the destination was the pilgrimage? This understanding runs contrary to a contemporary emphasis on the journey over the destination.

3. See, e.g., *Random House Kernerman Webster's College Dictionary*.

4. "Andar por tierras extrañas" (*Diccionario de la lengua española*).

5. *Merriam-Webster*.

6. See https://www.lexico.com/en/definition/pilgrimage (Oxford Dictionary) (accessed July 17, 2019).

7. "En algunas religiones, vivir entendiendo la vida como un camino que hay que recorrer para llegar a una vida futura en unión con Dios después de la muerte" (*Diccionario de la lengua española*).

8. "3. (1835) Voyage fait avec l'intention de rendre hommage à un lieu, à un grand homme qu'on vénère" (*Le Nouveau Petit Robert*).

9. See https://www.dictionary.com/browse/pilgrimage (accessed July 17, 2019).

10. "2. f. Fiesta popular que con meriendas, bailes, etc., se celebra en el campo inmediato a alguna ermita o santuario el día de la festividad religiosa del lugar" (*Diccionario de la lengua española*).

11. "3. f. Gran número de gentes que afluye a un sitio" (*Diccionario de la lengua española*).

12. See their liminal essay "International Perspectives on Pilgrimage Studies: Putting Anglophone Perspective in Its Place," in *International Perspectives on Pilgrimage Studies: Itineraries, Gaps and Obstacles*, ed. Dionigi Albera and John Eade (New York: Routledge, 2015), 13.

13. Bauman identifies four postmodern styles, who followed the modern style of the pilgrim: the stroller, the vagabond, the tourist, and the player in Zygmunt Bauman, "From Pilgrim to Tourist—Or a Short History of Identity," in *Questions of Cultural Identity*,

ed. Stuart Hall and Paul du Gay (London: Sage Publications, 2011), 18–37.

14. In medieval and early modern "hospitals," pilgrims, the sick, the elderly, and local poor were mingled. Comparisons could be made between *albergues* of the Camino and contemporary emergency homeless shelters.

15. See, e.g., William T. Cavanaugh, "Migrant, Tourist, Pilgrim, Monk: Mobility and Identity in a Global Age," *Theological Studies* 69 (2008): 340–56. The contrast between pilgrim and tourist has been played out by many scholars. See, e.g., the final, liminal chapters of Ellen Badone and Sharon R. Roseman, eds., *Intersecting Journeys: The Anthropology of Pilgrimage and Tourism* (Urbana: University of Illinois Press, 2004).

16. Treks on the Appalachian Trail, e.g., are sometimes presented as pilgrimages through the prism of a Thoreauesque quality of observation and communion with nature. On the outdoors seen through the prism of pilgrimage, see Lynn Ross-Bryant, *Pilgrimage to the National Parks: Religion and Nature in the United States* (New York: Routledge, 2013).

17. See André Brouillette, "Pèlerin et migrant: Regards théologiques croisés," *Théologiques* 25, no. 2 (2017): 75–94.

18. Charles Thompson contrasted odyssey and pilgrimage by stressing that the odyssey is individual, and its journey aims at returning home (which is what we see in Homer), whereas pilgrimage is fundamentally about others. See Charles D. Thompson, "Border Odyssey," Lecture given at the 2016 Annual Symposium for Pilgrimage Studies, College of William and Mary, Williamsburg, VA, September 30, 2016.

19. Monasticism took root around the same time that pilgrimages emerged in the fourth century, and both bloomed in the Middle Ages. Monks take a vow of stability, in opposition to the temporary, mobile endeavor of the pilgrim. But both are driven by a spiritual quest. Monasteries often sprang up along pilgrimage routes or at shrines, facilitating the pilgrims' journey. In an interesting twist, in a workshop on pilgrimage that I offered to a group of French laypeople, many mentioned the experience of a spiritual retreat in a monastery as resonating with the *ethos* of pilgrimage (going away to a destination, sacred time, spiritual experience). Very concretely,

it reconnected the physical experience of a place with a deep spiritual experience, exteriority, and interiority.

20. Bauman, "From Pilgrim to Tourist," 18.

21. The frontier is easily crossed by pilgrims, but not migrants, whose mobility is regulated by national borders (Cavanaugh, "Migrant, Tourist, Pilgrim, Monk," 344).

22. Every Muslim who can afford the pilgrimage to Mecca should complete it once in his lifetime. Islam also has numerous other pilgrimage sites, e.g., to the tombs of marabouts or prophets.

23. See Simon Coleman and John Elsner, *Pilgrimage: Past and Present in the World Religions* (Cambridge, MA: Harvard University Press, 1995) for a general overview of pilgrimages in different religious settings. For the Japanese context, see Ian Reader, "Japanese Studies of Pilgrimage," in Albera and Eade, eds., *International Perspectives on Pilgrimage Studies*, 23–46.

24. Heather Walton, "Theological Perspectives on Christian Pilgrimage," in Avril Maddrell, Veronica della Dora, Alessandro Scafi, and Heather Walton, *Christian Pilgrimage, Landscape and Heritage: Journeying to the Sacred* (New York: Routledge, 2015), 23.

25. See Albera and Eade, "International Perspectives on Pilgrimage Studies," 1–22.

26. Victor Turner and Edith Turner, *Image and Pilgrimage in Christian Culture: Anthropological Perspectives* (New York: Columbia University Press, 1978), 249. Turner mentions the connection of the liminal state to various passage experiences: death, birth, wilderness.

27. Turner and Turner, *Image and Pilgrimage*, 250.

28. Alphonse Dupront, *Du sacré: Croisades et pèlerinages, images et langages* (Paris: Gallimard, 2012), 412–14.

29. Christof May, *Pilgern: Menschsein auf dem Weg* (Würzburg: Echter, 2004), 273. May then develops each step. The *Aufbruch und Motivation* (Departure and Motivation) is the movement out of oneself, toward alterity, conversion (May, *Pilgern*, 273–76). The *Auf dem Weg* (On the road), subtitled "Double movement of Jacob's ladder" is the way in which the fatigue, the pain, one's weakness, and grace meet, etching the sign of the cross in discipleship, in the unity sought between the inner and the outer life, the soul and the flesh (277–82). The moment of *Ankunft und Ziel* (Arrival and goal) highlights at once the *telos* of arrival: God, but also the

heavenly Jerusalem, which reminds that the arrival of the pilgrimage is not the final one (283–85). The liturgy, and in particular the Eucharist at the shrine, signifies the entrance into the community of the Father, Son, and Holy Spirit. Finally, the *Versöhnter Rückgang* (Reconciled movement of return) is comprised of the movement of return into ordinary life, while keeping the memory of the pilgrimage as a reminder that life is a pilgrimage (285–87).

30. "The very dynamics of pilgrimages clearly reveals some steps that pilgrims take. They become a paradigm of the whole life of faith; *departure* reveals the decision of pilgrims to go forward up to the destination and achieve the spiritual objectives of their baptismal vocation; *walking* leads them to solidarity with their brothers and sisters and to the necessary preparation for the meeting with the Lord; the *visit to the Shrine* invites them to listen to the Word of God and to sacramental celebration; the *return*, in the end, reminds them of their mission in the world, as witnesses of salvation and builders of peace. It is important that these steps in a pilgrimage, lived in groups or individually, are marked by acts of worship, which would reveal their authentic dimension, with the use of the texts recommended in liturgical books for this purpose" (Pontifical Council for the Pastoral Care of Migrants and Itinerant People, "The Pilgrimage in the Great Jubilee" [April 25, 1998], §32).

31. (1) The Point of Pilgrimage, (2) The Place of the Holy, (3) Preparing for the Journey, (4) The Company of Others, (5) A Hard Road, (6) Along the Way, (7) Saints Before, (8) The Journey Within, (9) Worship on the Way and on Arrival, (10) The Destination, (11) The Journey Beyond (Martin Robinson, *Sacred Places, Pilgrim Paths: An Anthology of Pilgrimage*, [London: HarperCollins, 1997]).

32. The aim is not to establish a typology of pilgrimages by outlining its various types.

33. In his early reflection on pilgrimage in the *Explanation of the Ninety-Five Theses*, Luther probes the motivation for the (literal) pilgrimage, deeming some unworthy (e.g., curiosity), while others are worthy (e.g., devotion), showing that the intentionality determines the genuineness of the pilgrim nature.

34. Consequently, our understanding of phenomenology is not limited to what can be grasped by the senses but extends even to the motivations.

35. Pontifical Council for the Pastoral Care of Migrants and Itinerant People, "The Pilgrimage," §32. Hence, Alphonse Dupront identifies the "will of power" (*volonté de puissance*)—most likely with Nietzschean overtones—as a characteristic of the anthropology of pilgrimage (Dupront, *Du sacré*, 414–15), the will to build and create one's life, along with a desire for the ultimate *transitus* into eternal life. I would not equate the intention with such "will of power," but more with a radical openness that unfolds in an assumed vulnerability.

36. Contrary to the "tourist" label—often bestowed upon others—the pilgrim label must be claimed personally, since no description of a journey would make it a pilgrimage without the pilgrim's personal assent. Children or youths can be dragged along as tourists, but not as pilgrims.

37. Brian Brendan O'Malley, *A Pilgrim's Manual: Saint David's* (Marlborough, UK: Paulinus Press, 1985), 7. Such logic of desire is displayed in the Gospel according to John when individuals who expressed a desire to know where Jesus was staying were invited to "come and see" (John 1:39). Their desire to know a place—and a person—led them to undertake a journey. The desire leads the journey.

38. Thomas Merton, *The Seven Storey Mountain* (New York, Harcourt, Brace and Co., 1948), 108, 110. The emphasis is mine.

39. N. T. Wright expresses a similar sentiment in the early pages of *The Way of the Lord* as he shares a profound spiritual experience that he had on Good Friday, 1989, at the Church of the Holy Sepulchre, in Jerusalem, after which he recognized that he "became" a pilgrim (N. T. Wright, *The Way of the Lord: Christian Pilgrimage Today* [Grand Rapids, MI: Wm. B. Eerdmans Publishing Co., 1999], 7).

40. "...a tourist is half a pilgrim, if a pilgrim is half a tourist. Even when people bury themselves in anonymous crowds on beaches, they are seeking an almost sacred, often symbolic, mode of *communitas*, generally unavailable to them in the structured life of the office, the shop floor, or the mine. Even when intellectuals, Thoreau-like, seek the wilderness in personal solitude, they are seeking the material multiplicity of nature, a life source" (Turner and Turner, *Image and Pilgrimage*, 20).

41. Turner and Turner, *Image and Pilgrimage*, 193, 195; Dominique Julia, "Identité pèlerine, identité du passage," in *Identités*

pèlerines: Actes du colloque de Rouen, 15–16 mai 2002, ed. Catherine Vincent (Rouen: Publications de l'Université de Rouen, 2004), 235. On penitential pilgrimages, see Diana Webb, *Pilgrims and Pilgrimages in the Medieval West* (London: I. B. Tauris, 1999), 51–63.

42. Robinson, *Sacred Places, Pilgrim Paths*, 61.

43. May gives the example of Queen Margarete of Denmark who put 2,000 Marks aside in her 1411 will to pay for 130 pilgrimages to 44 different places (May, *Pilgern*, 47n166, quoting N. Ohler, *Pilgerstab und Jakobsmuschel* [Zurich: Artemis und Winkler, 2000], 31).

44. An intention not embraced would nonetheless reduce the journey to a performance only shadowing pilgrimage.

45. For the current Church legislation regarding shrines as destination for pilgrims, see Catholic Church, *Code of Canon Law* (1983), canons 1230–34.

46. On the *besoin* (need) for pilgrimage expressed by the popular "masses," see Dupront, *Du sacré*, esp. 411.

47. In most instances, the Church approves *post factum* a pilgrimage, i.e., its divine origin, rather than initiating one. In that regard, the Church's role is similar to the recognition of a new charism in the Church through a religious community; the most common role of the Church in that regard is to discern and assess the validity of the inspiration, not to be the inspiration herself.

48. Many Enlightenment bishops of the seventeenth and eighteenth centuries did not favor pilgrimage (Dupront, *Du sacré*, 408).

49. Julia, "Identité pèlerine," 246.

50. Pontifical Council for the Pastoral Care of Migrants and Itinerant People, "The Pilgrimage," §2.

51. Christian pilgrimage finds its source in the desire to visit the sites blessed with the historical presence of Christ. Hence, it constitutes a refoundation of the pilgrimage phenomenon, and not simply an extension of the Old Testament institutions of pilgrimage.

52. The spirit of renewed commitment to Christ through pilgrimages permeates the letter of Pope John Paul II prior to his visit to the Holy Land, in the context of the Great Jubilee Year of 2000 (John Paul II, "Letter Concerning Pilgrimage to the Places Linked to the History of Salvation" [June 30, 1999], http://www.vatican.va/content/john-paul-ii/en/letters/1999/documents/hf_jp-ii_let_30061999_pilgrimage.html).

53. In the final lines of his "Guidelines for Pilgrims," Simão Rodrigues, one of the first Jesuit priests, exemplifies the devotion to the saint venerated at the shrine of destination, and the desire for ongoing divine support: "When I arrive at the church to which I am making my pilgrimage, I will take the saint to whom it is dedicated as one who does me special favours before the Lord. I will give Him great thanks for having brought me to the place in question, and ask for help to persevere in His service. And I will renew all my good purposes and specific intentions about God's service, calling on the saint whose house it is as a witness, asking them that they should always remember me especially before the Divine Majesty, seeing the obligation that I have to God" (Simão Rodrigues, "Guidelines for Pilgrims: Coimbra, Portugal 1546," *The Way* 42, no. 1 [2003]: 70).

54. Vatican documents always emphasize worship as part of the journey of pilgrimage, e.g., "Lived as a celebration of one's own faith, for the Christian, a pilgrimage is a manifestation of worship to be accomplished faithfully according to tradition, with an intense religious sentiment and as a fulfillment of his Paschal existence" (Pontifical Council for the Pastoral Care of Migrants and Itinerant People, "The Pilgrimage," §32).

55. On the Camino, one is struck by the small "shrines" or the emerging rituals (crosses on a fence, ribbons near a spring, pictures of individuals) whose meaning can be very personal—and not overseen by any authority.

56. Pontifical Council for the Pastoral Care of Migrants and Itinerant People, "The Shrine: Memory, Presence and Prophecy of the Living God" (May 8, 1999), §1.

57. Pontifical Council for the Pastoral Care of Migrants and Itinerant People, "The Shrine," §4. In a similar vein, the Pontifical Council on migrants and refugees states that "in the course of history, Christians have always walked to celebrate their faith in places that indicate a memory of the Lord or in sites representing important moments in the history of the Church. They have come to shrines honoring the Mother of God and to those that keep the example of the saints alive" (Pontifical Council for the Pastoral Care of Migrants and Itinerant People, "The Pilgrimage," §2).

58. As I mentioned earlier, it is even one of the spin-off definitions of *pilgrimage*.

59. See e.g., Chris Bohjalian, "A proud pilgrimage to my homeland," *New York Times*, December 7, 2016, A15, https://www.nytimes.com/2016/12/06/opinion/my-proud-pilgrimage-to-my-homeland.html. The article begins with this paragraph: "Very few Americans could find Nagorno-Karabakh on a map. (Very few of us, of course, could find Armenia and Azerbaijan, either.) I went there this summer for the same reason that I return every year to Armenia and the remnants of Armenian civilization that are scattered across eastern Turkey: This earth is in my blood, and my visits are a pilgrimage. I am an Armenian-American, but only at midlife did I understand the draw of this ancient land for me." For Irish American examples, see James Silas Rogers, "Secular Pilgrimages: Recent Irish-American Memoir and Journeys of Healing," in *Irish-American Autobiography* (Washington, DC: Catholic University of America Press, 2016), 143–64.

60. See the pilgrimage of an opera lover to revere Wagner's work in Germany: Zachary Woolfe, "Make a Pilgrimage to Munich for 'Tannhäuser,'" *New York Times*, May 23, 2017, https://www.nytimes.com/2017/05/23/arts/music/review-tannhauser-wagner-bayerische-staatsoper-bavarian-state-opera-wagner-munich-germany.html.

61. The memorialization of historical events or phenomena like slavery or the Shoah indicate that they are not simply historical facts but carry an emotional weight and involvement in the present—with an underlying ethical commitment to change.

62. See Dupront, *Du sacré*, 382.

63. The power of the place is then more memorial than magical; it relies not on the intrinsic quality of the place, but on the memory attached to it. As Sheldrake asserts, "The concept of place refers not simply to geographical location but to a dialectical relationship between environment and human narrative. Place is space that has the capacity to be remembered and to evoke what is most precious" (Philip Sheldrake, *Spaces for the Sacred: Place, Memory, and Identity* [Baltimore: The Johns Hopkins University Press, 2001], 1). On the creation of competing Protestant sites in the Holy Land, see Stephanie Stidham Rogers, *Inventing the Holy Land: American Protestant Pilgrimage to Palestine, 1895–1941* (Lanham, MD: Lexington Books, 2011), 8 (see also her chap. 5: "The Out-of-Doors

Gospel in Palestine: Protestants Encounter Catholic and Orthodox Shrines and Create Their Own Traditions").

64. Many relics moved, sometimes for good reasons (the body of St. Francis Xavier brought from far-off Sancian to the Portuguese settlement of Goa), others through negotiation (the body of St. Teresa of Avila was moved from Alba de Tormes, where she died, to Avila, where she established her first reformed Carmel, and then back), or through theft (the relics of St. Mark being brought from Egypt to Venice).

65. See, e.g., the "Tour des Martyrs" in Saint-Célestin, Canada, started by a local priest at the end of the nineteenth century. It housed thousands of relics of saints, from 1895 to 1975, when the building was destroyed (http://www.ipir.ulaval.ca/fiche.php?id=815, accessed July 19, 2019). It attracted some attention in the early twentieth century, but never rose to the level of the major shrines of Canada.

66. Brother André Bessette (1845–1937), canonized by Pope Benedict XVI in 2010, was a miracle worker and the founder of St. Joseph's Oratory, in Montreal, Canada. Padre Pio de Pietrelcina (1887–1968), was a Capuchin priest with the stigmata. He was canonized in 2002 by Pope John Paul II.

67. The example of the Sanctuary of Our Lady of Yagma, in Burkina Faso, among many others, is a case in point since it was created *ex nihilo* as a focal point outside the city for Christians to go and pray.

68. In the Ignatian spiritual tradition, this practice is not necessarily tied to the preparation for sacramental confession, though they share some characteristics, for the examen is not only centered on sin. Ignatius of Loyola mentions the practice early in his *Spiritual Exercises* (Ignatius of Loyola, *Spiritual Exercises*, §43, in Ignatius of Loyola, *Personal Writings* [London: Penguin, 1997], 293).

69. "The 'way' is a symbol of existence which is expressed in a wide range of actions like leaving and coming back, entrance and exit, descent and ascent, walking and resting. Since the very first moment of their appearance on the stage of the world, human beings have always walked in search of new goals, investigating earthly horizons and tending towards the infinite. They navigated rivers and seas, climbed sacred mountains on whose summit the earth ideally meets the sky. They walked through time marking it

with sacred dates. They considered birth as an entrance into the world and death as an exit to enter the womb of the earth or to be assumed into the divine regions" (Pontifical Council for the Pastoral Care of Migrants and Itinerant People, "The Pilgrimage," §1).

70. Even for the armchair pilgrimage, there should be a beginning of the journey.

71. This is a radical transformation for pilgrimage, and a potential challenge. But it is not the first: the development of mass transportation, to name only one, had also revolutionized the practice of pilgrimage.

72. Arnold van Gennep, *The Rites of Passage* (Chicago: University of Chicago Press, 1960).

73. Turner considers that "inside the Christian religious frame, pilgrimage may be said to represent the quintessence of voluntary liminality" (Turner and Turner, *Image and Pilgrimage*, 9).

74. Medieval pilgrimages to the Holy Land could last years, thus the possibility of never returning, though not planned, could not be ruled out (Robinson, *Sacred Places, Pilgrim Paths*, 51).

75. For pilgrimage understood in a spiritual sense as the metaphor of Christian life, the term of the pilgrimage, and its origin, can be set in the heavenly city, hence one becomes a pilgrim by nature, not for a time. *Homo viator*. This sense of "homelessness" of the Christian runs parallel to the actual pilgrimaging, which implies a return to the home that one left. Ludolph of Saxony, in his famed *Vita Christi*, an important Latin medieval spiritual text later translated into many European languages, wrote in an Augustinian fashion, "We who are pilgrims in this world...have no permanent city, but we seek one that is to come" (Pt. 2, chap. 76, p. 717, col. 2; quoted in Paul Shore, "The *Vita Christi* of Ludolph of Saxony and Its Influence on the Spiritual Exercises of Ignatius of Loyola," *Studies in the Spirituality of Jesuits* 30, no. 1 [1998]: 11).

76. Pontifical Council for the Pastoral Care of Migrants and Itinerant People, "The Shrine," §1.

77. Cavanaugh highlights as one distinction between the pilgrim and the tourist that the pilgrim moves toward the center, while the tourist is on the look for the exoticism of the periphery (Cavanaugh, "Migrant, Tourist, Pilgrim, Monk," 350).

78. It is especially clear in Rome, through the various basilicas, and in the Holy Land, which offers a multipolar geography.

79. Ignatius of Loyola mentioned the universal joy "that did not seem purely natural" and the great spiritual consolation experienced by his group of pilgrims at the sight of the city of Jerusalem (Ignatius of Loyola, *Testament*, §45, in Ignatius of Loyola, *Personal Writings* [London: Penguin Books, 1997], 34—under the title "Reminiscences").

80. See, e.g., the space around the Sanctuary of Fatima, or Lourdes.

81. The theme of the "center" of the pilgrimage, between person and place, through holiness, is further developed in chap. 2.

82. This hymn finds its roots in the biblical acclamations of Isa 6:3 and Rev 4:8.

83. In one of the Creation accounts in Genesis, the goodness of what is created is attested at multiple steps (Gen 1:9, 12, 18, 21).

84. In the vocabulary of soteriology especially beloved in Eastern Christianity, "divinization" highlights the desired sharing of God's very nature, of which holiness is key, by human beings.

85. At the heart of this centralization in early Judaism, see Deut 12.

86. The New Testament sometimes calls the members of the early Christian communities "saints" (e.g., Eph 1:1; Phil 1:1).

87. Council of Trent, Decree "On Invocation, Veneration and Relics of the Saints, and on Sacred Images" (Session 25, December 3–4, 1563), in *Decrees of the Ecumenical Councils*, ed. Norman P. Tanner, SJ, vol. 2, *Trent to Vatican II* (Washington, DC: Georgetown University Press), 774–76.

88. "All Christians are invited to join and take part in the great pilgrimage that Christ, the Church and humankind have accomplished and must continue accomplishing in history. The shrine towards which they must be directed is to become 'the Tent of Meeting,' as the Bible calls the tabernacle of the alliance. There, in fact, a fundamental meeting takes place, one that reveals various dimensions and is presented under numerous appearances" (Pontifical Council for the Pastoral Care of Migrants and Itinerant People, "The Pilgrimage," §32).

89. A concrete translation of this personal invitation is the prayer (usually partaking in the Eucharist) and sacramental reconciliation that is required for the granting of the indulgence of visiting a shrine.

90. Julia, "Identité pèlerine," 232.

91. For an interesting qualitative anthropological study of the pilgrims on the road to Compostela, see Nancy Louis Frey, *Pilgrim Stories: On and Off the Road to Santiago* (Berkeley: University of California Press, 1998).

92. Avril Maddrell, Veronica della Dora, Alessandro Scafi, and Heather Walton, *Christian Pilgrimage, Landscape and Heritage: Journeying to the Sacred* (New York: Routledge, 2015). They analyze Meteora, Subiaco, and the Isle of Man.

93. For example, pilgrims to the Scala Sancta, in Rome ascend on their knees, and those to the Sanctuary of Our Lady of Guadalupe in Mexico approach the basilica that way.

94. The Rosary procession is a mainstay of the shrine of Lourdes.

95. In the Basilica of Santiago de Compostela, pilgrims hug the statue of St. James.

96. In the region of Arica, in Chile, there is a tradition of pilgrimages centered on collective dances performed each year by organized groups. See Nelson Peña Antil, SJ, *Bailes religiosos de Arica: Valoración de su historia y tradición* (Santiago de Chile: Procultura, 2015).

97. Turner pointedly mentions that pilgrimage is not associated in the Roman Catholic Church with rites of passage (e.g., baptism, confirmation, ordination), which is what his concept of liminality would suggest, but with the Eucharist and penance, which are repeatable sacraments (Turner and Turner, *Image and Pilgrimage*, 31–32).

98. "...aujourd'hui encore, en Occident, il n'y a presque pas de pèlerinage, même mineur, sans reliques à vénérer" (Dupront, *Du sacré*, 385).

99. Ludolph of Saxony describes in the fourteenth-century *Vita Christi* the physical and emotional connection between pilgrims and the place/relic visited: "Who can describe how the many devout pilgrims in the Holy Land travel from site to site, and with burning zeal kiss the ground and embrace the places where they hear that Jesus sat or performed some deed? Beating their breasts, weeping, groaning, and sighing by turns, they express outwardly in their bodies the devotion they doubtless feel in their hearts, and their emotion moves many to tears, even among the Saracens"

(Ludolph of Saxony, *The Life of Jesus Christ*, vol. 1, trans. Milton T. Walsh [Athens, OH: Cistercian Publications, 2018], 18).

100. The "touching" of relics could take extreme forms: kissing, licking—the soil of Loreto's Santa Casa—or even biting—the body of John of Montfort (Julia, "Identité pèlerine," 233). The Catholic Reform tried to substitute a more devotional "seeing" to this brutal "touching" (Julia, "Identité pèlerine," 234). We could also add the sense of smell (e.g., incense), less often taste.

101. In its extreme form, the cult of relics led to an attribution of magic power to them (Turner and Turner, *Image and Pilgrimage*, 197).

102. On the importance of bringing something back, see Dupront, *Du sacré*, 405. In the Catholic tradition, there are three classes of relics: a first-class relic is an actual body part of a saint, a second-class relic is an object that was used by a saint, and a third-class relic is an object that has touched a first- or second-class relic. This latter category constitutes the expendable category.

103. May, *Pilgern*, 53.

104. Walton mentions the potential of the category of sacramentality to understand the special character in space and place of the pilgrimage (Walton, "Theological Perspectives," 25).

105. In the medieval Church, the Eucharist was sometimes placed among other relics. See Franklin Harkins, "Matter Matters," in *The Holy Spirit: Setting the World on Fire*, ed. Richard Lennan and Nancy Pineda-Madrid (Mahwah, NJ: Paulist Press, 2017), 27.

106. Egeria in her travels was careful to partake in the eucharistic celebration of the monks whenever possible (May, *Pilgern*, 51).

107. Cavanaugh astutely mentions that tourists tend to shape—unbeknownst to them—the environment around them, even as they desire to encounter it in its authenticity (Cavanaugh, "Migrant, Tourist, Pilgrim, Monk," 347). Rogers also mentions the *mise en scène* of the Holy Land at work in early Protestants pilgrimages, in which the lived reality of (contemporary) Arabs was subsumed under biblical categories (Rogers, *Inventing the Holy Land*, 8–9; see also her chap. 3: "Protestants, Arabs, and Islam in the Holy Land").

108. On the Camino, many of the pilgrims take the opportunity early to send home—or give away—items that they thought necessary, but whose weight made more cumbersome than useful.

109. Modern technology curtails vulnerability since we can Google anything. But even technology cannot entirely erase vulnerability.

110. A challenge that pilgrimage organizers offer to young pilgrims is to give up their smart phones for the length of their pilgrimage, which constitutes the most eloquent sign that they entered a different space inviting to new ways to relate to their environment, themselves, and their traveling companions.

111. Pierre Corneille, *Le Cid*, Act 2, Scene 2.

112. In a long pilgrimage on foot, one recommits to the effort every day.

113. For a discussion on the authentic pilgrim, see Frey, *Pilgrim Stories*, 125–36. Her observation is also that the effort consented to would be a point of distinction—and pride—for pilgrims between themselves and "tourists" (or cyclists).

114. Turner and Turner, *Image and Pilgrimage*, 9.

115. Rodrigues, "Guidelines," 65.

116. Julia, "Identité pèlerine," 234.

117. Julia, "Identité pèlerine," 235.

118. Robinson, *Sacred Places, Pilgrim Paths*, 76–77.

119. Dupront, *Du sacré*, 406.

120. Turner and Turner, *Image and Pilgrimage*, 250–51.

121. See Antil, *Bailes religiosos de Arica*. They function in a way similar to the Spanish confraternities of the Holy Week, or the New Orleans groups (krewes) that build carnival floats.

122. Leo Agung Sardi, *La prueba de la peregrinación en el noviciado de la Compañía de Jesús: Su actualidad para la formación en Indonesia*, doctoral thesis (Madrid: Universidad Pontificia Comillas, 2015).

123. Zygmunt Bauman describes the tourist in this way: "The purpose is new experience; the tourist is a conscious and systematic seeker of experience, of a new and different experience, of the experience of difference and novelty—as the joys of the familiar wear off and cease to allure. The tourists want to immerse themselves in a strange and bizarre element (a pleasant feeling, a tickling and rejuvenating feeling, like letting oneself be buffeted by sea waves)—on condition, though, that it will not stick to the skin and thus can be shaken off whenever they wish" (Bauman, "From Pilgrim to Tourist," 29).

124. Richard Roos, *Christwalk: The Journal of a Young Priest's 600-Mile Pilgrimage by Foot along the California Mission Trail* (New York: Paulist Press, 1985), 201. Turner also mentions that expectation of change: "It is true that the pilgrim returns to his former mundane existence, but it is commonly believed that he has made a spiritual step forward" (Turner and Turner, *Image and Pilgrimage*, 15).

125. Rogers, *Inventing the Holy Land*, 4–5. Cavanaugh highlights the transformation of the self expected of the pilgrim through penance and forgiveness (Cavanaugh, "Migrant, Pilgrim, Tourist, Monk," 349).

126. Frey laments the lack of attention given to the moment of "return" of the pilgrim (Nancy L. Frey, "Pilgrimage and its Aftermaths," in *Intersecting Journeys: The Anthropology of Pilgrimage and Tourism*, ed. Ellen Badone and Sharon R. Roseman [Urbana: University of Illinois Press, 2004], 89–109).

127. Catherine Mayeur-Jaouen, "L'identité pèlerine en terre d'islam: du *hajj* aux pèlerinages locaux," in Vincent, ed., *Identités pèlerines*, 188.

128. However, many young Catholic religious and priests can trace their vocations to a calling heard at a World Youth Day, the so-called "John Paul II Generation."

129. Frey noticed in her qualitative study of pilgrims on the Camino that "serial pilgrims," those who walk that road multiple times, show an erosion of the sense of transformation; it no longer appears as a motivation for their travel (Frey, "Pilgrimage and its Aftermaths," 104). The fifteenth-century *Imitatio Christi* by Thomas à Kempis makes the pithy observation that "those who make many pilgrimages seldom become holy" (Thomas à Kempis, *The Imitation of Christ*, trans. P. G. Zomberg [Rockland, ME: Dunstan, 1985], 39 [Book 1]).

130. See, e.g., the work of French sociologist Danièle Hervieu-Léger, *Le pèlerin et le converti*, 99–109. Her reflection focuses on the pilgrims to the ecumenical community of Taizé, in France.

131. Chaumonot named a Huron village he established "Lorette," as a memorial to his fateful pilgrimage. When the village had to move, it carried the name to "Nouvelle-Lorette." It still stands near Quebec City, Canada.

132. Pontifical Council for the Pastoral Care of Migrants and Itinerant People, "The Shrine," §6–7.

133. "A shrine is an impetus to solidarity, impelling us to be 'living stones' that support one another in the edifice built on the cornerstone which is Christ (1 Pet 2:4–5). It would be fruitless to experience the 'time of the shrine' if this does not then draw us to the 'time of the road,' the 'time of the mission,' and the 'time of service,' wherever God manifests himself as love for the weakest and poorest creatures" (Pontifical Council for the Pastoral Care of Migrants and Itinerant People, "The Shrine," §8).

134. Graham Tomlin, "Protestants and Pilgrimage," in *Explorations in a Christian Theology of Pilgrimage*, ed. Craig Bartholomew and Fred Hughes (Hants: Ashgate, 2004), 122.

CHAPTER 2: A PILGRIM PEOPLE AND CHRIST THE PILGRIM

1. The painting can be seen at https://www.musee-jacquemart-andre.com/fr/oeuvres/pelerins-demmaus.

2. The Vulgate qualifies the fellow traveler as *peregrinus*, the only occurrence of the word in all the Gospels. It reinforces the pilgrim idea, and the suggestion that the two disciples were also pilgrims on their way home.

3. The four verbs of *take, bless, break,* and *give* underline the eucharistic overtone of the meal with the risen Christ.

4. As we saw in chap. 1, at the core of the Christian pilgrimage experience stands a transcendental encounter, and this real presence is expressed in a tangible form through the communal experience of the Eucharist, since it gathers a people around Christ in the Spirit in a given place, making visible the horizontal encounter with one another, and the vertical encounter with God.

5. The Emmaus pilgrims model the "examen," a spiritual tool of prayerful review of one's daily experience promoted especially by Ignatian spirituality in the Christian realm. See Ignatius of Loyola, *Spiritual Exercises*, §43, in Ignatius of Loyola, *Personal Writings* (London: Penguin, 1997), 293.

6. The pilgrimage of Jacob to Bethel (Gen 35), and the Psalms of Ascents (Pss 120–34), among others, testify to the many instances of pilgrimage in the Old Testament.

7. Dyas underlines how "for medieval Christians the expulsion of Adam and Eve from the Garden of Eden for disobedience meant that all human beings were in effect involuntary exiles, condemned to wander the world, separated from God and deprived of their true home" (Dee Dyas, "Medieval Patterns of Pilgrimage: A Mirror for Today?" in *Explorations in a Christian Theology of Pilgrimage*, ed. Craig Bartholomew and Fred Hughes [Hants: Ashgate, 2004], 94).

8. The cloistered gardens of some medieval monasteries, high places of desire for union with God, acted as vivid reminders of the lost Eden of a pristine creation. The fountain in their midst symbolized at once the source of life of Paradise, and Christ as the source of life in baptism. See Naomi Muller, "Paradise Regained: Medieval Garden Fountains," in *Medieval Gardens*, ed. Elisabeth Blair MacDougall (Washington, DC: Dumbarton Oaks Research Library and Collection, 1986), 135–53.

9. Pontifical Council for the Pastoral Care of Migrants and Itinerant People, "The Pilgrimage in the Great Jubilee" (April 25, 1998), §4.

10. The promise of a land was reiterated also to Jacob (Gen 28:13) but fulfilled only at the end of the Book of Exodus, as attested by the beginning of Deuteronomy (Deut 1:8), though not yet in an exclusive way.

11. Danielle Vella, in a final reflection on "Abraham, the migrant," at the end of a book on contemporary migration experiences in Europe, bridges the potential gap between the migrant and pilgrim by claiming the faith dimension in the experience of migrants (Danielle Vella, *Journeys of Hope* [Brussels: JRS Europe, 2016], 84–87). On the centrality of Abraham's story for the theology of migration in the Abrahamic religions, see Dale T. Irvin, "Theology, Migration, and the Homecoming," in *Theology of Migration in the Abrahamic Religions*, ed. Elaine Padilla and Peter C. Phan (New York: Palgrave Macmillan, 2014), 9–10.

12. See my reflections on the topic: André Brouillette, "Pèlerin et réfugié: Regards théologiques croisés," *Théologiques* 25, no. 2 (2017): 75–94.

13. See, e.g., Gustavo Gutiérrez, *A Theology of Liberation* (Maryknoll, NY: Orbis, 1988), especially the chapter on "Liberation and Salvation" (83–105). Michael Walzer, a noted political philosopher, offers in *Exodus and Revolution* (New York: Basic Books, 1985) an insightful meditation on the exodus from the perspective of the people.

14. Pontifical Council for the Pastoral Care of Migrants and Itinerant People, "The Pilgrimage in the Great Jubilee," §6.

15. Walzer develops the role of the "murmuring" in the process (Walzer, *Exodus and Revolution*, 50–51).

16. Enrique Nardoni, *Rise Up, O Judge: A Study of Justice in the Biblical World*, trans. Seán Charles Martin (Peabody: Hendrickson, 2004), 42; see also 68.

17. This commandment is reiterated soon afterward in Exod 23:9. The command to care for sojourners would be regularly restated (e.g., Deut 10:19; cf. 24:17–18).

18. The clear centralization of the cult in Jerusalem is part of the theology of Deuteronomy.

19. The prophet Ezekiel was particularly forceful in his critique of the sins of Judah that he saw as the cause for the exile. See Andrew Mein, "Ezekiel: Structure, Themes, and Contested Issues," chap. 11 in *The Oxford Handbook of the Prophets*, ed. Carolyn J. Sharp (Oxford: Oxford University Press, 2016), 197–200.

20. "Les chemins de l'exode et de l'exil sont le passage obligé pour accéder à la vie en plénitude" (Jean-Marc Éla, "Un Dieu métis," in *Theological Reflections on Migration: A CCME Reader*, ed. Benz H. R. Schär et Ralf Geisler [Brussels: Churches' Commission for Migrants in Europe, 2000], 6–9, at 6. Originally published in the journal *Relations* [November 2004]: 32–34).

21. J. G. McConville, "Pilgrimage and 'Place': An Old Testament View," in Bartholomew and Hughes, eds., *Explorations in a Christian Theology of Pilgrimage*, 19.

22. Menahem Haran underlines the intrinsic connection between the pilgrim-feast and a temple, not simply an altar, as God's dwelling and place of encounter (Menahem Haran, "Pilgrim-Feasts and Family Festivals," in *Temples and Temple-Service in Ancient Israel: An Inquiry into Biblical Cult Phenomena and the Historical Setting of the Priestly School* [Winoma Lake, IN: Eisenbrauns, 1985], 290).

23. McConville, "Pilgrimage and 'Place,'" 23.

24. McConville, "Pilgrimage and 'Place,'" 23.

25. "The Pilgrimage in the Great Jubilee," §6.

26. See Michael B. Hundley, *Gods in Dwellings: Temples and Divine Presence in the Ancient Near East* (Atlanta: Society of Biblical Literature, 2013).

27. "The Pilgrimage in the Great Jubilee," §6. The text continues: "'Yahweh your God...has watched over your journeying through this vast wilderness. Yahweh your God has been with you these forty years and you have never been in want' (Deut 2:7). He 'preserved us all along the way we traveled' (Jos 24:17). He, in fact, remembers with nostalgia 'affection of your youth, the love of your bridal days: you followed me through the wilderness, through a land unsown' (Jer 2:2)."

28. The extent to which Jewish contemporaries of Jesus were making the pilgrimage to Jerusalem for each of these festivals, and whether it was perceived as prescribed by Torah, is the object of debate among scholars (Catherine Hezser, *Jewish Travel in Antiquity* [Tübingen: Mohr Siebeck, 2011], 365).

29. Shavuot and Sukkot had roots as agricultural festivals related to harvest in addition to theological motives. Along with Passover, they constitute the "pilgrim festivals" (see the article "Festivals," in *Encyclopedia Judaica*, ed. Fred Skolnik, vol. 6, 2nd ed. [Detroit: Macmillan Reference USA, 2007], 765–66).

30. Hezser, *Jewish Travel in Antiquity*, 377. Josephus claimed no less than three million participants in the Passover celebration in Jerusalem in the year 65 (Josephus, *Jewish Wars*, 2:280, quoted in the article "Passover," *Encyclopedia Judaica*, vol. 15, 678).

31. The Feast of the Dedication commemorated the 164 BCE purification and restoration of the Jerusalem temple after its desecration by Antiochus Epiphanes.

32. John 2:23; 5:1; 7:10; 10:22.

33. See also Mark 11:15–19; Matt 21:12–17; Luke 19:45–48.

34. Hezser, *Jewish Travel in Antiquity*, 366.

35. There are even more contemporary echoes, in the pilgrimage to Ars to visit Jean-Marie Vianney, or San Giovanni Rotondo to see Padre Pio, or Kolkata to encounter Mother Teresa.

36. The idea of taking the magi as models of subsequent pilgrims coming to Jesus from all nations is suggested in Pontifical

Council for the Pastoral Care of Migrants and Itinerant People, "The Pilgrimage in the Great Jubilee," §10.

37. See also Mark 3:7–8; Luke 5:17; 6:17.

38. See Matt 3:5; Mark 1:5.

39. See Luke 9:31, 51; 13:22; 17:11; 18:31; 19:11, 28, 41, prior to the arrival in Jerusalem for his ultimate Feast of Passover.

40. This movement was already present in Mark's Gospel: "'For Mark, the route to the cross of Golgotha is constantly marked by verbs and words of movement and by the symbol of the "way"' (Cfr. Mark 8, 27.34; 9, 33–34; 10, 17.21.28.32–33.46.52)" (Pontifical Council for the Pastoral Care of Migrants and Itinerant People, "The Pilgrimage in the Great Jubilee," §9).

41. The immediate Lukan context of this assertion of radical unboundedness is particularly interesting, since Jesus was on his way to Jerusalem in a resolute way—"set[ting] his face" (Luke 9:51). As he is going "along the road" (*hodos*), Jesus fields interactions with (failed?) would-be followers (Luke 9:57–62). These logia are located right before Luke's great commissioning of the Seventy (Luke 10:1–12). They highlight the radical freedom of movement entailed by the following of Jesus.

42. For example, the house of Martha and Mary (Luke 10:38; John 12:1–11).

43. For example, Zacchaeus (Luke 19:5–6).

44. Matt 16:21; 20:17–18; Mark 10:32–33; Luke 9:51; 13:22.

45. The Johannine leitmotiv of the "hour" has been developed theologically by Hans Urs von Balthasar, e.g., in his *Theo-Drama: Theological Dramatic Theory*, vol. 4: *The Action* (San Francisco: Ignatius Press, 1994), 231–40.

46. Matt 14:23; 26:39–44; Mark 1:35; 6:46; 14:32–39; Luke 5:16; 6:12; 9:18, 28–29; 22:41–44.

47. See, e.g., the call of the disciples in John to "come and see" (John 1:39).

48. A great example is that of the Gerasene freed from an unclean spirit who wanted to follow Jesus, but instead was sent to proclaim what had been done to him by the Lord (Mark 5:19), and did so (v. 20), becoming the first missionary in Mark's Gospel, since the mission of the Twelve is narrated later (6:7–12).

49. Matt 26:26–29; Mark 14:22–25; Luke 22:14–20. "Why are Christians not reminded more often that the Eucharist was born of

a *pilgrimage*? It was born during the Passover pilgrimage to Jerusalem. Remember: Jerusalem was full of pilgrims. And Jesus' enemies feared that crowd....Jesus himself had come up to Jerusalem *as a pilgrim* for the feast of Passover.... In fact, in the Gospel of Luke, Jesus' risky ascent and last pilgrimage to Jerusalem begins much earlier, at the end of chapter 9: Jesus knows that his enemies are lying in wait for him, but 'he resolutely takes the road to Jerusalem' (Luke 9:51). This pilgrim's way therefore runs through the whole Gospel, and the Last Supper is the high point of the journey....Only for that reason—since it was at that supper that the Eucharist was instituted—each Mass we celebrate with the desire to identify with the sentiments of Christ Jesus must be lived with a pilgrim soul" (Francis Bourdeau, "Pilgrimage, Eucharist, Reconciliation," *Lumen Vitae* 39 [1984]: 395–96, quoted in Robinson, *Sacred Places, Pilgrim Paths*, 54).

50. Matt 28:18–20; Mark 16:15; Luke 24:47.

51. Pontifical Council for the Pastoral Care of Migrants and Itinerant People, "The Pilgrimage in the Great Jubilee," §10.

52. See the movement of kenosis highlighted in the ancient hymn of Phil 2:5–11.

53. See the discussion on sacred vs. holy in chap. 1, characteristic 5 (destination).

54. However, in Gal 1:17, Paul mentions that he did not go first to Jerusalem, but to Arabia, to preach, waiting for three years to go to Jerusalem to meet the apostles (Gal 1:18).

55. The first visit of Paul in Jerusalem, in Acts 9:26–29, does narrate only preaching and the visit to the apostles.

56. Matt 24:1; Mark 13:1–2; Luke 21:5–6.

57. Even a place as important as the Holy Sepulcher did not "replace" the Jerusalem temple.

58. For example, Acts 2:46; 3:1; 5:21, 42.

59. Hezser mentions that Egyptian Jews were not coming on a yearly basis to Jerusalem for the festivals, unlike many Palestinian Jews (Hezser, *Jewish Travel in Antiquity*, 376–78). One of the main reasons was an economical one. It also restricted potential Christian pilgrimages to Jerusalem.

60. The Jewish Diaspora similarly had to reinvent its festivals related to the temple after its destruction.

61. The abstention from "things polluted by idols and from fornication and from whatever has been strangled and from blood" (Acts 15:20).

62. Walker, "Pilgrimage in the Early Church," 83.

63. Protestant scholars, in particular, underline the new status of the holy place as being Christ (see Heather Walton, "Theological Perspectives on Christian Pilgrimage," in *Christian Pilgrimage, Landscape and Heritage: Journeying to the Sacred*, by Avril Maddrell, Veronica della Dora, Alessandro Scafi, and Heather Walton [New York: Routledge, 2015], 25, 32).

64. John Paul II, "Letter Concerning Pilgrimage to the Places Linked to the History of Salvation" (June 29, 1999), §3.

65. Matt 27:51; Mark 15:38; Luke 23:45.

66. Walton would also emphasize the incarnation as a primary theological locus for Christian pilgrimage (Walton, "Theological Perspectives on Christian Pilgrimage," 24), giving it a strong New Testament character, as opposed to a genealogical approach recounting the Abraham story. Walker, for his part, argues that the New Testament itself does not follow the line of development from "high doctrine of Incarnation" to "high doctrine of 'holy places'" (Walker, "Pilgrimage in the Early Church," 84). It is right that the New Testament does not realize in itself that line of thought, but this does not preclude the possible use of the doctrine of the incarnation to assess anew the importance of creation or space in faithfulness to the biblical testimony.

67. John Paul II, "Letter Concerning Pilgrimage to the Places Linked to the History of Salvation," §3.

68. Walker, "Pilgrimage in the Early Church," 87.

69. The nonreification of the divine had been a hallmark of Judaism, and in its wake Christianity, since the Decalogue.

70. For example, Acts 9:13; Rom 12:13; 16:15; 1 Cor 6:1–2.

71. John Paul II, "Letter Concerning Pilgrimage to the Places Linked to the History of Salvation," §3.

72. Stephanie Stidham Rogers, *Inventing the Holy Land: American Protestant Pilgrimage to Palestine, 1895–1941* (Lanham, MD: Lexington Books, 2011), 2.

73. "Contemporary Protestants have also adopted a notion of 'thin places' as a communicative metaphor; in a thin place God can

be *seen and heard* more clearly" (Walton, "Theological Perspectives on Christian Pilgrimage," 34–35).

74. On the Church as the *mystical* Body of Christ, see Pius XII, Encyclical Letter on the Mystical Body of Christ *Mystici Corporis Christi* (June 29, 1943).

75. The Eucharist can be celebrated anywhere, but it is most often celebrated in designated worship spaces. The memorial dimension, and the "installed" one, is emphasized in the Roman Catholic tradition of integrating relics of saints into the altar stone of the altar table used for the celebration of the Eucharist, be they fixed or mobile (Catholic Church, *Code of Canon Law* (1983), Canon 1237 §2).

76. The collective holiness is affirmed as one of the ecclesial attributes of the Nicene Creed of 325: The Church is one, holy, catholic, and apostolic.

77. Paul uses the image of the body (of Christ) quite frequently (see e.g., 1 Cor 12:27; Rom 12:5; Eph 4:4). The Second Vatican Council drew on that language in its constitution on the Church (Second Vatican Council, "Dogmatic Constitution on the Church *Lumen Gentium*," §7).

78. Chap. 5 of the Dogmatic constitution on the Church is entitled "The Universal Call to Holiness in the Church" (*Lumen Gentium* 39–42). This call is also echoed in Pope Francis's exhortation *Gaudete et exsultate* whose purpose, affirmed in the full title, is to address "the call to holiness in today's world" (Pope Francis, *Apostolic Exhortation* Gaudete et exsultate *on the Call to Holiness in Today's World* (March 19, 2018).

79. The prayers after communion, in particular, highlight the hoped-for transformation of the participants (Catholic Church, *Roman Missal* [2010]).

80. The connection between Eucharist and social commitment was not lost in the ancient world either. St. John Chrysostom in a homily on the Gospel of Matthew, prioritized the care for the poor over even the adornment of the Church, underlining that the eucharistic participants should not leave aside the care of the body of the poor for the adornment of the eucharistic table (John Chrysostom, "Homily 50," §4, in *A Select Library of the Nicene and Post-Nicene Fathers of the Christian Church*, ed. Philip Schaff, vol. 10: *Homilies on the Gospel of Saint Matthew* [Grand Rapids, MI: Eerdmans, 1956],

313). The concern for the ecological implications of the faith have gained traction in a special way by the publication of the encyclical *Laudato Si'* (2015) by Pope Francis.

81. The "final declaration" of the document "Pilgrimages and Shrines, Gifts of God-Love in Asia Today," from the Second Asian Congress on Pilgrimages and Shrines (Seoul, Korea, November 21–23, 2005), not only emphasizes the encounter with God, but also the necessary care for migrants and promotion of movements supporting life and human dignity.

82. French theologian Christoph Theobald has suggested a reimagination of Christianity as a "style" (see his two-volume *Le Christianisme comme style: Une manière de faire de la théologie en postmodernité* [Paris: Cerf, 2007–8]).

83. There are multiple accounts of the sending of the Twelve (Matt 10:1–42; Mark 6:7–13; Luke 9:1–6), but only in Luke's Gospel do we see a mission of the seventy or seventy-two (the various manuscripts offer competing numbers). See Dennis Hamm, "Luke," in *The Paulist Biblical Commentary*, ed. José Enrique Aguilar Chiu et al. (Mahwah, NJ: Paulist Press, 2018), 1065. The narrative is often thought of as an expansion of the missioning of the Twelve.

84. Later, in Luke 10:30–37, Jesus tells the story of the Good Samaritan, suggesting that he is most likely near Samaria, if not there. Martha's village is identified in John's Gospel as Bethany, in Judea (John 11:1, 18).

85. There was hostility in the Samaritan context (Hamm, "Luke," 1065), which is different from the more welcoming Galilean context evoked earlier in Luke 9 for the mission of the Twelve.

86. Acts 9:2; 18:25–26; 19:9, 23; 22:4; 24:14, 22.

87. Simão Rodrigues, the first Jesuit provincial of Portugal and one of the early companions of St. Ignatius of Loyola, encouraged novices who were on pilgrimage to consider on the road the labors of St. Paul (Simão Rodrigues, "Guidelines for Pilgrims: Coimbra, Portugal 1546," *The Way* 42, no. 1 [2003]: 64). He would also encourage them to make their presence to others as fruitful as that of Philip with the Eunuch—or to go alone!

88. My concern is centered on the "pilgrim style" of mission, which is distinct from the issues of Paul's consideration on pilgrimage to Jerusalem, and the place of its temple. For a discussion on the

latter, see Steve Motyer, "Paul and Pilgrimage," in Bartholomew and Hughes, *Explorations in a Christian Theology of Pilgrimage*, 50–69.

89. Most of Paul's letters were addressed to communities that he established himself, except for letters addressed to individuals or that to the community in Rome.

90. See 2 Tim 4:7; 1 Cor 9:24.

91. The ultimate step for Paul was to claim his authority directly from Christ, as in Gal 1:1, and not because he had been missioned by another church. See Jerome Murphy-O'Connor, *Paul: His Story* (Oxford: Oxford University Press, 2004), 112.

92. Rom 11:13; see Gal 2:7–8; 1 Tim 2:7.

93. Theirs was also a community effort done after Paul had left. In Corinth, according to Murphy-O'Connor, Paul avoided receiving contributions because of their personal nature, and the distortion it would bring by creating a client relationship (Murphy-O'Connor, *Paul: His Story*, 94).

94. Acts 18:2–3; Rom 16:3; 1 Cor 16:19; 2 Tim 4:19.

95. For example, Rom 16:1—15:23; 1 Cor 1:1; 2 Cor 1:1; 1 Thess 1:1; 2 Tim 4:11—12:21.

96. For example, breath (John 20:22), fire (Acts 2:3).

97. For a classic overview of the Spirit in the Scriptures and the history of the Church, see Yves Congar, *I Believe in the Holy Spirit*, vol. 1, *The Holy Spirit in the "Economy"* (New York: Crossroad, 1983).

98. The Creed of Constantinople (381) proclaims the Spirit as the Lord and "Giver of Life." For a life-filled Pneumatology, see Jürgen Moltmann, *The Spirit of Life: A Universal Affirmation* (Minneapolis: Fortress Press, 1992).

99. For an interesting example of the relationship between the Spirit and Christ, here from a christological perspective, see Frank D. Macchia, *The Spirit Baptizer: Christology in Light of Pentecost* (Grand Rapids, MI: Eerdmans, 2018).

100. "The Holy Spirit fell upon (*epipiptō*) all who heard the word" (Acts 10:44). See also Acts 11:15; 19:6.

101. Recognized even a posteriori through the bestowal of baptism (e.g., Acts 10:48).

102. Philip had been sent there at the invitation of the angel of the Lord (Acts 8:26).

103. There are also other instances of divine intervention (through an angel or God, e.g., Acts 5:19; 10:3; 12:7) that are not directly ascribed to the Spirit. Furthermore, other events, like the *dispersion* from Jerusalem (Acts 8:1, 4; 11:19), can appear providential a posteriori, but they are not linked directly to the Holy Spirit.

104. A famous example is that of the medieval Irish monks who had a tradition of internal pilgrimage, and also ventured to England and continental Europe, spreading their distinct take on Christianity. See William R. Cook and Ronald B. Herzman, *The Medieval World View: An Introduction* (New York: Oxford University Press, 2012), 158–63. The *Rule of Benedict* has a provision to receive traveling monks (*The Rule of Saint Benedict* [Collegeville, MN: Liturgical Press, 2001], §61), but the aim, even in their case, is stability. If the monk is good, an invitation would be extended for him to integrate the community. Monks of the monastery who must go on a journey for legitimate purposes are called to keep it to the minimum, atone at their return, and give an account of their travel (*Rule of Saint Benedict*, §67).

105. This is especially clear in the example of the Franciscans who have a special devotion for Lady Poverty. Chapters 4 and 5 of the Franciscan "Later Rule of 1223" deal in particular with poverty. See "Later Rule of 1223 (Regula Bullata)," in *The Writings of Francis of Assisi: Rules, Testament, and Admonitions*, ed. Michael W. Blasstic, OFM, Jay M. Hammond, PhD, J.-A. Wayner Hellmann, OFM Conv, Studies in Early Franciscan Sources (St. Bonaventure, NY: Franciscan Institute Publications, 2001), 2:163–203. For the Latin edition, see "Regula II," *Opuscula Sancti Patris Francisci Assisiensis*, 2nd ed. (Quaracchi, Florence: Collegium S. Bonaventurae, 1941), 63–74.

106. "Later Rule of 1223," Chap. 3.

107. "Later Rule of 1223," Chap. 6.

108. "Later Rule of 1223," Chap. 6.

109. In the sixteenth century, e.g., the Society of Jesus would be inspired by the *vita apostolica*.

110. The interplay of those references will be expounded in chap. 4, as we will discuss the theme of the Pilgrim Church.

111. The main Greek works related, to various degrees, to the notion of pilgrim (in its foreigner-like quality) are numerous: *parepidēmos* (Heb 11:13; 1 Pet 1:1; 2:11), *paroikeō* (Luke 24:18;

Heb 11:9), *paroikia* (Acts 13:17; 1 Pet 1:17); *paroikos* (Acts 7:6, 29; Eph 2:19; 1 Pet 2:11), and *xenos* (Matt 25:35, 38, 43–44; 27:7; Acts 17:18, 21; Rom 16:23; Eph 2:12, 19; Heb 11:13; 13:9; 1 Pet 4:12; 3 John 1:5). Other expressions correlate the idea of the home (*oikia*) or its absence (e.g., 2 Cor 5).

112. Luke 24:18; 2 Cor 5:6, 8; 8:19; Heb 11:13; 13:9; 1 Pet 2:11; 4:12; 3 John 1:5. The Wycliffe Bible even has 16 occurrences, adding to the Vulgate references 1 Pet 1:17 in the epistles (and subtracting Heb 13:9), and Matt 21:33; 25:14; 27:7; Mark 12:1; 13:34; Luke 15:13; 20:9 for the Gospels.

113. Heb 11:13; 1 Pet 2:11. The American Standard Version has the same occurrences.

114. Cognates of *oikos* (house/home) are present in Eph 2:22: *sunoikodomeisthe* (build up) and *katoikētērion* (dwelling).

CHAPTER 3: THE MODERN PILGRIM

1. Ignacio Iparraguirre, SJ, and Manuel Ruiz Jurado, SJ, "Introducción general," in San Ignacio de Loyola, *Obras* (Madrid: Biblioteca de Autores Cristianos, 2014), lxv.

2. The more than 6,800 letters of Ignatius are published in 12 volumes of the *Monumenta Historica Societatis Iesu*. Ignatius's epistolary output is the largest of any sixteenth-century author. See John Padberg, "Introduction," in Ignatius of Loyola, *Letters and Instructions* (St. Louis: Institute of Jesuit Sources, 2006), ix.

3. References to the *Testament*, the narrative about his life that Ignatius confided in a companion in 1553–55, are given in the text in parentheses, introduced by a *T*, using the paragraph number, since there are multiple editions and translations. The edition of reference, in the original Spanish and Italian, has been published under the title "Acta Patris Ignatii de Loyola," in Dionysius Fernandez Zapico, SJ, and Candidus de Dalmases, SJ, eds., *Fontes Narrativi de S. Ignatio de Loyola et de Societatis Iesu Initiis*, vol. 1, *Narrationes Scriptae Ante Annum 1557* (Rome: Monumenta Historica Societatis Iesu, 1943), 364–506 (henceforth referred to as *Fontes Narrativi* I for the whole volume). All translations to English are mine, unless noted otherwise. For all Ignatian texts with multiple editions, reference will be given to the standard paragraph numbering (and

sometimes to the book), and not the page (except for introductions, or footnotes).

4. The vow of obedience was added later when the companions decided to establish a religious order.

5. This vow to go on pilgrimage to Jerusalem was also taken by the companions who aggregated themselves in subsequent years (1535, 1536), as the early companions renewed their commitment. That vow, however, was not carried over into the religious community they established, although the experience of the pilgrimage would be a constitutive one of formation.

6. The medieval and early modern "hospital" was a shelter for the homeless, the sick, the pilgrims, the elderly, unlike our modern-day establishments of health care.

7. Ignatius had to navigate the competing demands of his noble brother, who could not fathom letting him leave his native place by foot. In a stay in his hometown after his studies, Ignatius had refused to reside at the family castle, preferring the local hospital (*T* 87), however, he agreed to ride on horseback out of the province, accompanied by family members (*T* 89–90).

8. The *Constitutions* mention it as the default way of journeying (St. Ignatius of Loyola, *The Constitutions of the Society of Jesus*, trans. with an intro. and a com. by George E. Ganss, SJ (St. Louis: Institute of Jesuit Sources, 1970), §625, cf. also §§609–10). A narrative depiction of the same appears in Ribadeneyra's *Vita*: "Pues viene a propósito, no quiero (aunque de passo) dexar de dezir la manera cómo en aquel tiempo embiava nuestro B. P. a nuestros hermanos a tierras y provincias tan apartadas. Yvan peregrinando a pie, y aunque no todos de un ábito, todos pobremente vestidos. Yvan pidiendo limosna y della vivían. Recogíanse a los hospitales, donde los avía, Quando no hallavan de limosna qué comer o dónde dormir, socorríanse con algún dinerillo que para este fin y para semejante necessidad llevavan guardado. Predicavan en las plaças, según la oportunidad y tiempo que hallaban" (Pedro de Ribadeneyra, *Vita Ignatii Loyolae*, ed. Candidus de Dalmases, SJ, series *Fontes Narrativi de S. Ignatio de Loyola et de Societatis Iesu Initiis*, vol. 4 [Rome: Monumenta Historica Societatis Iesu, 1965], bk. 3, §18; henceforth quoted as *Vita*). The model was on the one hand the journeys of Ignatius and his early companions, but also what was understood of apostolic life, in imitation of the disciples. It exemplified both

the availability of Jesuits for missions, and their freedom regarding money or comfort.

9. See chap. 2 of this book. In the *Chronicon Societatis Iesu*, detailing the early years of the Society of Jesus throughout the world, Juan Alfonso de Polanco documents various instances of missions made in the style of pilgrims and accompanied by preaching, emphasizing the apostolic dimension of the pilgrimage. The original text of the *Chronicon*, in Latin, was published in 6 volumes under the general title *Vita Ignatii Loiolae et Rerum Societatis Iesu Historia* (Madrid: Monumenta Historica Societatis Iesu, 1894–98). A full translation was done in French and is now accessible online, see https://archive.org/details/textesignaciens (assessed June 26, 2019). A partial English translation is also available: Juan Alfonso de Polanco, *Year by Year with the Early Jesuits (1537–1556): Selections from the "Chronicon" of Juan De Polanco, SJ*, ed. John Patrick Donnelly (St. Louis: Institute of Jesuit Sources, 2004).

10. See the "embodiment" category in chap. 1.

11. See my development of the three pilgrimages in Ignatius's narrative of his life: André Brouillette, "Le pèlerinage ignatien: Entre ascèse, identité et mystique," *Nouvelle Revue Théologique* 140 (2018): 91–106.

12. In the Christian tradition, a vocation is a call from God to orient one's life and gifts to edify God's kingdom. Such call needs to be heard and discerned, then confirmed and lived out. In its sixteenth-century understanding, it usually referred to a committed state of life (e.g., marriage, priesthood, religious life). It can also extend to other important commitments or ways to live out a commitment (e.g., a particular way to live one's married or priestly life).

13. This biography was constantly reedited, well into the nineteenth century. See, e.g., a Spanish edition of 1891, by the Brothers Subirana, in Barcelona, or the French biography by Charles Clair, SJ, *La Vie de Saint Ignace de Loyola d'après Pierre Ribadeneira, son premier historien* (Paris: Plon, 1891), largely based on Ribadeneira's *Vita*. The critical edition of the *Vita*, in Latin and Spanish, is that of the Monumenta Historica Societatis Iesu, already mentioned.

14. The first Latin edition dates from 1572, and a Spanish edition, by the same author, was released in 1583. The *Vita* has been edited and translated in different languages for the last four centuries. However, with the rediscovery of Ignatius's own narrative

throughout the twentieth century, it fell out of favor. Nonetheless, a new English translation of the Latin version was realized by Claude Pavur of the Institute of Jesuit Sources in 2014 (Pedro de Ribadeneira, SJ, *The Life of Ignatius of Loyola* [St. Louis: Institute of Jesuit Sources, 2014]).

15. The *Vita* included the material from Ignatius's narrative and expanded it with sections about his style of governance, the early years of the Society of Jesus, or his spiritual and human portrait, up to the miracles he performed. The framework was different, but Ribadeneira did not use the opportunity to remove some embarrassing episodes from Ignatius's life (e.g., his idea of killing a man who had, in his opinion, insulted the Virgin Mary—Ribadeneyra, *Vita*, bk. 1, §15).

16. Jerónimo Nadal's "Praefatio," §2 (*Fontes Narrativi* I, 355–57). There are two ancient prefaces for the *Testament*: one by Luis Gonçalves da Câmara, and the other by Jerónimo Nadal, who was one of the initiators of the project.

17. Nadal, "Praefatio," §§1–2 (*Fontes Narrativi* I, 354–55).

18. One of the early Spanish manuscripts—the original has been lost—is titled *Vida de Nro. P.^{e} Ignatio de Sta memoria, como él la dictó al P.^{e} Luis Glis. de Cámara*, underlying the "dictation" of the text by Ignatius to Câmara (*Fontes Narrativi* I, 333).

19. Luis Gonçalves da Câmara, "Praefatio," §5 (*Fontes Narrativi* I, 363).

20. Nadal, "Praefatio," §4 (*Fontes Narrativi* I, 361).

21. Câmara wrote down his observations of Ignatius and table conversations or little events around him that happened when he was the minister of the house where Ignatius lived, signaling the extreme importance for him of everything related to Ignatius. That text is known as the "Memoriale" (*Fontes Narrativi* I, 527–752).

22. Among the Jesuits who saw the text early stand Jerónimo Nadal, who wrote a preface to the work, and Pedro de Ribadeneira, who was the first official biographer of Ignatius.

23. An earlier letter (June 16, 1547) by Diego Laínez, one of the first companions and the successor of Ignatius as superior general, already relates many of the episodes of Ignatius's life, as he shared them with him, or as Laínez saw them ("Epistola Patris Laynez de P. Ignatio" [Bologna, June 16, 1547], in *Fontes Narrativi* I, 70–145). This letter is in factual agreement with Câmara's text. The

uniqueness of the latter is that it is coming from Ignatius himself, and offers his perspective.

24. See the editors' preface to the *Testament* (*Fontes Narrativi* I, 327).

25. O'Rourke Boyle suggests reading dual voices in the text: the humble voice of Ignatius emphasizing his sinfulness, and the hagiographical voice of Câmara, characterized respectively as "recitation" and "intervention" (Marjorie O'Rourke Boyle's *Loyola's Acts: The Rhetoric of the Self* [Berkeley: University of California Press, 1997], 17). Such hermeneutical hypothesis dichotomizes the text too strongly, but her book offers an erudite study of the *Testament* in the context of the rhetoric of its time.

26. Active measures were taken under the generalate of Francisco Borja to remove copies of the *Testament* from circulation, when Ribadeneira's *Vita* was produced (*Fontes Narrativi* I, 345).

27. *Fontes Narrativi* I, 348–49.

28. A final edition of the original text was realized in 1943, found in *Fontes Narrativi* I, 364–506.

29. *The Testament of Ignatius Loyola: Being "Sundry Acts of Our Father Ignatius, under God, the First Founder of the Society of Jesus Taken Down from the Saint's Own Lips by Luis Gonzales,"* trans. E. M. Rix (London: Sands, 1900), and *The Autobiography of St. Ignatius*, ed. J. F. X. O'Conor (New York: Benzinger Brothers, 1900). See *Fontes Narrativi* I, 349.

30. St. Ignatius of Loyola, *A Pilgrim's Journey: The Autobiography of Ignatius of Loyola*, trans. Joseph N. Tylenda (Wilmington, DE: Michael Glazier, 1985); in French: *Le récit du pèlerin: Autobiographie de S. Ignace de Loyola*, trans. Eugène Thibaut, 2nd ed. (Bruges: Charles Beyaert, 1924); in German: *Der Bericht Des Pilgers*, trans. Burkhart Schneider (Freiburg: Verlag Herder, 1956); in Spanish: *El Relato del Peregrino: Autobiografía de Ignacio de Loyola* (Bilbao: Mensajero, 2011).

31. The title "Autobiografía" (Autobiography) is the standard title (see, e.g., the catalogue of the Bibliothèque nationale de France, at https://catalogue.bnf.fr/ark:/12148/cb16211738d [accessed June 16, 2019]).

32. The authors of these two important monographs on Ignatius's text in English chose that option: O'Rourke Boyle's *Loyola's Acts*, already mentioned, and John M. McManamon's *The Text and*

Contexts of Ignatius' Loyola's "Autobiography" (New York: Fordham University Press, 2013), in which McManamon reads the *Testament* through the lens of the writings of St. Luke (Gospel and Acts of the Apostles).

33. St. Ignatius of Loyola, "Reminiscences," in *Personal Writings*, ed. Joseph A. Munitiz and Philip Endean (London: Penguin, 1997), 13–64. On the contrary, Diego Laínez, one of Ignatius's early companions, wrote proper reminiscences in a letter dated June 16, 1547, in which he aggregates various memories or stories shared by Ignatius over time, witnessed by Laínez, or simply reported to him: "En quanto la memoria nos sirviere, fiel y sencillamente diremos en pocas palabras lo que ocurriere en lo que toca a las cosas de nuestro P.ᵉ M.º Ignacio, refiriendo lo que por edificación nuestra o de otros presentes, a tiempo y lugar le habremos oído decir y de sus palabras colegido. En lo demás que toca a los principios de la Compañía, hablando como testigos, parte de oídas, parte de vista; y en lo uno y en lo otro refiriéndome a la verdad y al buen juicio que esperamos en nuestro Señor le dará, para tomar o dexar, según a gloria de su Magestad y edificación del próximo le parecerá más conveniente" ("Epistola Patris Laynez de P. Ignatio," §1 [*Fontes Narrativi* I, 70]).

34. Ignatius of Loyola, *The Testament of Ignatius Loyola*, trans. E. M. Rix (London: Sands, 1900). This title was also chosen for the 2006 edition by the Institute of Jesuit Sources: Ignatius of Loyola, *A Pilgrim's Testament: The Memoirs of Saint Ignatius of Loyola*, trans. Parmananda R. Divarkar (St. Louis: Institute of Jesuit Sources, 2006).

35. Only parts of those notes, most likely by Ignatius's own volition, came to us. They constitute the *Spiritual Diary* covering the period of February 1544 to February 1545. The Spanish original has been published under the title "Ephemeris S. P. N. Ignatii," in Ignatii de Loyola, *Constitutiones Societatis Jesus*, vol. 1: *Monumenta Constitutionum Praevia* (Rome: Monumenta Historica Societatis Jesu, 1934), 86–158.

36. On the integrity of the text, see the introduction in *Fontes Narrativi* I, 330–31.

37. Câmara, "Praefatio," §2 (*Fontes Narrativi* I, 358–59).

38. The division in 101 paragraphs is standard since the edition by the Bollandists, in 1731, whereas the division of the material

in chapters varies from one edition to the other. I follow the division in 11 chapters found in the edition of the Monumenta Historica Societatis Iesu.

39. This search does not imply that Ignatius had no clue about what God was calling him to do. There is a constant desire to "help souls," a continuum of studies geared toward the priesthood, companions along the way, trials and errors regarding poverty. Ignatius also experienced pushbacks. Only at the end of that period did a spiritual confirmation occur that set firmly Ignatius on a trajectory that would be his for the rest of his life.

40. Ribadeneyra, *Vita*, bk. 1, §1.

41. Ignatius was not alone is using the third person singular for an autobiographical narrative; see, e.g., the *Interior Castle* by Teresa of Avila, or the *Book of Margery Kempe*.

42. Letter to Inès Pascual in 1525, the oldest one we have from Ignatius. This is the only letter in which he signs "*El pobre peregrino, Iñigo*" (St. Ignatius of Loyola, *Epistolae et Instructiones*, vol. 1 [Madrid: Monumenta Historica Societatis Iesu, 1903], 73).

43. Barton T. Geger, SJ, in "Ten Things That St. Ignatius Never Said or Did," *Studies in the Spirituality of Jesuits* 50, no. 1 (2018): 1–44, argues against the "myth" that "St. Ignatius habitually referred to himself as 'the pilgrim'" (27). His argument is convincing for the "habitually" part; there is no evidence that Ignatius called himself constantly "the pilgrim." However, pilgrimage represented an important component of Ignatius's life. His early pilgrimage to Jerusalem takes up most of the first half of the *Testament*, demonstrating how defining a moment this pilgrimage was in his life. He then used pilgrimage as a formation tool for training future Jesuits. Given the circumstances of redaction of the *Testament* exposed earlier and the unique nature of this document, it is most likely that the adoption of the title "pilgrim," which figures so prominently, comes from Ignatius himself (or was authorized by him), and not simply from a redaction choice by Câmara.

44. Francisco José Ruiz Pérez, *Teología del Camino: Une aproximación antropológico-teológica a Ignacio de Loyola* (Bilbao/Santander: Mensajero/Sal Terrae, 2000), 157.

45. The act of "naming," or assuming a new name for a new reality, is important, from the biblical story of Adam naming the animals (Gen 2:19–20), to the religious custom of popes or members

of some religious orders of receiving a new name to reflect their new state of life.

46. Ribadeneyra, *Vita*, bk. 1, §15.

47. In the *Spiritual Exercises*, the important mediations of the "Call of the King," and the "Two Standards" are replete with chivalric images.

48. Diego Laínez, who accompanied Ignatius on the road to Rome, connects clearly, in his recollections, the vision of the Storta with the insistence of Ignatius on the name of Jesus. Since the Father told Jesus to take Ignatius as servant, which he did, Ignatius developed a great devotion to the name of Jesus: "*per questo, pigliando gran devotione a questo santissimo nome, volse nominare la congregatione: la Compagnia di Gesù*" (Diego Laínez, "Lectione Prima" [July 2, 1559], §7, in *Fontes Narrativi de S. Ignatio de Loyola et de Societatis Iesu Initiis*, vol. 2, *Narrationes Scriptae Annis 1557–1574*, ed. Candidus de Dalmases, SJ [Rome: Monumenta Historica Societatis Iesu, 1951], 133, cited as "*Fontes Narrativi* II").

49. In the *Spiritual Diary*, the importance of the daily celebration of the Eucharist by Ignatius is paramount. It occupies the nexus of his discernment and his prayer life, being accompanied frequently by tears (see *Spiritual Diary*, e.g., §1.4.5.6.).

50. The purpose of the *Vita* by Ribadeira was clearly to portray Ignatius in a way fitting a saint (though the main miracle was the creation of the Society of Jesus per se—Ribadeneyra, *Vita*, bk. 5, §203).

51. That situation is now completely reversed, since many recent statues of Ignatius of Loyola, e.g., on the campuses of Georgetown University and St. Louis University, and at the Guelph Retreat Center in Canada, show Ignatius as a pilgrim, whereas traditionally depiction of Ignatius as the founder, the priest, or the writer were more prevalent.

52. Câmara, "Praefatio," §5 (*Fontes Narrativi* I, 363).

53. Nothing is said on early travels; not much on travels for fundraising in Low Countries and England (*T* 76). On the contrary, the pilgrimage to Rouen to visit a sick person (*T* 79), or the many travels in Italy in the decisive months leading to the foundation of the Society are detailed (*T* 93–96).

54. Other expressions also appear, though less frequently, such as *seguir* (about 6 times) or *proseguir* (to follow/to continue).

55. Ruiz Pérez, *Teología del Camino*, 169.

56. On the importance of desire in Ignatian spirituality, see the enlightening article by Michel de Certeau: "L'espace du désir ou le 'fondement' des Exercices spirituels," *Christus* 20, no. 77 (1973): 118–28.

57. These writings have been lost.

58. These options mirror the dichotomy underlined by the ascription of the *res* and the image of pilgrimage according to Protestant and Catholic theologies, between pilgrimage as first and foremost an interior moment (that could be exemplified by the still place of the monastery) or an embodied endeavor (a physical pilgrimage, here to Jerusalem).

59. Diego Laínez, "Lectione Prima" (July 2, 1559), §7 (*Fontes Narrativi* II, 133).

60. The poor man to whom Ignatius gave his clothes was suspected of robbery (*T* 18).

61. Ignatius's ritual echoed the vesting of the habit in religious community, as well as the medieval ritual of the taking of habit of the pilgrims. In the Middle Ages, rituals developed that involved the blessing of the pilgrims' pouch and mantel, and the presentation (Jonathan Sumption, *Pilgrimage—An Image of Medieval Religion* [1975], 172–74, quoted in Martin Robinson, *Sacred Places, Pilgrim Paths: An Anthology of Pilgrimage* [London: HarperCollins, 1997], 56–57).

62. At the beginning of his studies in Barcelona, since he had recovered from the failing health he had in Manresa, he restarted his penances, reaching the point where he would walk without soles on his shoes (*T* 55). Although Ignatius would later indulge in some penances at times, in general, he subsequently adopted a more measured approach.

63. It pertains to the third time of election, in which the retreatant relies on his natural faculties, and not spiritual consolations and desolations (Ignatius of Loyola, *Spiritual Exercises*, §177).

64. A leitmotif that Ignatius had already foreseen in Manresa (*T* 26) would eventually take the central stage: *ayudar a las ánimas/almas* (helping souls). It became clearer around the Jerusalem pilgrimage (*T* 45.50) and would take greater prominence once the studies were completed (*T* 88), and with the creation of the Society of Jesus (*T* 98).

65. Laínez even mentions that Ignatius, uncharacteristically, brought no relics back from his pilgrimage to Jerusalem ("Epistola Patris Laynez de P. Ignatio," §21, in *Fontes Narrativi* I, 90).

66. *T* 96. Ignatius introduces this event by recalling that he decided, despite being already ordained to the priesthood, to wait to celebrate the Eucharist, and had prayed Mary that he might be placed with her son. The vision is presented as a response to his prayer. The importance of the vision is such that he does not even mention his first Mass, celebrated later at the basilica of St. Mary Major, despite the importance of the celebration of the Eucharist in his life.

67. Interestingly enough, Rome was treated only very briefly, and even slighted, in his account of his pilgrimage to Jerusalem (*T* 36.39.40), as it played a merely functional role in the later part of the narrative, prior to that scene.

68. The pages of the Ignatius spiritual diary that reached us (1544–45) pertain to the thorny issue of whether the churches of the Society of Jesus could have endowments (or "benefices"). This is an issue that Ignatius had to wrestle with as he was writing the Constitutions of the new order. Houses of formation could have an endowment, whereas communities of formed Jesuits could not. The issue was to determine where would churches fall in that regard.

69. *T* 73; cf. also *T* 35.

70. Especially upon his return to his native land (*T* 89). On the way to Jerusalem, he disposed of his donkey at the Abbey of Montserrat (*T* 17).

71. See the final rules on poverty in the *Constitutions* (pt. 6, chap. 2, §§553–81).

72. Ignatius once passed for a fool because of his frankness... and it finally helped him to move beyond warring armies (*T* 51–53).

73. *T* 38. Ignatius fended off the aggressors and escaped with the threatened pilgrims.

74. *T* 13; cf. also *T* 73, for his departure for Paris.

75. Contrary to what was expected of pilgrims to Jerusalem (O'Rourke Boyle, *Loyola's Acts*, 153).

76. The Parisian group renewed their vows at Montmartre on August 15, 1535 and 1536, under the leadership of Peter Faber, as Ignatius was away, adding new members each time (Ribadeneyra, *Vita*, bk. 2, §§20–21).

77. A similar enlargement of horizon was witnessed in chap. 2 of this book.

78. The *Legenda aurea*, by Jacobus de Voragine, originated in the thirteenth century as a compilation of saints' lives. It was extremely popular in the late medieval and early modern period. The book had been translated from the original Latin into various European languages, including Spanish. Hence, it is not surprising that it was one of the two books found in the Loyola family castle during Ignatius's convalescence.

79. On the potential impact of the stay in Montserrat on Ignatius, see Javier Melloni Ribas, SJ, "Las influencias cisnerianas de los Ejercicios," in *Las fuentes de los Ejercicios espirituales de San Ignacio: Actas del Simposio Internacional (Loyola, 15–19 septiembre 1997)*, ed. Juan Plazaola (Bilbao: Mensajero, 1998), 353–77.

80. *T* 21.22.34.37 (at which point Ignatius mentioned that he lost his eagerness to look for spiritual people).

81. The first mention of the *peregrino* comes in the subsequent paragraph, as Ignatius realized that he had to move forward.

82. Consolation and desolation constitute the two basic elements of the spiritual grammar of Ignatius. He uses *consolation* to describe when "any interior movement is produced in the soul that leads her to become inflamed with the love of her Creator and Lord, and when, as a consequence, there is no created thing on the face of the earth that we can love in itself, but we love it only in the Creator of all things. Similarly, I use the word 'consolation' when one sheds tears that lead to love of one's Lord, whether these arise from grief over one's sins, or over the Passion of Christ Our Lord, or over other things expressly directed towards His service and praise. Lastly, I give the name 'consolation' to every increase of hope, faith and charity, to all interior happiness that calls and attracts a person towards heavenly things and to the soul's salvation, leaving the soul quiet and at peace in her Creator and Lord" (Ignatius of Loyola, *Spiritual Exercises*, §316). *Desolation*, for its part, designates "everything contrary to what is in Rule 3, e.g., darkness and disturbance in the soul, attraction towards what is low and of the earth, anxiety arising from various agitations and temptations. All this tends to a lack of confidence in which the soul is without hope and without love; one finds oneself thoroughly lazy, lukewarm, sad, and as though cut off from one's Creator and Lord. For just as consolation

is contrary to desolation, so the thoughts born of consolation are contrary to the thoughts born of desolation" (Ignatius of Loyola, *Spiritual Exercises* [Munitiz/Endean edition], §317).

83. On the centrality of the election for Ignatian spirituality, see Javier Melloni, *The Spiritual Exercises of Saint Ignatius Loyola in the Western Tradition* (Leominster: Gracewing, 2000), 50.

84. *T* 60–62 (Alcalá); 64–70 (Salamanca); 81.86 (Paris).

85. This would continue. Ignatius would often ask to receive the judgement in writing. He later sought approval for the *Spiritual Exercises* from the Holy See when he reached Rome.

86. The final paragraphs (*T* 99–101) also show such suspension from the regular narrative, which ended when Ignatius said that Nadal could tell the rest of the story (*T* 98). It shows final questions by Câmara, and final comments by Ignatius.

87. For example, Ignatius uses that device to share that by an encounter (*visitación*) with the Virgin Mary carrying the baby Jesus, he gained such disgust for the "things of the flesh" (*cosas de la carne*) of his past life that he never assented to them again, up to the present (*T* 10). In another instance, he mentions that the vision that occurred in Manresa had a lasting impact in his life in terms of the spiritual knowledge imparted (*T* 30).

88. For a further discussion, see Barton T. Geger, SJ, "The 'First' First Companions: The Continuing Impact of the Men Who Left Ignatius," *Studies in the Spirituality of Jesuits* 44, no. 2 (2012). In the *Vita*, Ribadeneira does not pursue these digressions about the early companions, simply mentioning that they did not regroup with Ignatius in Paris as planned (Ribadeneyra, *Vita*, bk. 2, §18). Their fate is not mentioned.

89. In the *Spiritual Exercises*, Ignatius suggests using the perspective of one's (hypothetical) last breath to look back at a given decision (to be made in the present) and ponder what choice would have been better to make (Ignatius of Loyola, *Spiritual Exercises*, §186).

90. San Ignacio de Loyola, *Obras* (Madrid: Biblioteca de Autores Cristianos, 2014), 47n18.

91. Especially through the movement of the Spirit of God—and that of the devil—at Loyola (*T* 8). On the difficulty of speaking too explicitly about the Spirit in sixteenth-century Spain, with fears of *alumbradismo*, see José María Lera Monreal, SJ, *La pneumatología*

de los Ejercicios espirituales: Una teología de la crux traducida a la vida (Madrid: Universidad Pontificia Comillas, 2016), 136–48.

92. As Ignatius settled some debts owed to him on his way to Montserrat, he paid for the restoration of an image of the Virgin (*T* 13).

93. Ignatius had previously discovered those movements in himself (*T* 8).

94. Even though he feared such apparition when a spiritual woman he met wished him that Christ appear to him (*T* 21).

95. A few lines later, Ignatius explains that he had seen Our Lady in a similar fashion, without distinguishing body parts.

96. At the beginning of his studies in Barcelona, he also realized that not every spiritual thought is inspired by God, especially when it is detrimental to his mission, which was then to study (*T* 54).

97. For example, one must distinguish the consolation itself and its aftermath (Ignatius of Loyola, *Spiritual Exercises*, §336). There are also consolations whose origin is not God (*Spiritual Exercises*, §331).

98. This confirmation of Ignatius's vocation by the vision can be likened to a first-time election, in which the exercitant can have no doubt (*sin dubitar ni poder dubitar*) about God's will (*Spiritual Exercises*, §175). Here also, Ignatius indicates that there could be no doubt (*dubitare*) on his part (*T* 96).

99. Personal glimpses of the mystical journey of Ignatius can be found in his (fragmentary) *Spiritual Diary*.

100. Ignatius's narrative choice can be compared to the scope of the Spiritual Exercises. While they set the retreatant on a journey of discovery and confirmation of his/her vocation, centered on the election, they end with a final contemplation to attain love, but do not offer a roadmap for future spiritual development. Similarly, in the Jesuit *Constitutions*, Ignatius does not mandate any spiritual practice for formed Jesuits (Ignatius of Loyola, *Constitutions*, §582). In that regard, the pedagogy of spiritual development is different from that of St. Teresa of Avila or St. Marie de l'Incarnation, who shared eloquently their own spiritual summits as ways to help fellow spiritual travelers. Ignatius only mentions the final place of the last leg of his journey, without developing it.

101. "Determinationes Societatis" (1539), §9, in Sancti Ignatii de Loyola, *Constitutiones Societatis Jesus*, vol. 1, 12. In Jesuit parlance, an "experiment" is an activity prescribed to a novice over a period of time and aimed at testing him and honing certain skills. As a formation program, the experiments were specifically meant to shape the religious life of young Jesuits; however, given the renewed understanding of the universal call to holiness in the wake of the Second Vatican Council, they can also be adapted for broader use, e.g., in Ignatian educational institutions. It is already the case with the Spiritual Exercises and ministry to the poor, but less frequently with pilgrimage.

102. Ignatius of Loyola, *Constitutions*, §§65–70.

103. Câmara, "Memoriale," §137 (*Fontes Narrativi* I, 610).

104. Ignatius of Loyola, *Constitutions*, §67.

105. We find here an echo of the invitation to "indifference," or radical inner freedom, found in the text of the Principle and Foundation, at the beginning of the *Spiritual Exercises*, in which the retreatant is invited to look at all created things through the lens of their congruence with God's will (Ignatius of Loyola, *Spiritual Exercises*, §23).

106. Câmara, "Memoriale," §137 (*Fontes Narrativi* I, 610).

107. For a recent study integrating contemporary elements to the reflection on the practice of the noviciate pilgrimage (in this case Indonesia), see Leo Agung Sardi, *La prueba de la peregrinación en el noviciado de la Compañía de Jesús: Su actualidad para la formación en Indonesia* (PhD diss., Madrid: Universidad Pontificia Comillas, 2015).

108. Most of the instances where Ignatius uses pilgrimages and for which the context is clear can be found in the *Memoriale* by Câmara. In other instances, it is known that Ignatius sent or encouraged people to go on pilgrimage, but without being given reasons. There is also evidence of Ignatius's own devotional pilgrimages in Rome, e.g., at Santa Maria Maggiore, where he celebrated his first Mass.

109. Câmara, "Memoriale," §§336–38 (*Fontes Narrativi* I, 717–18). Loreto, the usual destination of Italian pilgrimages ordered by Ignatius, is a late medieval Marian sanctuary that claims to have the "Holy House" (*Santa Casa*) of the family of Jesus in Nazareth, transported by angels from Palestine to Italy.

110. Ignatius also undertook himself a similar journey while he was a student in Paris. Hearing that a compatriot was sick in Rouen, he undertook traveling there as in a pilgrimage, without eating, to secure the healing of his friend (*T* 79).

111. Câmara, "Memoriale," §403 (*Fontes Narrativi* I, 738); see nn. 10 and 11 (about Francisco Ferrares and Thomaso), who might have talked about things heard in confession and were sent on a three-month pilgrimage. Ignatius wrote to the superiors of the houses of Perugia, Éverard Mercurian, and Loreto, Olivier Manare, where the two young Jesuits were sent (Sancti Ignatii de Loyola, *Epistolae et Instructiones*, vol. 9 [Madrid: Monumenta Historica Societatis Iesu, 1909], 30 [Letter 5360, May 2, 1555], and 49 [Letter 5374, May 18, 1555]). See also the story of the brother who was required to accomplish a 400-league pilgrimage to atone (Câmara, "Memoriale," §58 [*Fontes Narrativi* I, 563]).

112. This episode of February 16, 1555, can be found in Câmara, "Memoriale," §§127–29 (*Fontes Narrativi* I, 603–5).

113. Câmara, "Memoriale," §128 (*Fontes Narrativi* I, 604).

114. Câmara, "Memoriale," §128 (*Fontes Narrativi* I, 604–5).

115. A certain Lazaro was also given permission by Ignatius to undertake a pilgrimage for his spiritual benefit, first to Loreto (Câmara, "Memoriale," §371 (*Fontes Narrativi* I, 729). His final fate is unknown.

116. Câmara, "Memoriale," §61 (*Fontes Narrativi* I, 566).

117. Câmara, "Memoriale," §61 (*Fontes Narrativi* I, 566). For other examples, see §235 (*Fontes Narrativi* I, 664).

CHAPTER 4: THE PILGRIM CHURCH

1. Dee Dyas, "Medieval Patterns of Pilgrimage: A Mirror for Today?" in *Explorations in a Christian Theology of Pilgrimage*, ed. Craig Bartholomew and Fred Hughes (Hants: Ashgate, 2004), 102.

2. The Second Vatican Council renewed this self-definition of the Church by drawing on the stock of biblical and patristic images, e.g., "people of God" (Dogmatic Constitution on the Church *Lumen Gentium* [November 21, 1964], §13; hereafter, *LG*), and "Body of Christ" (*LG* 7), already highlighted by Pius XII who had issued an encyclical on the Mystical Body of Christ (June 29, 1943).

3. In the title of chap. 7 of *Lumen Gentium*. The standard translation is "Pilgrim Church." Grammatically, the Latin present participle (*peregrinans*), closely based on the verb (*peregrinor*), underlines the continuous action deployed. For the documents produced by the Holy See, the translations, when available, and original texts used are those provided on the website of the Vatican (http://www.vatican.va/content/vatican/en.html).

4. Other important liturgical innovations were introduced in different parts of the world in the wake of the Council, e.g., the Zairian rite, but only one Eucharistic Prayer with local origins came to be adopted worldwide.

5. *LG* 8 references St. Augustine, *De civ. Dei*, XVIII, 51, 2. Regarding the theme of pilgrimage, the Second Vatican Council often refers to biblical texts as inspiration, but Augustine is the only theologian called to the fore.

6. The twenty-two books that comprise the *City of God* were not written at once. The earliest date of composition given for the first books is 412, while the latest date given for the completion of the whole project is 426/7. The date of writing of the latest books is particularly subject to divergence of assessments among scholars.

7. Augustine, *City of God*, Book 1, preface. The emphasis is mine. I will quote the *City of God* as: *CG* book:chapter. The Latin text can be found in Migne's *Patrologia Latina* 41:13–804. A common English translation is that of Marcus Dods in St. Augustine, *City of God and Christian Doctrine*, A Select Library of the Nicene and Post-Nicene Fathers of the Christian Church, ed. Philip Schaff, vol. 2 (New York: Charles Scribner's Sons, 1899).

8. The notion of *peregrinatio* itself, but also its cognates (*peregrinus, peregrinor*).

9. M. A. Claussen, "'Peregrinatio' and 'Peregrini' in Augustine's 'City of God,'" *Traditio* 46 (1991): 43. Claussen addresses in this article the complex reality of *peregrinatio, peregrinor, peregrinus* in Augustine's works—the *City of God* in particular, but also other works.

10. Sarah Stewart-Kroeker, *Pilgrimage as Moral and Aesthetic Formation in Augustine's Thought* (Oxford: Oxford University Press, 2017), 1, 5. Claussen nonetheless warns that the *peregrinatio* of the *City of God* is a collective enterprise (Claussen, "Peregrinatio," 43).

11. Claussen, "Peregrinatio," 33. This is out of 800 references in the whole Augustinian corpus (Claussen, "Peregrinatio," 62). English translations mask that prevalence because of the absence of a verbal cognate of *pilgrim* to translate *peregrinor*. Only the substantive *pilgrim* remains, while the verbs *journey* or *sojourn* translate the Latin *peregrinor*.

12. Claussen, "Peregrinatio," 66.

13. Christian pilgrimages to the Holy Land had started in earnest in the early fourth century.

14. Claussen, "Peregrinatio," 42. Claussen would later acknowledge the potential (limited) influence of the practice of pilgrimage on Augustine's thought (Claussen, "Peregrinatio," 73).

15. Claussen, "Peregrinatio," 42.

16. Augustine qualifies the *peregrinatio* as "miserable" (*aerumnosa*; *CG* 17:13). See also, e.g., *CG* 1:35.

17. Claussen, "Peregrinatio," 63. Referring to various passages in the Augustinian corpus, Claussen notices characteristics associated with *peregrinatio*: "It is filled with labors and burdens, it is uncertain and long, it is hunger and thirst, sedition and temptation, a desert, filled with sighing, weeping, wailing, and tribulations," though some of the most punitive edges are softened in the *City of God*, compared to other writings, according to Claussen. See also Stewart-Kroeker, *Pilgrimage*, 4.

18. See Stewart-Kroeker, *Pilgrimage*, 1. Without responding to those criticisms, her study of Augustine softens that concern by underlying the ethical dimension of Augustine's use of *peregrinatio*.

19. *CG* 19:17.

20. See, e.g., *CG* 1:pref.; 5:16; 19:17.

21. For example, peace (*CG* 19:17), divine consolation (*CG* 18:51), hope (*CG* 15:18), joy (*CG* 14:9).

22. Claussen, "Peregrinatio," 43.

23. A question remains as to the extension of the *peregrini*; who is excluded? Do all reach the destination? (Claussen, "Peregrinatio," 74). It seems that not everybody in the Church would make it to the eternal city (*CG* 1:35).

24. Claussen, "Peregrinatio," 74.

25. The struggle to harmonize the biblical material around pilgrimage will also play out in the texts of the Second Vatican Council, as we will later see.

26. Claussen, "Peregrinatio," 44. See, e.g., *CG* 11:28; 15:1.

27. Claussen, "Peregrinatio," 71–73.

28. Hence the reluctance of some Augustinian scholars to even translate *peregrinatio* by *pilgrimage* (Stewart-Kroeker, *Pilgrimage,* 11). However, we have already seen in chap. 1 how multifaceted the concept of pilgrimage is.

29. "The political and civil rights of the *peregrinus* were restricted. He could enter into only certain kinds of contracts, his testatory and marriage rights were limited, he could not sue for personal damages. In the same way, he could never have *dominium,* or use civil processes of acquisition and transfer" (Claussen, "Peregrinatio," 36).

30. Claussen, "Peregrinatio," 43.

31. Augustine uses the adjective, whereas the Second Vatican Council settles for the present participle.

32. An image of the Christian journey to God (Stewart-Kroeker, *Pilgrimage,* 14).

33. Claussen, "Peregrinatio," 44.

34. Stewart-Kroeker, *Pilgrimage,* 2. The project of her book is to unravel that process.

35. Claussen, "Peregrinatio," 49–50.

36. Claussen, "Peregrinatio," 46.

37. Stewart-Kroeker, *Pilgrimage,* 16.

38. Claussen, "Peregrinatio," 51, 57–58.

39. *CG* 18:1–2.

40. *Peregrinantem in hoc mundo ciuitatem Dei* ("the city of God that sojourns in this world"; *CG* 18:51).

41. Translated in *LG* 8 as, "The Church, 'like a stranger in a foreign land, presses forward amid the persecutions of the world and the consolations of God,'" while a more regular English translation renders pilgrimage in a substantive form: "the Church has gone forward on pilgrimage amid the persecutions of the world and the consolations of God" (St. Augustine, *City of God and Christian Doctrine,* trans. Marcus Dods, 392).

42. *CG* 18:51.

43. Claussen, "Peregrinatio," 74n210.

44. See Yves Congar, "Moving Toward a Pilgrim Church" for an analysis of preference of the language of a "new People of God" and a "Pilgrim Church" over the more juridical language—favored

in the nineteenth and early twentieth centuries—of the Church as *societas* (*perfecta, inaequalis, hierarchica*), in *Vatican II Revisited by Those Who Were There*, ed. Alberic Stacpoole (Minneapolis, MN: Winston Press, 1986), 129–52.

45. See, e.g., George H. Tavard, *The Pilgrim Church* (New York: Herder and Herder, 1967) written in the aftermath of the Council.

46. Second Vatican Council, Pastoral Constitution on the Church in the Modern World *Gaudium et Spes* (1965), §1 (henceforth: *GS*).

47. "Sacred theology rests on the written word of God, together with sacred tradition, as its primary and perpetual foundation" (Second Vatican Council, *Dogmatic Constitution on Divine Revelation* Dei Verbum [November 18, 1965], §24).

48. See, e.g., *LG* 9 for the Old Testament references to the wandering people. As mentioned earlier, most references are made to the epistles regarding pilgrimage.

49. The conciliar fathers mention pilgrimages to Lourdes, Rome, etc.—see, e.g., *Acta Synodalia Sacrosancti Concilii Oecumenici Vaticani Secundi, Vol. I: Periodus prima* (Rome: Typis Polyglottis Vaticanis, 1970), 317, 322, 474, 518, 650, in the context of the discussion of the language for liturgy.

50. See the first footnote in *LG* 50.

51. Congar, "Moving Toward," 130–35. See also Richard R. Gaillardetz, *The Church in the Making:* Lumen Gentium, Christus Dominus, Orientalium Ecclesiarum (Mahwah, NJ: Paulist Press, 2006), 100.

52. See Pius XII, Encyclical *Mystici corporis Christi* (June 29, 1943), http://www.vatican.va/content/pius-xii/en/encyclicals/documents/hf_p-xii_enc_29061943_mystici-corporis-christi.html.

53. See, e.g., the *Catechism of the Council of Trent*, Part 1: Exposition of the Creed, Article IX (*Catechismus ex Decreto Concilii Tridentini ad Parochos* (Rome: Congregatio de Propaganda Fide, 1871), 87).

54. Pope John XXIII, Address on the Occasion of the Solemn Opening of the Most Holy Council *Gaudet Mater Ecclesia* (October 11, 1962). See https://w2.vatican.va/content/john-xxiii/la/speeches/1962/documents/hf_j-xxiii_spe_19621011_opening-council.html for the Latin original.

55. John XXIII, *Gaudet Mater Ecclesia*, §5.

56. For example, the official Spanish translation (also on the Vatican website) renders affirmatively *peregrinos sobre esta tierra* (pilgrims on this earth), https://w2.vatican.va/content/john-xxiii/es/speeches/1962/documents/hf_j-xxiii_spe_19621011_opening-council.html.

57. John XXIII, *Gaudet Mater Ecclesia*, §4.

58. John XXIII, *Gaudet Mater Ecclesia*, §5.

59. Some dictionaries contain *pilgrimage* as a verb (to designate going on a pilgrimage—e.g., *Merriam Webster Unabridged*, https://unabridged.merriam-webster.com/unabridged/pilgrimage), but it is not broadly used, and could lead to a restrictive understanding of the underlying Latin *peregrinor*.

60. For example, in *Lumen Gentium*, out of the fourteen Latin references to pilgrimage (through cognates), only six are translated as *pilgrim/pilgrimage*.

61. In *LG* 49–50, there are three references to *viator* (traveler). For an overarching reading of the theology of the Second Vatican Council through the lens of pilgrimage, see Jeffrey G. Sobosan, "Pilgrimage Theology in the Documents of Vatican II," ThD thesis (Berkeley: Graduate Theological Union, 1977). My focus is on the explicit recourse to pilgrimage vocabulary and its immediate context.

62. Second Vatican Council, Constitution on the Sacred Liturgy *Sacrosanctum Concilium* (December 4, 1963), §2 (henceforth: *SC*).

63. *SC* 8.

64. *Oxford Latin Dictionary* (London: Oxford University Press, 1968), 1335.

65. The proximity with Christ is underlined by the triple repetition in the sentence of the Latin prefix "con-/com-" (*consociamur, compatientes, conglorificemur*), reminiscent of the Pauline *syn* (with), called forth by the explicit reference to Rom 8:17.

66. The glory to be shared with Christ is located in the future (i.e., *ut cum Eo conglorificemur*).

67. The official English translation emphasizes again "alienation" by rendering *ecclesia peregrinando* as "The Church, like a stranger in a foreign land."

68. Quoting Augustine, *The City of God*, XVIII, 51, 2 (*Patrologia Latina* 41:614). In that passage, Augustine talks about the long-term

journey of the Church of God from the time of Abel to the end of the world.

69. Biblical resources are alluded to at this point of *LG* but are not explored in depth.

70. *Peregrinans* is a present participle, the literal translation of which is "pilgrimaging," and not a substantive or an adjective, which would be *peregrinus*, "pilgrim." It is a verbal form of *peregrinor*, whereas *coelestis*, used to qualify the Church of heaven (*Ecclesia coelestis*), is an adjective.

71. See Otto Semmelroth, "Dogmatic Constitution on the Church: Chapter VII," in *Commentary on the Documents of Vatican II*, ed. Herbert Vorgrimler (New York: Herder and Herder, 1967), 1:280. Umberto Betti states that this addition on the relationship between the Church in heaven and the Pilgrim Church was asked at the second session of the Council, but that the idea had already been voiced by Pope John XXIII in February 1961, before being endorsed by Pope Paul VI in 1963 (Umberto Betti, "Histoire chronologique de la constitution," in *L'Église de Vatican II : Études autour de la Constitution conciliaire sur l'Église*, ed. Guilherme Baraúna [Paris: Cerf, 1967], 2:72, 76–77).

72. A three-part distinction is sometimes used, adding the "suffering" Church (in purgatory) as the second term. *LG* 49 can lend itself to such reading when it lists, "some [*alii*] of His disciples are exiles on earth, some [*alii*] having died are purified, and others [*alii*] are in glory beholding 'clearly God Himself triune and one, as He is' (Conc. Florentinum, Decretum pro Graecis: Denz. 693 (1305)." However, in the title and a few lines later, the distinction is bipartite, between "the wayfarers" and "the brethren who have gone to sleep in the peace of Christ" (*LG* 49).

73. *Oxford Latin Dictionary*, 1109; 1979.

74. Semmelroth, e.g., does not highlight the importance of the change in language, simply using the equivalent trilogy of militant, suffering, and triumphant (Semmelroth, "Chapter VII," 280–84). On the contrary, years later, Dennis Doyle highlighted the dramatic significance of the change from militant to pilgrim (Dennis M. Doyle, *The Church Emerging from Vatican II* [Mystic, CT: Twenty-Third Publications, 1992], 192–93).

75. The official Vatican translation renders *Ecclesia viatorum* as "Pilgrim Church" (*LG* 50), whereas *viatorum*, used independently, is translated as "wayfarers" (*LG* 49, 50).

76. It is translated in that section as "exiles," in keeping with the earlier mention (*LG* 48) of the "exile from the Lord" (*peregrinamur a Domino*) from 2 Cor 5:6.

77. A more explicit trinitarian development will be seen in *Gaudium et Spes*.

78. Rom 8:23, cited in *LG* 48.

79. This theme is further developed in the epilogue.

80. The connection between Mary and pilgrimage would be further developed in subsequent pontifical documents. See, e.g., John Paul II, "Bull of induction of the Great Jubilee of the Year 2000 *Incarnationis Mysterium*" (November 29, 1998), §14, https://w2.vatican.va/content/john-paul-ii/en/jubilee/documents/hf_jp-ii_doc_19981129_bolla-incarnationis-mysterium.html.

81. I correct here the online Vatican translation, which renders (inexplicably) the Latin *angustiis* by "cultics," instead of "difficulties."

82. The English translation emphasizes the distinction between the two places by specifying the "on earth" of the current journey as opposed to the ultimate place (*patria*, "homeland") that is happy.

83. Title of part 5 of chap. 8 of *LG*. This line is taken from *LG* 68. As an expression, it combines two important images used for the Church in *LG*, namely, people of God and Pilgrim Church.

84. Dogmatic Constitution on Divine Revelation *Dei Verbum* (November 18, 1965), quoted as *DV*.

85. Pastoral Constitution on the Church in the Modern World *Gaudium et Spes* (December 7, 1965), quoted as *GS*.

86. *DV* 7, referring to 1 John 3:2.

87. The original translation states "men" (*hominum*) to imply all human beings. I replaced "men" with "people," "man" with "person," and "mankind" with "humankind."

88. *GS* 45, with two occurrences.

89. *GS* 45, quoting Eph 1:10 for the last part.

90. *Peregrinitas* means "foreignness," or the "alien status" (*Oxford Latin Dictionary*, 1335). I use it here in a different understanding, as

the overarching concept pertaining to the pilgrim nature or character of the Church.

91. "Eucharistic Prayer III," *The Roman Missal*, English translation according to the Third Typical Edition (Totowa, NJ: Catholic Book Publishing Corp., 2011), 502–7.

92. On the history of the postconciliar developments of Eucharistic Prayers, see Walter von Arx, "Das Hochgebet die Kirche in der Schweiz: ein liturgiegeschichtliches Ereignis," *Zeitschrift für schweizerische Kirchengeschichte* 71 (1977): 279–80.

93. Sacred Congregation for Divine Worship, *Eucharistiae participationem* (April 27, 1973). See Vincenzo Raffa, *Liturgia Eucaristica: Mistagogia della Messa: dalla storia e dalla teologica alla pastorale pratica* (Rome: Edizioni Liturgiche, 2003), 782.

94. Raffa, *Liturgia Eucaristica*, 783. On the progressive geographical and linguistic reach of the prayer, see Corrado Maggioni, "Coordinate spazio-temporali della Preghiera Eucaristica 'Synode '72,'" *Notitiae* 301, no. 27 (1991): 464–71.

95. On the history of this Eucharistic Prayer's text, see Richard E. McCarron, "History of the Text," in *A Commentary on the Order of Mass of* The Roman Missal, ed. Edward Foley, John F. Baldovin, Mary Collins, and Joanne M. Pierce (Collegeville, MN: Liturgical Press, 2011): 549–56.

96. "Vielmehr muß das Hochgebet als Ganzes in der Sprache unserer Zeit verfaßt sein" (Arx, "Das Hochgebet," 285). Arx is summarizing the argument of the letter, not quoting it verbatim.

97. "Tutte le parti variabili si ispirano, in maniera più o meno palese, all'idea del pellegrinaggio" (Raffa, *Liturgia Eucaristica*, 793).

98. Raffa attributes mostly to the local circumstances of the Synod the choice of the pilgrimage theme (Raffa, *Liturgia Eucaristica*, 793). However, as shown by the subsequent requests from other episcopal conferences, this theme resonated much more broadly than only for a national Church event.

99. Anton Hänggi, "Das Hochgebet "Synode '72" für die Kirche in der Schweiz," *Notitiae* 301, no. 27 (1991): 452.

100. The German and French versions were approved together on August 8, 1974, and the Italian version on November 14 of the same year. The Latin *editio typica* was prepared in the aftermath of the success of the prayers and approved in 1991 to be used as the basis for further translations (Raffa, *Liturgia Eucaristica*, 783–84).

101. For the text of the 1991 Latin version, see Congregatio de Cultu Divino et Disciplina Sacramentorum, "Acta," *Notitiae* 301, no. 27 (1991): 391–99. The title of the prayer, which was previously in flux, was also normalized as *Prex Eucharistica quae in Missis pro variis necessitatibus adhiberi potest*, whereas it had previously been known under various titles, even for a single language.

102. Pere Tena, "Commentarium," *Notitiae* 301, no. 27 (1991): 419.

103. Regarding the changes to the prayer, Paul de Clerk applauds them in general for the French version, though he regrets the disappearance of a reference to the "way" (*chemin*) in the petition to accept the offerings, since it provided a nice reminder of the Emmaus story (Paul de Clerck, "La révision de la prière eucharistique suisse," *La Maison-Dieu* 191 [1992]: 68).

104. For an excellent synoptic presentation of the Latin text with the three original versions in German, French, and Italian prior to their harmonization with the Latin, see Congregatio de Cultu Divino et Disciplina Sacramentorum, "Acta," *Notitiae* 301, no. 27 (1991): 400–415.

105. The English translation of the prayer mentions "the disciples" for which Jesus opened the Scriptures and broke the bread, in a wording similar to the French version. However, the Italian version and the German version (in parenthesis) indicate explicitly that the prayer refers to the *Emmaus* disciples (Luke 24:13–35).

106. The first paragraph is different is each of the four variants of this Eucharistic Prayer. The following two paragraphs are common to all four versions.

107. "Eucharistic Prayer for Various Needs," *The Roman Missal*, 624–47. The emphasis is mine.

108. "Hochgebete für Messen für besondere Anliegen" (1974/1994).

109. "Prière eucharistique pour des circonstances particulières" (1974/1996).

110. "Preghiera Eucaristica V" (1974/?).

111. "Prex Eucharistica quae in Missis pro variis necessitatibus adhiberi potest" (1991).

112. The Latin version having come later, the analysis focuses on the three original versions, although in their harmonized forms.

113. The concept of God's dwelling place signals a location (e.g., in heaven), whereas that of the kingdom (of God) is more dynamic, as exemplified in the preaching of Jesus (see Matt 4:17). *Basileia* (kingdom) appears close to a hundred times in the Gospels.

114. Preface I: "The Church on the Path of Unity" (*Ecclesia in viam unitatis progrediens*), III: "Jesus, the Way to the Father" (*Iesus via ad Patrem*), and IV: "Jesus, Who Went About Doing Good" (*Iesus pertransiens benefaciendo*). The 1974 original titles did not display the same emphasis.

115. "Preface II: God Guides His Church along the Way of Salvation," in the "Eucharistic Prayer for Various Needs," *The Roman Missal*, 630–31.

116. There is no usual adjective in French for *pilgrim*, although *pèlerin/pèlerine* is sometimes used, which explains the expression: "[ton Église] dans sa marche" ([Your Church] in her journey).

117. Other allusions to pilgrimage or journey in the liturgical norms can be found, for example, in the funeral liturgies, from an individual perspective. See National Conference of Catholic Bishops, *Order of Christian Funerals*, Study Guide Edition (Chicago: Liturgy Training Publications, 1990), 11 (§43), 76 (§148), 161.

118. Catholic Church, *Code of Canon Law* (1983), can. 400.

119. Popes had traveled internationally before, but often under duress (e.g., Popes Pius VI and Pius VII were forcibly brought to France in the late eighteenth and early nineteenth centuries). Paul VI was the first modern pope to travel to a different continent.

120. Many examples of important papal gestures—beyond any magisterial statements—come to mind, such as Pope Francis washing the feet of prisoners during the Holy Thursday liturgy, Benedict XVI visiting a mosque in Istanbul, and Pope John Paul II praying at the Western Wall in Jerusalem.

121. Loreto is a pilgrimage site, mentioned in our previous chapter, whose main relic is the house of the Holy Family purportedly transported miraculously from Nazareth to Italy in the Middle Ages.

122. Pope John XXIII, "Discorso presso il Santuario di Loreto" (October 4, 1962), http://www.vatican.va/content/john-xxiii/it/speeches/1962/documents/hf_j-xxiii_spe_19621004_santuario-loreto.html. Note: for texts available only in a language other than English, all translations are mine.

123. "Di fatto siamo tutti pellegrini sulla terra, con una effusione di preghiera sulle labbra, che, pur nelle sue molteplici espressioni, è comune a tutti: andiamo verso la patria" (John XXIII, *Discorso presso Loreto*).

124. John XXIII, *Discorso presso Loreto.*

125. The connection between incarnation and pilgrimage can be circumstantial insofar as the sanctuary of Loreto is associated with Nazareth, because of the Santa Casa. In his discourse, the pope developed the theme of the incarnation, the family, and labor, in light of Mary's role, and Jesus's hidden life of thirty years before he embarked on his public ministry.

126. Paul VI, "Solenne chiusura della seconda sessione del concilio: Allocuzione del Santo Padre" (December 4, 1963), §29, https://w2.vatican.va/content/paul-vi/la/speeches/1963/documents/hf_p-vi_spe_19631204_chiusura-concilio.html. Although the title is in Italian, the reference is to the Latin original. The paragraph numbers can be found only in the Italian version.

127. See, e.g., Paul VI, "Saluto al Presidente della Repubblica Italiana alla partenza da Rome" (January 4, 1964), https://w2.vatican.va/content/paul-vi/it/speeches/1964/documents/hf_p-vi_spe_19640104_partenza-fiumicino.html; "Address to the King of Jordan" (January 4, 1964), https://w2.vatican.va/content/paul-vi/en/speeches/1964/documents/hf_p-vi_spe_19640104_jordania.html; "Discours aux communautés catholiques de rites orientaux" (January 4, 1964), http://www.vatican.va/content/paul-vi/fr/speeches/1964/documents/hf_p-vi_spe_19640104_riti-orientali.html; "Votre Excellence le sait, et Dieu Nous en est témoin, Nous ne sommes guidé dans cette visite par aucune considération qui ne soit d'ordre purement spirituel. Nous venons en pèlerin; Nous venons vénérer les Lieux-Saints; Nous venons pour prier" ("Discours au 'Peuple de l'Alliance'" [January 5, 1964]), https://w2.vatican.va/content/paul-vi/fr/speeches/1964/documents/hf_p-vi_spe_19640105_peuple-alliance.html.

128. Paul VI, "Solenne chiusura" (1963), §30.

129. Paul VI, "Solenne chiusura" (1963), §30. However, the Italian translation provided by the Vatican website omits the "penitential" dimension.

130. Paul VI, "Prière au Saint Sépulcre" (January 4, 1964), https://w2.vatican.va/content/paul-vi/fr/speeches/1964/documents/hf_p-vi_spe_19640104_santo-sepolcro.html.

131. Paul VI, "Solenne chiusura" (1963), §30.

132. Paul VI, "Discours au 'Peuple de l'Alliance.'"

133. Paul VI, "Discorso al Sacro Collegio" (January 6, 1964), https://w2.vatican.va/content/paul-vi/it/speeches/1964/documents/hf_p-vi_spe_19640106_sacro-collegio.html.

134. Paul VI, "Discorso al Sacro Collegio" (January 6, 1964).

135. Paul VI, "Discorso al Sacro Collegio" (January 6, 1964).

136. Paul VI, "Discorso al Sacro Collegio" (January 6, 1964).

137. Paul VI, "Discorso al Sacro Collegio" (January 6, 1964).

138. Paul VI, "Discorso al Sacro Collegio" (January 6, 1964).

139. Paul VI, "Discorso al Sacro Collegio" (January 6, 1964).

140. Lubac mentions that the parallel between John's pilgrimage to Loreto and Paul's to the Holy Land was not lost on many observers (Henri de Lubac, "Paul VI, Pilgrim to Jerusalem," in *The Church: Paradox and Mystery*, trans. James R. Dunne [Staten Island, NY: Alba House, 1969], 97).

141. Lubac, "Paul VI, Pilgrim to Jerusalem," 98–101.

142. The famous trip to the General Assembly of the United Nations in October 1965, also during the Council, was not labeled as a "pilgrimage." In Paul VI's whole pontificate, only eight trips are considered as such (see the list of travels at https://w2.vatican.va/content/paul-vi/en/travels.index.1.html). The pilgrimage to the Holy Land was Paul VI's first pilgrimage and the one to India his second.

143. Paul VI, "Discours au Corps diplomatique" (December 3, 1964), http://w2.vatican.va/content/paul-vi/fr/speeches/1964/documents/hf_p-vi_spe_19641203_corps-diplomatique.html.

144. Paul VI, "Discours au Corps diplomatique" (December 3, 1964).

145. Paul VI, "Address at the Welcome Ceremony at the Airport of Bombay" (December 2, 1964), http://www.vatican.va/content/paul-vi/en/speeches/1964/documents/hf_p-vi_spe_19641202_arrival-india.html.

146. Paul VI, "Discours du Pape Paul VI à l'Organisation des Nations-Unies à l'occasion du 20e anniversaire de l'organisation"

(October 4, 1965), https://w2.vatican.va/content/paul-vi/fr/speeches/1965/documents/hf_p-vi_spe_19651004_united-nations.html.

147. Paul VI, "Discours à l'Organisation des Nations-Unies" (1965).

148. See http://www.vatican.va/news_services/press/documentazione/documents/viaggi/viaggi_santo_padre_statistiche_fuori-italia_elenco_cronologico_it.html#105.

149. John Paul II, "Bull of Indiction of the Great Jubilee of the Year 2000 *Incarnationis Mysterium*" (November 29, 1998), see esp. §7, https://w2.vatican.va/content/john-paul-ii/en/jubilee/documents/hf_jp-ii_doc_19981129_bolla-incarnationis-mysterium.html.

150. Pontifical Council for the Pastoral Care of Migrants and Itinerant People, "The Pilgrimage in the Great Jubilee" (April 25, 1998), http://www.vatican.va/roman_curia/pontifical_councils/migrants/documents/rc_pc_migrants_doc_19980425_pilgrimage_en.htm.

151. Pontifical Council for the Pastoral Care of Migrants and Itinerant People, "The Shrine: Memory, Presence and Prophecy of the Living God" (May 8, 1999), http://www.vatican.va/roman_curia/pontifical_councils/migrants/documents/rc_pc_migrants_doc_19990525_shrine_en.html.

152. Pope John Paul II, "Letter Concerning Pilgrimage to the Places Linked to the History of Salvation" (June 29, 1999), http://w2.vatican.va/content/john-paul-ii/en/letters/1999/documents/hf_jp-ii_let_30061999_pilgrimage.html.

153. Pontifical Council for the Pastoral Care of Migrants and Itinerant People, "The Pilgrimage," §26.

154. Pontifical Council for the Pastoral Care of Migrants and Itinerant People, "The Pilgrimage," §30.

155. Pontifical Council for the Pastoral Care of Migrants and Itinerant People, "The Pilgrimage," §25.

156. Pontifical Council for the Pastoral Care of Migrants and Itinerant People, "The Pilgrimage," §2.

157. Pontifical Council for the Pastoral Care of Migrants and Itinerant People, "The Pilgrimage," §§ 23, 38, mentions that pilgrimage "may also be *the tent of meeting with charity*," calling for the care of the poor, and a special attention to the sick—called to be not simply "objects" of compassion, but also subjects of "commitment and of action."

158. Pontifical Council for the Pastoral Care of Migrants and Itinerant People, "The Pilgrimage," §2.

159. Pontifical Council for the Pastoral Care of Migrants and Itinerant People, "The Pilgrimage," §21.

160. Pontifical Council for the Pastoral Care of Migrants and Itinerant People, "The Pilgrimage," §37.

161. Pontifical Council for the Pastoral Care of Migrants and Itinerant People, "The Pilgrimage," §§32–33.

162. Pontifical Council for the Pastoral Care of Migrants and Itinerant People, "The Shrine: Memory, Presence and Prophecy of the Living God" (May 8, 1999), §1.

163. Pontifical Council for the Pastoral Care of Migrants and Itinerant People, "The Shrine," §§6–8.

164. Pontifical Council for the Pastoral Care of Migrants and Itinerant People: "The Shrine," §8.

165. Pontifical Council for the Pastoral Care of Migrants and Itinerant People, "The Shrine," §§10–12. Despite the very ecclesial character of the document (e.g., the emphasis on sacrament), there is also an openness that extends beyond the Church (e.g., §12), in learning from non-Christians, the foreigner, etc.

166. Pontifical Council for the Pastoral Care of Migrants and Itinerant People, "The Shrine," §16.

167. Pontifical Council for the Pastoral Care of Migrants and Itinerant People, "The Shrine," §13–15.

168. John Paul II, "Letter Concerning Pilgrimage," §1.

169. John Paul II, "Letter Concerning Pilgrimage," §3.

170. John Paul II, "Letter Concerning Pilgrimage," §10.

171. John Paul II, "Letter Concerning Pilgrimage," §8.

172. John Paul II, "Letter Concerning Pilgrimage," §12.

173. The interiority of the journey of pilgrimage can be seen, e.g., in a greater personal awareness about God's presence and action in the world. See John Paul II, "Letter Concerning Pilgrimage," §10.

174. John Paul II, "Letter Concerning Pilgrimage," §12.

175. John Paul II, "Speech at the Welcome Ceremony in Israel" (March 21, 2000), §1, http://w2.vatican.va/content/john-paul-ii/en/speeches/2000/jan-mar/documents/hf_jp-ii_spe_20000321_israel-arrival.html.

176. John Paul II, "Angelus" (March 26, 2000), http://w2.vatican.va/content/john-paul-ii/en/angelus/2000/documents/hf_jp-ii_ang_20000326_jerusalem.html.

177. John Paul II, "Speech at the Welcome Ceremony in Israel," §3.

178. For example, John Paul II, "Speech at the Visit to the President of Israel" (March 23, 2000), http://w2.vatican.va/content/john-paul-ii/en/speeches/2000/jan-mar/documents/hf_jp-ii_spe_20000323_presidente-israele.html; John Paul II, "Greeting to the Consuls General" (March 25, 2000), http://w2.vatican.va/content/john-paul-ii/en/speeches/2000/jan-mar/documents/hf_jp-ii_spe_20000325_general-consuls.html.

179. John Paul II, "Speech at the Welcome Ceremony in Israel," §4. See especially the meeting of John Paul II with leaders of various faith communities (John Paul II, "Address at the Interreligious Meeting at the Notre Dame Pontifical Institute" [March 23, 2000], http://w2.vatican.va/content/john-paul-ii/en/speeches/2000/jan-mar/documents/hf_jp-ii_spe_20000323_jerusalem-notre-dame.html).

180. This image was the counterpart to that of the encounter of Pope Paul VI with Ecumenical Patriarch Athenagoras, in 1964.

181. John Paul II, "Speech during the Visit to the Refugee Camp of Dheisheh" (March 22, 2000), §1, http://w2.vatican.va/content/john-paul-ii/en/speeches/2000/jan-mar/documents/hf_jp-ii_spe_20000322_deheisheh-refugees.html.

182. Turner had noted the connection of pilgrimage with confession and the Eucharist, i.e., repeatable sacraments, and not unique events like baptism. This connection underlines the continuous aspect of pilgrimage.

183. See Michael W. Twomey, "Homo Viator," in *Encyclopedia of Medieval Pilgrimage*, ed. Larissa J. Taylor et al. (Leiden: Brill, 2010), 265–67.

184. While it defines *synodality* as "the specific *modus vivendi et operandi* of the Church, the People of God, which reveals and gives substance to her being as communion when all her members journey together, gather in assembly and take an active part in her evangelising mission" (§6), the International Theological commission also underlines the role of the Spirit at the core of synodality, since it declares that "the principle of synodality is the action of the

Spirit in the communion of the Body of Christ and in the missionary journey of the People of God" (International Theological Commission, "Synodality in the Life and Mission of the Church" [March 2, 2018], §46).

185. The consideration of the pilgrim paradigm can explicate the opposition faced by Pope Francis from some sectors of the Church who view immutability as the sign of truth, the Church of yesterday as the Church of always. Pope Francis's consent to in-depth discussions that led divergent voices to be heard is compared to a "confusion" that is opposed to the "clarity" of an immutable discourse. The underlying question is whether the Church has "arrived" or is still on a quest.

186. See Pope Francis's appointment of cardinals from the outskirts (and not necessarily from traditional cardinalate sees).

187. In his case, it was more than a symbol since he is the pope who, in the wake of the Second Vatican Council, simplified or eliminated pontifical paraphernalia (e.g., the tiara and the *sedia gestatoria*), and famously relinquished pontifical jewelry to give the proceeds to the poor, while inviting fellow bishops to do likewise.

188. The early Christian community undertook that process by discerning what was essential of the Jewish faith in light of the gospel, especially in the so-called Council of Jerusalem (Acts 15).

189. That path taken by Pope John Paul II met strong oppositions from certain sectors of the Church, since it was perceived as an admission of weakness that could taint the image of the Church as holy—mistakenly understood in that case as "perfect."

190. See, in particular, the Declaration *Dominus Iesus* on the Unicity and Salvific Universality of Jesus Christ and the Church by the Congregation for the Doctrine of Faith (August 6, 2000).

EPILOGUE: PILGRIMAGE AND THE HOLY SPIRIT

1. John Paul II, "Letter Concerning Pilgrimage to the Places Linked to the History of Salvation" (June 29, 1999), §12.

2. The last few decades have witnessed a rapid growth of Christian movements associated with the Holy Spirit. In the 1970s, the Charismatic Renewal spread across the Catholic Church, remaining strong in some places such as Africa. Neo-Pentecostal

churches are on the rise in the Global South. Regarding pilgrimage, I highlighted in the introduction both the popular interest in pilgrimage, even for nonreligious reasons, and the academic interest.

3. Two of the most famous traditional texts praising the Spirit are the hymn *Veni Creator Spiritus* and the Pentecost sequence *Veni Sancte Spiritus*. Hymns and prayers to Christ, e.g., display a broader range, but often focus on the person of Christ without assigning specific action to him.

4. The Nicene Creed of 325 affirms the belief "and in the Holy Spirit." The Council of Constantinople (381) fleshed out the understanding of the person of the Spirit.

5. The Constantinopolitan Creed mentions that the Spirit has spoken through the prophets, emphasizing the unicity and eternity of the Spirit.

6. Ignatius would obviously not have stated that himself, but a reader would know of his contemporary fame and his later official recognition as a saint.

7. See my work on the Spirit as the "*Incarnator*" of salvation in *Le lieu du salut: Une pneumatologie d'Incarnation chez Thérèse d'Avila* (Paris: Cerf, 2014), available in English as *Teresa of Avila, the Holy Spirit, and the Place of Salvation* (Mahwah, NJ: Paulist Press, 2021).

8. From the Constantinopolitan Creed (381).

9. Second Vatican Council, Pastoral Constitution on the Church in the Modern World *Gaudium et Spes* (December 7, 1965).

Bibliography

CHURCH DOCUMENTS

Second Vatican Council

Constitution on the Sacred Liturgy *Sacrosanctum Concilium* (December 4, 1963). https://www.vatican.va/archive/hist_councils/ii_vatican_council/documents/vat-ii_const_19631204_sacrosanctum-concilium_en.html.

Dogmatic Constitution on the Church *Lumen Gentium* (November 21, 1964). https://www.vatican.va/archive/hist_councils/ii_vatican_council/documents/vat-ii_const_19641121_lumen-gentium_en.html.

Dogmatic Constitution on Divine Revelation *Dei Verbum* (November 18, 1965). https://www.vatican.va/archive/hist_councils/ii_vatican_council/documents/vat-ii_const_19651118_dei-verbum_en.html.

Pastoral Constitution on the Church in the Modern World *Gaudium et Spes* (December 7, 1965). https://www.vatican.va/archive/hist_councils/ii_vatican_council/documents/vat-ii_const_19651207_gaudium-et-spes_en.html.

Acta Synodalia Sacrosancti Concilii Oecumenici Vaticani Secundi, vol. I: Periodus prima. Rome: Typis Polyglottis Vaticanis, 1970.

Church Documents on Pilgrimage

Pontifical Council for the Pastoral Care of Migrants and Itinerant People. "The Pilgrimage in the Great Jubilee" (April 25, 1998).

https://www.vatican.va/roman_curia/pontifical_councils/migrants/documents/rc_pc_migrants_doc_19980425_pilgrimage_en.htm.

Pope John Paul II. "Bull of Induction of the Great Jubilee of the Year 2000 *Incarnationis Mysterium*" (November 29, 1998). https://www.vatican.va/jubilee_2000/docs/documents/hf_jp-ii_doc_30111998_bolla-jubilee_en.html.

Pontifical Council for the Pastoral Care of Migrants and Itinerant People. "The Shrine: Memory, Presence and Prophecy of the Living God" (May 8, 1999). https://www.vatican.va/roman_curia/pontifical_councils/migrants/documents/rc_pc_migrants_doc_19990525_shrine_en.html.

Pope John Paul II. "Letter Concerning Pilgrimage to the Places Linked to the History of Salvation" (June 29, 1999). https://www.vatican.va/content/john-paul-ii/en/letters/1999/documents/hf_jp-ii_let_30061999_pilgrimage.html.

Second Asian Congress on Pilgrimages and Shrines. "Final Document" (November 23, 2005). https://www.vatican.va/roman_curia/pontifical_councils/migrants/documents_1/rc_pc_migrants_doc_21112005_IIcong-sant-seul-finaldoc_en.html.

Papal Discourses

Pope John XXIII. "Discorso presso il Santuario di Loreto" (October 4, 1962). http://www.vatican.va/content/john-xxiii/it/speeches/1962/documents/hf_j-xxiii_spe_19621004_santuario-loreto.html.

Pope John XXIII. "Address on the Occasion of the Solemn Opening of the Most Holy Council *Gaudet Mater Ecclesia*" (October 11, 1962). https://w2.vatican.va/content/john-xxiii/la/speeches/1962/documents/hf_j-xxiii_spe_19621011_opening-council.html.

Pope Paul VI. "Solenne chiusura della seconda sessione del concilio: Allocuzione del Santo Padre" (December 4, 1963). https://w2.vatican.va/content/paul-vi/la/speeches/1963/documents/hf_p-vi_spe_19631204_chiusura-concilio.html.

Pope Paul VI. "Address to the King of Jordan" (January 4, 1964). https://w2.vatican.va/content/paul-vi/en/speeches/1964/documents/hf_p-vi_spe_19640104_jordania.html.

Pope Paul VI. "Discours aux communautés catholiques de rites orientaux" (January 4, 1964). http://www.vatican.va/content/paul-vi/fr/speeches/1964/documents/hf_p-vi_spe_19640104_riti-orientali.html.

Pope Paul VI. "Saluto al Presidente della Repubblica Italiana alla partenza da Rome" (January 4, 1964). https://w2.vatican.va/content/paul-vi/it/speeches/1964/documents/hf_p-vi_spe_19640104_partenza-fiumicino.html.

Pope Paul VI. "Discours au 'Peuple de l'Alliance'" (January 5, 1964). https://w2.vatican.va/content/paul-vi/fr/speeches/1964/documents/hf_p-vi_spe_19640105_peuple-alliance.html.

Pope Paul VI. "Prière au Saint Sépulcre" (January 4, 1964). https://w2.vatican.va/content/paul-vi/fr/speeches/1964/documents/hf_p-vi_spe_19640104_santo-sepolcro.html.

Pope Paul VI. "Discorso al Sacro Collegio" (January 6, 1964). https://w2.vatican.va/content/paul-vi/it/speeches/1964/documents/hf_p-vi_spe_19640106_sacro-collegio.html.

Pope Paul VI. "Address at the Welcome Ceremony at the Airport of Bombay" (December 2, 1964). http://www.vatican.va/content/paul-vi/en/speeches/1964/documents/hf_p-vi_spe_19641202_arrival-india.html.

Pope Paul VI. "Discours au Corps diplomatique" (December 3, 1964). http://w2.vatican.va/content/paul-vi/fr/speeches/1964/documents/hf_p-vi_spe_19641203_corps-diplomatique.html.

Pope Paul VI. "Discours du Pape Paul VI à l'Organisation des Nations-Unies à l'occasion du 20e anniversaire de l'organisation" (October 4, 1965). https://w2.vatican.va/content/paul-vi/fr/speeches/1965/documents/hf_p-vi_spe_19651004_united-nations.html.

Pope John Paul II. "Speech at the Welcome Ceremony in Israel" (March 21, 2000). http://w2.vatican.va/content/john-paul-ii/en/speeches/2000/jan-mar/documents/hf_jp-ii_spe_20000321_israel-arrival.html.

Pope John Paul II. "Speech During the Visit to the Refugee Camp of Dheisheh" (March 22, 2000). http://w2.vatican.va/content/john-paul-ii/en/speeches/2000/jan-mar/documents/hf_jp-ii_spe_20000322_deheisheh-refugees.html.

Pope John Paul II. "Address at the Interreligious Meeting at the Notre Dame Pontifical Institute" (March 23, 2000). http://

w2.vatican.va/content/john-paul-ii/en/speeches/2000/jan-mar/documents/hf_jp-ii_spe_20000323_jerusalem-notre-dame.html.

Pope John Paul II. "Speech at the Visit to the President of Israel" (March 23, 2000). http://w2.vatican.va/content/john-paul-ii/en/speeches/2000/jan-mar/documents/hf_jp-ii_spe_20000323_presidente-israele.html.

Pope John Paul II. "Greeting to the Consuls General" (March 25, 2000). http://w2.vatican.va/content/john-paul-ii/en/speeches/2000/jan-mar/documents/hf_jp-ii_spe_20000325_general-consuls.html.

Pope John Paul II, "Angelus" (March 26, 2000). http://w2.vatican.va/content/john-paul-ii/en/angelus/2000/documents/hf_jp-ii_ang_20000326_jerusalem.html.

Other Church Documents

Catholic Church. *The Code of Canon Law.* Washington, DC: Canon Law Society of America, 1983.

———. *The Roman Missal.* English translation according to the third typical edition. Totowa, NJ: Catholic Book Publishing, 2011.

Council of Trent. Decree "On Invocation, Veneration and Relics of the Saints, and on Sacred Images" (Session 25, December 3–4, 1563). In *Trent to Vatican II,* ed. Norman P. Tanner, SJ, 774–76. Vol. 2 of *Decrees of the Ecumenical Councils.* Washington, DC: Georgetown University Press, 1990.

International Theological Commission. "Synodality in the Life and Mission of the Church" (March 2, 2018). http://www.vatican.va/roman_curia/congregations/cfaith/cti_documents/rc_cti_20180302_sinodalita_en.html.

Pope Francis. Apostolic Exhortation *Gaudete et Exsultate* on the Call to Holiness in Today's World (March 19, 2018). http://www.vatican.va/content/francesco/en/apost_exhortations/documents/papa-francesco_esortazione-ap_20180319_gaudete-et-exsultate.html.

Pope Pius XII. Encyclical Letter on the Mystical Body of Christ *Mystici Corporis Christi* (June 29, 1943). http://www.vatican

.va/content/pius-xii/en/encyclicals/documents/hf_p-xii_enc_29061943_mystici-corporis-christi.html.

JESUIT PRIMARY SOURCES

Câmara, Luís Gonçalves da. "Acta Patris Ignatii de Loyola." In *Narrationes Scriptae Ante Annum 1557*, ed. Dionysius Fernandez Zapico, SJ, and Candidus de Dalmases, SJ, 364–506. Vol. 1 of *Fontes Narrativi de S. Ignatio de Loyola et de Societatis Iesu Initiis*. Rome: Monumenta Historica Societatis Iesu, 1943.

———. "Memoriale." in *Narrationes Scriptae Ante Annum 1557*, ed. Dionysius Fernandez Zapico, SJ, and Candidus de Dalmases, SJ, 527–752. Vol. 1 of *Fontes Narrativi de S. Ignatio de Loyola et de Societatis Iesu Initiis*. Rome: Monumenta Historica Societatis Iesu, 1943.

Ignatius of Loyola. *Epistolae et Instructiones*. 12 vols. Madrid: Monumenta Historica Societatis Iesu, 1903–11. A selection has been translated as *Letters and Instructions*. St. Louis: The Institute of Jesuit Sources, 2006.

———. "Ephemeris S. P. N. Ignatii." In *Constitutiones Societatis Jesus*, vol. 1: *Monumenta Constitutionum Praevia*, 86–158. Rome: Monumenta Historica Societatis Jesu, 1934 (known as the *Spiritual Diary*).

———. *Obras*. Madrid: Biblioteca de Autores Cristianos, 2014.

———. *Personal Writings*. London: Penguin, 1997.

———. *The Constitutions of the Society of Jesus*. Translated by George E. Ganss, SJ. St. Louis: The Institute of Jesuit Sources, 1970.

Laínez, Diego. "Adhortationes in librum examinis." In *Narrationes Scriptae Annis 1557–1574*, ed. Candidus de Dalmases, SJ, 127–140. Vol. 2 of *Fontes Narrativi de S. Ignatio de Loyola et de Societatis Iesu Initiis*. Rome: Monumenta Historica Societatis Iesu, 1951.

———. "Epistola Patris Laynez de P. Ignatio." In *Narrationes Scriptae Ante Annum 1557*, ed. Dionysius Fernandez Zapico, SJ, and Candidus de Dalmases, SJ, 70–145. Vol. 1 of *Fontes Narrativi de S. Ignatio de Loyola et de Societatis Iesu Initiis*. Rome: Monumenta Historica Societatis Iesu, 1943.

Polanco, Juan Alfonso de. *Vita Ignatii Loiolae et Rerum Societatis Iesu Historia*. 6 vols. Madrid: Monumenta Historica Societatis Iesu, 1894–1898. Partially translated as *Year by Year with the Early Jesuits (1537–1556): Selections from the "Chronicon" of Juan De Polanco, S.J.* Edited by John Patrick Donnelly. St. Louis: Institute of Jesuit Sources, 2004.

Ribadeneyra, Pedro de. *Vita Ignatii Loyolae*. Edited by Candidus de Dalmases, SJ, *Fontes Narrativi de S. Ignatio de Loyola et de Societatis Iesu Initiis*, vol. 4. Rome: Monumenta Historica Societatis Iesu, 1965. English translation: Pedro de Ribadeneira. *The Life of Ignatius of Loyola*. Translated by Claude Pavur. St. Louis: Institute of Jesuit Sources, 2014.

GENERAL BIBLIOGRAPHY

Albera, Dionigi, and John Eade, eds. *International Perspectives on Pilgrimage Studies: Itineraries, Gaps and Obstacles*. New York: Routledge, 2015.

———. *New Pathways in Pilgrimage Studies*. New York: Routledge, 2017.

Arx, Walter von. "Das Hochgebet die Kirche in der Schweiz: Ein liturgiegeschichtliches Ereignis." *Zeitschrift für schweizerische Kirchengeschichte* 71 (1977): 279–293.

Augustine. *City of God and Christian Doctrine*. Translated by Marcus Dods. Vol. 2 of *A Select Library of the Nicene and Post-Nicene Fathers of the Christian Church*, edited by Philip Schaff. New York: Charles Scribner's Sons, 1899.

Badone, Ellen, and Sharon R. Roseman, eds. *Intersecting Journeys: The Anthropology of Pilgrimage and Tourism*. Urbana: University of Illinois Press, 2004.

Balthasar, Hans Urs von. *Theo-Drama: Theological Dramatic Theory*. Vol. 4, *The Action*. San Francisco: Ignatius Press, 1994.

Bartholomew, Craig, and Fred Hughes, eds. *Explorations in a Christian Theology of Pilgrimage*. Hants: Ashgate, 2004.

Bauman, Zygmunt. "From Pilgrim to Tourist—Or a Short History of Identity." *Questions of Cultural Identity*, edited by Stuart Hall and Paul du Gay, 18–37. London: Sage Publications, 2011.

Bibliography

Benedict. *The Rule of Saint Benedict*. Edited by Timothy Fry. Collegeville, MN: Liturgical Press, 2001.

Betti, Umberto. "Histoire chronologique de la constitution." In *L'Église de Vatican II: Études autour de la Constitution conciliaire sur l'Église*, edited by Guilherme Baraúna, 57–83. Vol. 2. Paris: Cerf, 1967.

Blasstic, Michael W., Jay M. Hammond, and J.-A. Wayner Hellmann, eds. *The Writings of Francis of Assisi: Rules, Testament, and Admonitions*. Vol. 2, *Studies in Early Franciscan Sources*. St. Bonaventure, NY: Franciscan Institute Publications, 2001.

Brouillette, André. *Le lieu du salut: Une pneumatologie d'Incarnation chez Thérèse d'Avila*. Paris: Cerf, 2014. Translated into English as *Teresa of Avila, the Holy Spirit, and the Place of Salvation*. Mahwah, NJ: Paulist Press, 2021.

———. "Le pèlerinage ignatien: Entre ascèse, identité et mystique." *Nouvelle Revue Théologique* 140, no. 1 (2018): 91–106.

———. "Pèlerin et réfugié: Regards théologiques croisés." *Théologiques* 25, no. 2 (2017): 75–94.

Cavanaugh, William T. "Migrant, Tourist, Pilgrim, Monk: Mobility and Identity in a Global Age." *Theological Studies* 69 (2008): 340–56.

Certeau, Michel de. "L'espace du désir ou le 'fondement' des Exercices spirituels." *Christus* 20, no. 77 (1973): 118–28.

Claussen, M. A. "'Peregrinatio' and 'Peregrini' in Augustine's 'City of God.'" *Traditio* 46 (1991): 33–75.

Clerck, Paul de. "La révision de la prière eucharistique suisse." *La Maison-Dieu* 191 (1992): 61–68.

Coleman, Simon, and J. Eade. *Reframing Pilgrimage: Cultures in Motion*. London: Routledge, 2004.

Coleman, Simon, and J. Elsner. *Pilgrimage Past and Present: Sacred Travel and Sacred Space in the World Religions*. Cambridge, MA: Harvard University Press, 1995.

Congar, Yves. *I Believe in the Holy Spirit*. Vol. 1, *The Holy Spirit in the "Economy."* New York: Crossroad, 1983.

———. "Moving Toward a Pilgrim Church." In *Vatican II Revisited by Those Who Were There*, edited by Alberic Stacpoole, 129–152. Minneapolis, MN: Winston Press, 1986.

Cook, William R., and Ronald B. Herzman. *The Medieval World View: An Introduction*. New York: Oxford University Press, 2012.

Davies, J. G. *Pilgrimage Yesterday, and Today: Why? When? How?* London: SCM, 1988.

Doyle, Dennis M. *The Church Emerging from Vatican II: A Popular Approach to Contemporary Catholicism.* Mystic, CT: Twenty-Third Publications, 1992.

Dupront, Alphonse. *Du sacré: Croisades et pèlerinages, images et langages.* Paris: Gallimard, 2012.

Eade, John, and Michael J. Sallnow, eds. *Contesting the Sacred: The Anthropology of Christian Pilgrimage.* New York: Routledge, 1991.

Egeria. *The Pilgrimage of Egeria: A New Translation of the* Itinerarium Egeriae *with Introduction and Commentary.* Translated by Anne McGowan and Paul F. Bradshaw. Collegeville, MN: Liturgical Press Academic, 2018.

Éla, Jean-Marc. "Un Dieu métis." In *Theological Reflections on Migration: A CCME Reader,* edited by Benz H. R. Schär and Ralf Geisler, 6–9. Brussels: Churches' Commission for Migrants in Europe, 2000.

Foley, Edward, John F. Baldovin, Mary Collins, and Joanne M. Pierce, eds. *A Commentary on the Order of Mass of* The Roman Missal. Collegeville, MN: Liturgical Press, 2011.

Frey, Nancy Louise. *Pilgrim Stories: On and Off the Road to Santiago.* Berkeley: University of California Press, 1998.

Gaillardetz, Richard R. *The Church in the Making:* Lumen Gentium, Christus Dominus, Orientalium Ecclesiarum. Mahwah, NJ: Paulist Press, 2006.

Geger, Barton T. "Ten Things that St. Ignatius Never Said or Did." *Studies in the Spirituality of Jesuits* 50, no. 1 (2018).

———. "The 'First' First Companions: The Continuing Impact of the Men Who Left Ignatius." *Studies in the Spirituality of Jesuits* 44, no. 2 (2012).

Gennep, Arnold van. *The Rites of Passage.* Chicago: University of Chicago Press, 1960.

Grégoire de Nysse. *Lettres.* Translated by Pierre Maraval. *Sources chrétiennes,* no. 363. Paris: Cerf, 1990.

Gutiérrez, Gustavo. *A Theology of Liberation.* Maryknoll, NY: Orbis, 1988.

Hänggi, Anton. "Das Hochgebet 'Synode '72' für die Kirche in der Schweiz." *Notitiae* 301, no. 27 (1991): 436–459.

Haran, Menahem. "Pilgrim-Feasts and Family Festivals." In *Temples and Temple-Service in Ancient Israel: An Inquiry into Biblical Cult Phenomena and the Historical Setting of the Priestly School*, 289–316. Winona Lake, IN: Eisenbrauns, 1985.

Harkins, Franklin. "Matter Matters." In *The Holy Spirit: Setting the World on Fire*. Edited by Richard Lennan and Nancy Pineda-Madrid, 24–32. Mahwah, NJ: Paulist Press, 2017.

Hervieu-Léger, Danièle. *Le pèlerin et le converti: La religion en mouvement*. Paris: Flammarion, 1999.

Hezser, Catherine. *Jewish Travel in Antiquity*. Tübingen: Mohr Siebeck, 2011.

Hundley, Michael B. *Gods in Dwellings: Temples and Divine Presence in the Ancient Near East*. Atlanta: Society of Biblical Literature, 2013.

Irvin, Dale T. "Theology, Migration, and the Homecoming." In *Theology of Migration in the Abrahamic Religions*. Edited by Elaine Padilla and Peter C. Phan, 7–25. New York: Palgrave Macmillan, 2014.

Jansen, Willy, and Catrien Notermans, eds. *Gender, Nation and Religion in European Pilgrimage: Old Routes, New Journeys*. Burlington, VT: Ashgate, 2012.

John Chrysostom. *Homilies on the Gospel of Saint Matthew*. Vol 10, *A Select Library of the Nicene and Post-Nicene Fathers of the Christian Church*, edited by Philip Schaff. Grand Rapids, MI: Eerdmans, 1956.

Julia, Dominique. *Le voyage aux saints: Les pèlerinages dans l'Occident moderne: XVe–XVIIIe siècle*. Paris: Seuil/EHESS/Gallimard, 2016.

Lera Monreal, José María. *La pneumatología de los Ejercicios espirituales: Una teología de la crux traducida a la vida*. Madrid/Santander/Bilbao: Universidad Pontificia Comillas/Sal Terrae/Mensajero, 2016.

Lubac, Henri de. *The Church: Paradox and Mystery*. Translated by James R. Dunne. Staten Island, NY: Alba House, 1969.

Ludolph of Saxony. *The Life of Jesus Christ*. Translated by Milton T. Walsh. Athens, Ohio: Cistercian Publications; Collegeville, MN: Liturgical Press, 2018.

Macchia, Frank D. *The Spirit Baptizer: Christology in Light of Pentecost*. Grand Rapids, MI: Eerdmans, 2018.

Maddrell, Avril, Veronica della Dora, Alessandro Scafi, and Heather Walton. *Christian Pilgrimage, Landscape and Heritage: Journeying to the Sacred*. New York: Routledge, 2015.

Maggioni, Corrado. "Coordinate spazio-temporali della Preghiera Eucaristica 'Synode '72.'" *Notitiae* no. 301, 27 (1991): 460–479.

May, Christof. "'Mal weg' sein—ob das ausreicht?: Pilgern als Chance christlicher Verkündigung." *Geist und Leben* 81, no. 3 (2008): 174–185.

———. *Pilgern: Menschsein auf dem Weg*. Würzburg: Echter, 2004.

McManamon, John M. *The Text and Contexts of Ignatius Loyola's "Autobiography."* New York: Fordham University Press, 2013.

Melloni, Javier. *The Spiritual Exercises of Saint Ignatius Loyola in the Western Tradition*. Leominster: Gracewing, 2000.

Melloni Ribas, Javier. "Las influencias cisnerianas de los Ejercicios." In *Las fuentes de los Ejercicios espirituales de San Ignacio: Actas del Simposio Internacional (Loyola, 15–19 septiembre 1997)*, edited by Juan Plazaola, 353–77. Bilbao: Mensajero, 1998.

Merton, Thomas. *The Seven Storey Mountain*. New York: Harcourt, Brace and Co., 1948.

Moltmann, Jürgen. *The Spirit of Life: A Universal Affirmation*. Minneapolis: Fortress, 1992.

Muller, Naomi. "Paradise Regained: Medieval Garden Fountains." In *Medieval Gardens*, edited by Elisabeth Blair MacDougall, 135–53. Washington, DC: Dumbarton Oaks Research Library and Collection, 1986.

Murphy-O'Connor, Jerome. *Paul: His Story*. Oxford: Oxford University Press, 2004.

Nardoni, Enrique. *Rise Up, O Judge: A Study of Justice in the Biblical World*. Translated by Seán Charles Martin. Peabody: Hendrickson, 2004.

O'Malley, Brian Brendan. *A Pilgrim's Manual: Saint David's*. Marlborough: Paulinus Press, 1985.

O'Rourke Boyle, Marjorie. *Loyola's Acts: The Rhetoric of the Self*. Berkeley: University of California Press, 1997.

Peña Antil, Nelson. *Bailes religiosos de Arica: Valoración de su historia y tradición*. Santiago de Chile: Procultura, 2015.

Pentkovsky, Aleksei, ed. *The Pilgrim's Tale*. New York: Paulist Press, 1999.

Raffa, Vincenzo. *Liturgia Eucaristica: Mistagogia della Messa: dalla storia e dalla teologica alla pastorale pratica*. Rome: Edizioni Liturgiche, 2003.

Robinson, Martin. *Sacred Places, Pilgrim Paths: An Anthology of Pilgrimage*. London: HarperCollins, 1997.

Rodrigues, Simão. "Guidelines for Pilgrims: Coimbra, Portugal 1546," *The Way* 42, no. 1 (2003): 58–70.

Rogers, James Silas. "Secular Pilgrimages: Recent Irish-American Memoir and Journeys of Healing." In *Irish-American Autobiography*, 143–64. Washington, DC: Catholic University of America Press, 2016.

Rogers, Stephanie Stidham. *Inventing the Holy Land: American Protestant Pilgrimage to Palestine, 1895–1941*. Lanham, MD: Lexington Books, 2011.

Roos, Richard. *Christwalk: The Journal of a Young Priest's 600-Mile Pilgrimage by Foot along the California Mission Trail*. New York: Paulist, 1985.

Rosenberger, Michael. *Wege, die bewegen: Eine kleine Theologie der Wallfahrt*. Würzburg: Echter, 2005.

Ross-Bryant, Lynn. *Pilgrimage to the National Parks: Religion and Nature in the United States*. New York: Routledge, 2013.

Ruiz Pérez, Francisco José. *Teología del Camino: Una aproximación antropológico-teológica a Ignacio de Loyola*. Bilbao/Santander: Mensajero/Sal Terrae, 2000.

Sardi, Leo Agung. "La prueba de la peregrinación en el noviciado de la Compañía de Jesús: Su actualidad para la formación en Indonesia." Doctoral diss. Universidad Pontificia Comillas (Madrid), 2015.

Semmelroth, Otto. "Dogmatic Constitution on the Church: Chapter VII." In *Commentary on the Documents of Vatican II*, edited by Herbert Vorgrimler, vol. 1. New York: Herder and Herder, 1967.

Sheldrake, Philip. *Spaces for the Sacred: Place, Memory, and Identity*. Baltimore: The John Hopkins University Press, 2001.

Shore, Paul. "The Vita Christi of Ludolph of Saxony and its Influence on the Spiritual Exercises of Ignatius of Loyola." *Studies in the Spirituality of Jesuits* 30, no. 1 (1998).

Sobosan, Jeffrey G. "Pilgrimage Theology in the Documents of Vatican II." ThD diss. Graduate Theological Union (Berkeley, CA), 1977.

Stewart-Kroeker, Sarah. *Pilgrimage as Moral and Aesthetic Formation in Augustine's Thought.* Oxford: Oxford University Press, 2017.

Tavard, George H. *The Pilgrim Church.* New York: Herder and Herder, 1967.

Theobald, Christoph. *Le Christianisme comme style: Une manière de faire de la théologie en postmodernité.* 2 vols. Paris: Cerf, 2007–2008.

Thomas à Kempis. *The Imitation of Christ.* Translated by P. G. Zomberg. Rockland, ME: Dunstan, 1985.

Turner, Victor, and Edith Turner. *Image and Pilgrimage in Christian Culture: Anthropological Perspectives.* New York: Columbia University Press, 1978.

Vélez, Karin. *The Miraculous Flying House of Loreto: Spreading Catholicism in the Early Modern World.* Princeton, NJ: Princeton University Press, 2019.

Vella, Danielle, ed. *Journeys of Hope.* Brussels: JRS Europe, 2016.

Vincent, Catherine, ed. *Identités pèlerines: Actes du colloque de Rouen, 15–16 mai 2002.* Rouen: Publications de l'Université de Rouen, 2004.

Walzer, Michael. *Exodus and Revolution.* New York: Basic Books, 1985.

Webb, Diana. *Pilgrims and Pilgrimages in the Medieval West.* London: I. B. Tauris, 1999.

Whalen, Brett Edward, ed. *Pilgrimage in the Middle Ages: A Reader.* Toronto: University of Toronto Press, 2011.

Wilkinson, John. *Jerusalem Pilgrims before the Crusades.* Warminster, England: Aris & Phillips, 2002.

Wright, N. T. *The Way of the Lord: Christian Pilgrimage Today.* Grand Rapids, MI: Eerdmans, 1999.

Index

Page numbers in **bold** refer to section titles

Abraham, 48–49, **50–52**, 53, 55, 60, 86, 88, 199, 204
Adam, 49, **50**, 53, 60, 88, 162, 199, 215
Albera, Dionigi, 15, 181, 183, 185
Alterity, 11, 19, 35, **41–42**, 84, 101, 106, **107–9**, 171, 185
Apostle(s), 2, 25, 28, 32, 34, 68, 69, 71, 75–77, 79–81, 83, 88, 108, 131, 151, 156, 161, 174, 203; Apostolic, 49, 75, 78, 83–84, 96, 103, 107, 110, 125, 157, 161, 169, 205, 210, 211
Arx, Walter von, 231
Asceticism, 8, 15, 92, 96, 108, 114, 120, 122–24. *See also* Effort
Augustine, 12, 127, 128–32, 137, 146, 224–26, 228; *City of God*, 12, 127, **128–32**, 167, 224–26, 228

Badone, Ellen, 181, 184
Balthasar, Hans Urs von, 202
Bartholomew, Craig, 9, 177, 180
Bauman, Zygmunt, 7, 180, 183, 185, 186
Benedict, 4, 208
Betti, Umberto, 229
Body. *See under* Embodiment
Body of Christ, 32, 37–38, 67, 71–74, 133, 171, 205, 223, 239. *See also* Eucharist
Bohjalian, Chris, 190
Boniface VIII, Pope, 3
Bourdeau, Francis, 203
Bowman, Glenn, 180
Brouillette, André, 184, 199, 211
Bunyan, John, 6–8

Câmara, Luís Gonçalves da, 93–95, 101, 118–22, 212–16, 220, 222–23
Cavanaugh, William T., 184–85, 192, 195, 197
Certeau, Michel de, 217
Chaucer, Geoffrey, 4, 8
Church, 1–4, 6–8, 10, 12, 23–24, 28–29, 37, 42, 74–75, 77, 80, 83–85, 89, 125, 126–41, 143–44, 146–50, 152–59, 161,

163–64, 166–71, 173–76, 177, 183, 188–89, 193–95, 205, 207–8, 223, 225–31, 233, 237–40; Church (building), 21, 29, 32, 43, 74, 187, 189, 205, 218. *See also* Shrine
Claussen, M. A., 132, 224–26
Clerck, Paul de, 232
Code of Canon Law, 188, 205, 233
Coelho, Paulo, 5–6
Coleman, Simon, 181, 185
Congar, Yves, 207, 226–27
Congregation for the Doctrine of Faith, 239
Cook, William R., 208
Corneille, Pierre, 196
Council of Trent, 5, 33, 178, 193, 227

Davies, John Gordon, 10, 178–79
Departure, 11, 18–19, **30–32**, 35, 43, 53, 55, 67, 80, 108, 169, 185–86, 218
Destination, 1, 8, 11, 14–17, 19, 22, 27–28, 30, **32–35**, 38, 43, 47, 49–51, 53–57, 60–64, 72, 76–79, 81, 84, 86–88, 91, 97, 101–2, **104–5**, 109, 114, 116, 118–19, 121–23, 128–30, 135, 138–39, 145, 147, 152, 158, 163, 169–70, 174–76, 183–84, 186, 188–89, 203, 222, 225
Discernment, 24, 98–99, 101, 104–6, 109–14, 116–17, 119, 121–24, 141, 147, 154, 169, 174–76, 188, 211, 216, 239
Disciple, 46–48, 62, 65–66, 72–73, 75–81, 83, 88, 91, 108, 123, 148, 150, 161, 174, 198, 202, 210, 229, 232. *See also* Apostle(s)
Discipleship, 25, 108, 185
Dora, Veronica della, 9, 194
Doyle, Dennis M., 229
Dupront, Alphonse, 180–81, 185, 187–88, 190, 194–96
Dyas, Dee, 126, 128, 199, 223

Eade, John, 15, 181, 183
Effort, 11, 19, 35, **40–41,** 53, 66, 77, 80, 84, 136, 166, 196
Egeria, 2, 9, 178, 195
Éla, Jean-Marc, 56, 200
Elsner, John, 181, 185
Embodiment, 1, 7–8, 11–12, 18–19, 24–25, 27, 31, 33–34, **35–38,** 40, 43–44, 49, 56, 60, 61, 64, 66, 67–75, 78–80, 84, 87–88, 92, 97, 100, 106, 109, 120, 123–24, 127, 135–36, 143, 145, 147, 152, 156, 160, 161, 167, 169–71, 175–76, 211, 217; Body, 4, 35–37, 40–41, 57, 67, 70, 87, 103, 116, 131, 133, 136, 142, 165–67, 169–71, 191, 195, 205, 221; Embodied holiness, 34, **67–75,** 170, 175. *See also* Body of Christ

Emmaus (disciples), **46–48**, 73, 78–79, 148, 150, 198, 232
Eucharist, 26, 29, 36–38, 47, 49, **73–75**, 148, 150, 155, 160, 163–64, 166, 168, 171, 174, 186, 193–95, 198, 202–3, 205, 216, 218, 238; Eucharistic Prayers, 127, 132, 147, **148–55**, 167, 224, 231–33
Eve, 49, **50**, 53, 60, 88, 199
Exodus, 11, 48–49, **52–54**, 55–59, 61–62, 74, 88, 125, 127, 129, 139, 154, 162, 199–200

Fatima, 5, 26, 29, 32, 193
Felkai, Peter, 181
Formation, 11, 88, 89, 92, 106, 108, **119–23**, 130, 175, 210, 215, 218, 222, 224
Francis, Pope, 169, 205–6, 233, 239
Francis of Assisi, 83–84, 110, 208
Frey, Nancy Louise, 40, 194, 196–97

Gaillardetz, Richard R., 227
Ganss, George E., 210
Geger, Barton T., 215, 220
Gennep, Arnold van, 31, 43, 192
Gregory of Nyssa, 3, 178, 180
Gutiérrez, Gustavo, 200

Hajj, 1, 181, 197
Hajji, 43
Hamm, Dennis, 206
Hänggi, Anton, 150, 231
Haran, Menahem, 200
Harkins, Franklin, 195
Hervieu-Léger, Danièle, 181, 197
Herzman, Ronald B., 208
Hezser, Catherine, 201, 203
Holy/Holiness, 3, 8, 20, **33–34**, 36–37, 42–44, 49, 56, 58, 60–61, 63–65, 67–69, **70–73**, 74–75, 78, 86–88, 105, 109, 124, 140–41, 160, 165, 170, 175–76, 186, 193, 197, 203–5, 222, 233, 239. *See also* Embodiment: Embodied holiness; Holy Spirit
Holy Land, 2–3, 5, 7, 17, 25, 28, 32, 35, 56, 65, 71–72, 90–91, 157–65, 173, 179–80, 188, 190, 192, 194–95, 225, 235; Jerusalem, 1, 3, 5–7, 9, 27, 32, 35, 47, 49, 56–57, 60, 62–70, 75–76, 78–82, 89–92, 96–97, 99–100, 102, 104–5, 107, 109–12, 114–19, 121, 135, 138, 159, 164, 166, 170, 171, 175, 177–78, 180, 186–87, 193, 200–203, 206, 208, 210, 215, 217–18, 233, 235, 239. *See also* Temple: Jerusalem temple
Holy Spirit, 12, 62, 72, 74–75, 77–79, **81–83**, 84, 89, 114, 115, 141, 144–45, 147, 150, 153–55, 167, 169, 171,

173–76, 186, 195, 198, 207–8, 220, 238–40
Home, 7, 16, 30–32, 35, 37, 42–43, 52, 63, 65, 67, 78–79, 87, 89, 128, 130, 135–36, 142, 170, 184, 192, 195, 198–99, 209
Homeland, 86, 133, 142, 157–58, 166, 190, 230
Hughes, Fred, 9, 177, 180
Hundley, Michael B., 201

Identity, 4, 11, 16, 44, 46, 55, 89, 92, 97–100, 103, 106, 109, 120, 124, 126, 175, 177, 180, 184, 190
Ignatius of Loyola, 11, 44, 88, 89–124, 174–76, 191–93, 198, 206, 209–23, 240; *Constitutions*, 90, 93, 120, 210, 218, 221; *Spiritual Diary*, 100, 214, 216, 218, 220–21; *Spiritual Exercises*, 89–91, 93, 96, 101–2, **109–12**, 120, 123–24, 175, 191–92, 198, 216, 217, 219–22; *Testament*, 11, 89, **92–119**, 120, 123–24, 179, 193, 209–10, 212–15
Intention, 4, 11, 15–16, 19, **20–24**, 30–31, 40–41, 44, 80, 84, 102, 159, 168, 183, 186–88
International Theological Commission, 238–39
Iparraguirre, Ignacio, 209
Irvin, Dale T., 199

Jansen, Willy, 181
Jerome, 3, 178
Jesus Christ, 11, 15, 25, 28–29, 33, 37, 40, 46–49, 60–82, 84–85, 88, 91, 99, 104–5, 108, 115, 117–18, 123, 141–45, 150–51, 153, 158–59, 161, 164, 167, 169, 173–75, 181, 187, 193–95, 197, 201–3, 205–7, 216, 220, 222, 232–34, 239, 240
John Chrysostom, 205
John Paul II, Pope, 6–7, 12, 27, 69, 71, 127, 157, 161–66, 171, 173, 180, 182, 188, 191, 197, 204, 230, 233, 236–39
John XXIII, Pope, 133–34, 156–61, 166, 175, 227–29, 233–34
Jubilee, 3, 6, 8, 10, 18, 27, 67, 157, **161–66**, 167, 171, 173, 178, 180, 182, 188
Julia, Dominique, 24, 34, 178, 181, 187–88, 194–96

Kempe, Margery, 8, 215

Laínez, Diego, 102, 108, 212, 214, 216–18
Lambert, Bernard, 177
Lera Monreal, José María, 220–21
Lincoln, Andrew T., 179–80
Loreto, 3, 44, 121–22, 157–59, 178, 195, 222–23, 233–35
Lourdes, 1, 5, 8, 26, 36, 38, 193–94, 227

Lubac, Henri de, 160, 235
Ludolph of Saxony, 192, 194–95
Luther, Martin, 4–5, 178, 186

Macchia, Frank D., 207
Maddrell, Avril, 9, 194
Maggioni, Corrado, 231
Maraval, Pierre, 177
Martin, James, 9, 181
Mary (mother of Jesus), 15, 25–26, 28, 62, 64–65, 90, 99, 103, 108, 115, 117, 142–43, 147, 151, 175, 212, 218, 220–21, 230, 234
Mary (sister of Martha), 202
Mary Magdalen, 4
May, Christof, 9, 18, 37, 177, 182, 185, 188, 195
Mayeur-Jaouen, Catherine, 197
McCarron, Richard E., 231
McConville, J. Gordon, 56–58, 200–201
McManamon, John M., 213–14
Mein, Andrew, 200
Melloni Ribas, Javier, 219–20
Memory, 4, 11, 14, 19–20, **26–30**, 34, 36–37, 42, 50, 53, 57, 61, 70, 73–74, 84, 141, 160, 162–64, 166, 168, 174, 182, 186, 189–90, 205; Memorial, 27, 58, 72–74, 88, 197
Merton, Thomas, 21, 187
Migrant, 10, 16, 50–51, 55, 86, 162, 165, 169–70, 184–85, 199, 206. *See also* Refugee
Miracle, 3–4, 29, 54, 178, 191, 212, 216, 233
Mission, 11, 18, 48–49, **75–84**, 88, 90–91, 123, 137, 141–42, 144, 147, 161, 163, 168, 174, 186, 198, 202, 206–7, 211, 221, 238–39
Moltmann, Jürgen, 207
Monasticism (Monk), 4, 8, 16, 83, 112, 168, 184, 195, 208
Moses, 52, 54, 59, 88
Motyer, Steve, 207
Muller, Naomi, 199
Murphy-O'Connor, Jerome, 207

Nadal, Jerónimo, 94–95, 108, 212, 220
Nardoni, Enrique, 200
National Conference of Catholic Bishops, 233
Notermans, Catrien, 181

O'Malley, Brian Brendan, 20, 187
O'Rourke Boyle, Marjorie, 213, 218

Padberg, John, 209
Paul, 25, 28, 68–69, 74, 78, **79–81**, 82, 84–85, 87–88, 108, 129, 136, 141, 156, 175, 203, 205, 206–7, 228
Paula, 3
Paul VI, Pope, 12, 127, 139, 156–62, 164–66, 170–71, 229, 233–36, 238
Peña Antil, Nelson, 41, 194, 196
Penance, 1, 4, 40–41, 103, 110, 121, 123, 136, 159, 166, 194, 197, 217

Peter, 25, 28, 32, 82, 85, 87, 108, 156, 159
Philip, **78–79**, 81–82, 206–7
Pilgrim's Tale (or *The Way of the Pilgrim*), 8, 181
Pius VI, Pope, 178–79
Pius VII, Pope, 179
Pius XII, Pope, 133, 205, 223, 227
Polanco, Juan Alfonso de, 211
Pontifical Council for the Pastoral Care of Migrants and Itinerant People, 24, 44, 58, 162, 182, 186–89, 192–93, 198–200, 202–3, 236–37
Poverty, 83–84, 91, 96, 100, 105–7, 121, 170, 208, 215, 218
Protestantism, 2, 4–7, 104, 160, 178–79, 190, 195, 204, 217

Raffa, Vincenzo, 149, 231
Reader, Ian, 185
Refugee, 16, 30, 32, 65, 129, 165, 167, 169, 170, 238. *See also* Migrant
Relics, 2–5, 28, 33, **37–38**, 72, 91, 124, 170, 178, 191, 193–95, 205, 218, 233
Return, 18, 20, 26, 30–32, 41–44, 47, 50, 52–53, 56, 58, 62, 67, 70, 73, 77–80, 86, 90–91, 96, 102–3, 105, 110, 112–13, 130, 159, 164, 168, 174, 184, 186, 190, 192, 197, 208, 218
Ribadeneira (or Ribadeneyra), Pedro de, 92, 94, 98–99, 210–13, 215–16, 218, 220
Robinson, Martin, 18, 186, 188, 192, 196
Rodrigues, Simão, 40, 189, 196, 206
Rogers, James Silas, 190
Rogers, Stephanie Stidham, 179, 190–91, 195, 197, 204
Rome, 2–3, 5, 6, 21, 25, 28, 32, 36, 44, 68, 79, 81, 90, 92, 95–97, 99–100, 102–3, 105, 112, 117–18, 121, 128, 129, 156–59, 176, 179–80, 192, 194, 207, 216, 218, 220, 222, 227
Roos, Richard, 43, 197
Roseman, Sharon R., 181, 184
Rosenberger, Michael, 182
Ross-Bryant, Lynn, 184
Ruiz Jurado, Manuel, 209
Ruiz Pérez, Francisco José, 102, 215, 217

Sacred, 1, 5, 7, 9, 13–14, 17, 20, 22, **32–33**, 37, 53, 59, 61, 67, 69, 71, 73, 104, 122, 164, 179–81, 184, 186–87, 190–92, 203, 227
Sacred Congregation for Divine Worship, 231
Saint, 5, 15, 25, 28, 30, 33–34, 37, 42, 49, 70–74, 85, 88, 92, 99–100, 108–9, 130, 139–41, 147, 151–52, 168, 170, 178, 181, 186, 189, 191, 193, 195, 205, 216,

219, 240. *See also* Holy/ Holiness
Sallnow, Michael J., 181
Sanctuary, 3–4, 15, 21, 26, 28–29, 34, 36, 60, 90, 157, 191, 193–94, 222, 234. *See also* Shrine
Santiago de Compostela, 3, 5, 28, 34, 179, 194; Camino (de Santiago), 6, 9, 13, 17, 23, 29, 36, 40, 179, 181, 184, 189, 194–95, 197
Sardi, Leo Agung, 42, 196, 222
Scafi, Alessandro, 9, 194
Second Asian Congress on Pilgrimages and Shrines, 206
Second Vatican Council, 1, 10, 12, 74, 126–28, 130–49, 155–57, 160–61, 166–67, 171, 175, 178, 205, 222–30, 234, 239–40; *Acta Synodalia Sacrosancti Concilii Oecumenici Vaticani Secundi,* 227; *Dei Verbum,* 134, **143**, 227, 230; *Gaudium et Spes,* 133–34, **143–45**, 146, 155, 175, 227, 230, 240; *Lumen Gentium,* 128, 132–34, **135–43**, 152, 155, 158, 163, 166, 177, 205, 223–24, 226–30; *Sacrosanctum Concilium,* **134–35**, 138, 228
Semmelroth, Otto, 229
Sheldrake, Philip, 190
Shore, Paul, 192
Shrine, 1–3, 5, 17, 21, 26–28, 32, 34, 37, 42, 44, 72–74, 91, 148, 157–58, 162–63, 166–67, 177, 184, 186, 188–89, 191, 193–94, 198, 206. *See also* Sanctuary
Sobosan, Jeffrey G., 10, 228
Society of Jesus (=Jesuits), 11, 42, 4, 89–90, 92–93, 95–96, 98, 100, 108, 112, 119–24, 181, 189, 206, 208, 211–12, 215–18, 221–23
Stewart-Kroeker, Sarah, 128, 224–26
Sumption, Jonathan, 217

Tavard, George H., 227
Temple, 21, 59–60, 68–69, 72, 86, 164, 175, 200–201; Jerusalem temple, 7, 33, 56–57, 60–63, 65, 68–71, 164, 201, 203, 206
Tena, Pere, 232
Teresa of Avila, 191, 215, 221, 240
Theobald, Christoph, 206
Thomas à Kempis, 197
Thompson, Charles D., 184
Tomlin, Graham, 44, 178, 180, 198
Tourist, 16, 21–23, 26, 162, 180–81, 183–84, 187, 192, 195–96
Transcendence, 11, 19–20, 22, **24–26**, 38, 41, 84, 164, 168
Transformation, 8, 11, 20, 23, 30–32, 38, **42–44**, 46–48, 51, 54, 58, 61, 66, 74, 79, 84, 99, 101, **103–4**, 105, 108, 159, 171, 174–76, 192, 197, 205

Trinity, 37, 115, 144–45, 147, 154–55, 169, 173–75, 186, 230; Father (God), 144, 154, 173, 174, 186, 216, 233. *See also* Holy Spirit; Jesus Christ
Turner, Victor and Edith, 9, 17, 22, 31, 40–41, 178, 180–81, 185, 187, 192, 194–97, 238
Twomey, Michael W., 238

Vélez, Karin, 178
Vella, Danielle, 199
Voragine, Jacobus de, 219
Vulnerability, 11, 19, 24, 35, **38–40**, 77, 80, 84, 101, **106–7**, 166, 170–71, 174, 187, 196

Walker, Peter W. L., 69, 71, 177, 204
Walton, Heather, 7, 9, 179–80, 185, 194–95, 204–5
Walzer, Michael, 200
Webb, Diana, 188
Wilkinson, John, 178
Woolfe, Zachary, 190
World Youth Day, 6, 27, 36, 43, 179–80, 197
Wright, N. T., 180, 187

Zacchaeus, 202

Disputing New France

MCGILL-QUEEN'S FRENCH ATLANTIC WORLDS SERIES

SERIES EDITORS: NICHOLAS DEW AND JEAN-PIERRE LE GLAUNEC

The French Atlantic world has emerged as a rich and dynamic field of historical research. This series will showcase a new generation of scholarship exploring the worlds of the French Atlantic – including West Africa, the greater Caribbean region, and the continental Americas – from the sixteenth century to the mid-nineteenth century. Books in the series will explore how the societies of the French Atlantic were shaped and connected by trans-oceanic networks of colonialism, how local and indigenous cultures and environments shaped colonial projects, and how the diverse peoples of the French Atlantic understood and experienced their worlds. Especially welcome are histories from the perspectives of the enslaved and dispossessed. Comparative studies are encouraged and the series will accept manuscript submissions in English and in French. Original works of scholarship are preferred, though translations of landmark books in the field will be considered.

Le monde atlantique français est devenu un domaine de recherche riche et dynamique au sein de la discipline historique. La présente collection a pour vocation d'accueillir une nouvelle génération d'ouvrages explorant les espaces de l'Atlantique français – y compris l'Afrique de l'Ouest, la grande région des Caraïbes et les Amériques continentales – du début du XVIe siècle jusqu'au milieu du XIXe siècle. Les œuvres qui y sont publiées explorent de quelles manières les sociétés de l'Atlantique français sont façonnées et reliées par les réseaux transocéaniques issus du colonialisme, de quelle manière les cultures locales et leurs environnements influencent les projets coloniaux, et comment les divers peuples de l'Atlantique français comprennent et expérimentent leurs mondes. Les ouvrages donnant la parole aux esclaves ou aux acteurs traditionnellement dominés sont particulièrement bienvenus, tout comme les recherches comparées. La collection est ouverte aux manuscrits rédigés en anglais ou en français, de préférence des monographies originales, ainsi qu'aux traductions de livres ayant marqué le domaine.

1 Architecture and Urbanism in the French Atlantic Empire
State, Church, and Society, 1604–1830
Gauvin Alexander Bailey

2 Flesh Reborn
The Saint Lawrence Valley Mission Settlements through the Seventeenth Century
Jean-François Lozier

3 Power and Subsistence
The Political Economy of Grain in New France
Louise Dechêne

4 Fruits of Perseverance
The French Presence in the Detroit River Region, 1701–1815
Guillaume Teasdale

5 The Cry of Vertières
Liberation, Memory, and the Beginning of Haiti
Jean-Pierre Le Glaunec

6 People, State, and War under the French Regime in Canada
Louise Dechêne

7 Disputing New France
Companies, Law, and Sovereignty in the French Atlantic, 1598–1663
Helen Dewar